T R
The menta

T0143850

The**inspirational**series™
Overcoming adversity and thriving

Mind Over Mountain
A Mental and Physical Climb to the Top

BY ROBBY KOJETIN

We are proud to introduce The**inspirational**series™.
Part of the Trigger family of innovative mental health books,
The**inspirational**series™ tells the stories of the people who have
battled and beaten mental health issues.

THE AUTHOR

Robby Kojetin lives in Johannesburg, South Africa and is a high-altitude adventurer. Since his accident in 2006 which resulted in him breaking both of his ankles, he has gone on to become one of only a handful of people to have stood on top of the world's highest mountain, Mount Everest. He has also climbed Kilimanjaro nine times, completed the Ironman triathlon, and scaled five of the Seven Summits. Known as an inspirational and engaging speaker on stage, he presents on the topics of failure, self-doubt and persisting against all odds, in the hopes of inspiring people of all ages and backgrounds facing the daunting mountains and obstacles in their own lives.

Robby is a proud husband and father who also coaches people to reach their personal summit goals. He is a regular contributor to a number of radio programmes, magazine articles and TV features, including Discovery Channel's *Everest: Beyond the Limit*.

First published in 2019
This edition published in 2023 by Trigger Publishing
An imprint of Shaw Callaghan Ltd

UK Office
The Stanley Building
7 Pancras Square
Kings Cross
London N1C 4AG

US Office
On Point Executive Center, Inc
3030 N Rocky Point Drive W
Suite 150
Tampa, FL 33607
www.triggerhub.org

A CIP catalogue record for this book is available upon request
from the British Library
ISBN: 978-1-83796-405-5
Ebook ISBN: 978-1-83796-406-2

Cover design and typeset by Fusion Graphic Design Ltd

A NOTE FROM THE SERIES EDITOR

The Inspirational range from Trigger brings you genuine stories about our authors' experiences with mental health problems.

Some of the stories in our Inspirational range will move you to tears. Some will make you laugh. Some will make you feel angry, or surprised, or uplifted. Hopefully they will all change the way you see mental health problems.

These are stories we can all relate to and engage with. Stories of people experiencing mental health difficulties and finding their own ways to overcome them with dignity, humour, perseverance and spirit.

In *Mind Over Mountain*, Robby explores the detrimental effect that breaking both his ankles, and therefore losing his sense of "identity" as a climber, had on his mental health. His honesty about his own anxiety and depression and the effect of his father's suicide is both raw and refreshing. Whilst this book highlights the fact that overcoming your mental barriers can be as difficult as overcoming physical ones, Robby provides hope in showing that he managed to overcome his mental health problems and went on to achieve every climber's dream – scaling the world's highest peaks.

This is our Inspirational range. These are our stories. We hope you enjoy them. And most of all, we hope that they will educate and inspire you. That's what this range is all about.

Lauren Callaghan,
Co-founder and Lead Consultant Psychologist at Trigger

For Tracey and Kendall,
The two best reasons to return home safely.

Trigger Warning: This book contains references to suicide and suicidal thoughts.

FOREWORD

It was late morning on 24th December 2003. We were well into our summit push on Aconcagua with only one major obstacle left – the infamous Canaleta, the final hurdle to the top of South America and the highest point outside of the Himalaya. We had been on the go for eight hours odd. I had been strong the whole expedition; Dirk – who had been totally wiped out only two days earlier and was unable to even assist with camp chores, had surged ahead and by now was nearly through the Canaleta. Yet I was now the one who was struggling, struggling as I had never done before, and I don't recall struggling that much on more than thirty expeditions since. I could barely progress one step at a time, yet I was determined not to turn around for the third time on this mountain. I had been beaten back once before by dangerous weather and once by illness; I could not face the prospect of coming to within 100 vertical metres of the summit and not succeeding. Robby, who had become my best friend and with whom I have shared almost all of my expeditions, was there, immediately behind or just in front of me. He literally urged, begged, pleaded and encouraged me through every step of that final section, which took extraordinarily long, much longer than it should have.

Almost fifteen years later, I still remember vividly how Robby metaphorically dragged me to the top of Aconcagua, just under 7000 metres high. That is who Robby is, and that is the type of climber and person that Robby has always been – someone who will risk their own success and endure additional discomfort and agony for someone else.

I shed a few tears on the summit and hugged Robby and Dirk before heading back to High Camp and then on to Base Camp that same evening, just in time to spend Christmas Eve in Base Camp. It was a memorably long and hard, yet fulfilling day.

Just over three years prior to our Aconcagua summit, Robby and I had embarked on an ambitious expedition with some friends to climb the three highest mountains in Africa in one trip, something that had yet to be accomplished by anyone. We did not succeed in the summit count department, but far more importantly, we did succeed in kindling a love of high places and bonds born in the mountains.

Many of our best friends were on that trip with us. One of my dearest memories of mountains was on Kilimanjaro summit night. Our team had an average age of under twenty; we were leading our own expedition, were gloriously naïve, green and out of our depth, but we soldiered on undeterred. It had been a tough day and we were all exhausted. Having been nominally appointed as expedition leader I felt the weight of expectation to motivate the team, but was struggling with my own confidence. Just before sunrise I got the feeling that everyone was on the cusp of throwing in the towel and heading down.

Robby and I, bent over our trekking poles, looked at each other, and I knew he was thinking the same as I was. I can't remember who said it, but it was a shared decision – "five more minutes". We climbed for another five minutes, and another five and eventually we summited Kilimanjaro. That "five minutes more" moment is more memorable to me than the summit. Had we turned back at that point, I believe our mountaineering careers would have gone no further than that. Many years later we have each climbed Kilimanjaro nine times and shared our deep love for the mountain with dozens of other people. Again, this is another one of Robby's passions – sharing his love, enthusiasm and knowledge with others. This is evident in his success on the speaking circuit and confirmed by his continued involvement in the Scout movement.

It was the Scout movement that introduced Robby and me, back in 1994, during a twelve-day Patrol Leader Training Unit course where Robby was a member of staff and I was a participant. We went on to fulfil staffing roles during many subsequent courses, and it was during one of these courses that the "Three Peaks Expedition" came up. I think that scouting had a lot to do with forming our approach – and that of many of our mountaineering mates – towards adventure, mountains, the outdoors, teamwork, hard work and the ability to cope and even thrive during tough times and gruelling environments. We, and many men, owe a debt of gratitude to the Scout movement.

Since we met back in 1994, Robby has climbed many of the highest mountains across the globe, some of them repeatedly. We have shared many hours on the same rope, same tent and same ledge together. Inevitably the successes and the summits are interspersed with disappointment, mistakes and expeditions with no summits. As the cliché goes, to experience the highs, you have to go through some lows. In between his highs such as the many summits he has achieved, the great travel opportunities, completing an Ironman and ticking many things off his bucket list (a theme he has now made a career òut of), Robby has had his share of lows.

Having been friends for well over twenty years, I can fairly safely say that Robby's lowest point was when he smashed both ankles during a mInor, ordinarily pedestrian fall at an indoor climbing gym. The actual smashing of bones was not the low point, but it was the long period that it preceded that would become a low phase in Robby's life. It impacted on him severely, both physically and mentally. The months of being wheelchair bound, the countless doctor's visits, operations, prolonged pain, physical limitations and everything associated with it would take a dire toll on Robby's job, finances, his engagement and most importantly his self-confidence. I have little doubt that the life lessons learnt in scouting and in the mountains – and Robby's desire to get back there – had a lot to do with Robby pulling himself out of what seemed like a very deep and dark hole at the time.

Robby's accomplishments since then are evidence of the man he is. He has climbed Mount Everest, the highest mountain on Earth; he has been on many other expeditions from the Himalaya to Alaska, Peru to Russia, Africa to Australia. He has married a wonderful woman, travelled the world, and got his dream career going. And he is just getting started.

This book gives us some insight and understanding into a collection of Robby's highest, lowest and most vulnerable moments. It is a great reflection of the challenges, albeit very different, that we all go through in our own lives.

A better friend and a better mountaineering partner is hard to find. It is a privilege to have been able to write this foreword for Robby's book. I hope you enjoy it as much as I did.

John Black

INTRODUCTION

The conquest of Everest, since its epic beginnings, has been a tale of triumph, victory and valour.

A golden cross is pinned on a hero's chest.

Trumpets sound while angels sing. Man conquers mountain.

The beast is slain. The battle is won.

This is not that story.

I must make it clear: in some of the photographs taken of the infamous Death Zone – in which strings of climbers wait anxiously at the bottleneck that has become the Hillary Step – I'm the guy in the red down suit at the back of the queue with my head in my hands.

I always arrived last into each camp, often several hours behind the other climbers, and I was described in the Discovery Channel's third season of *Everest: Beyond the Limit* as Russell Brice's "weakest climber".

If you were to ask me what I found most amazing about my experience of climbing to the top of Mount Everest, my answer would be this: it was the fact that I actually did it. It's almost absurd.

I don't say this in arrogance or self-flattery, but out of pure disbelief.

I am the crack in the bell, the flaw in the Cullinan diamond, the blemish on Mona Lisa's face.

I am the chink in the armour. I am the Achilles heel.

CHAPTER 1

CLIMB ON

Had I been aware of its significance and the role it would play in the story that would unfold, I would have framed that page from the *OutThere* magazine (page eighty-seven, circa 1996) and displayed it somewhere on a wall in my home. It featured an article about the mystical Kilimanjaro, Africa's highest mountain. On it was a photo no bigger than a playing card of a man walking between some small boulders, ankle-deep in white snow. The caption read "Yes, there is snow at the Equator."

My fantasy world was based on both this article and what I had seen in the countless volumes of the *National Geographic* magazines that crowded our next-door neighbour's bookshelves. They were a towering library of adventures from far-off mountain ranges to the frozen remains of the Austrian mummified "Ice Man." I was completely ignorant when it came to the actual topic of high-altitude climbing, the countless mountain pinnacles of the world and the immersive culture of mountaineering. But the inexplicable pull was there.

I cannot pinpoint a particular moment when I decided I wanted to be a mountaineer. I will admit to clowning around on the staircase en route to my third-floor biology class, pretending to be Edmund Hillary or Ed Viesturs. With each step I rasped as though wearing an oxygen mask, imagining the crunch of the steel teeth on my make-believe crampons strapped to my make-believe boots. I pictured them digging deep into the knee-deep snow and my hand slid up the banister as if it were the final length of rope securing me to summit pitch of some imaginary Himalayan peak.

And so it is safe to say that by the time I was a teenager my head was already up in the clouds, dreaming of the frozen vertical landscapes of Everest. My elder brother Dieter and I would horse around, making fun of Brad Pitt's phoney accent in his portrayal of Heinrich Harrer in the movie *Seven Years in Tibet*. "Ve are auf to Nanga Parbat! In de Heema-liar!" was about the only line we remembered from that movie.

In the mid-nineties, my older brother Mark was studying at WITS Technikon, now the University of Johannesburg. He had joined the rock-climbing club, a motley gang of scruffy, long-haired dental technology and electrical engineering students, their wiry arms racked with bracelets made from leather and worn pieces of nylon accessory cord. It would not be long before I found myself joining them on weekend trips to Waterval Boven in Mpumalanga and the Harrismith holiday resort, inexplicably named Mount Everest, in the flatness of the Free State.

After my brother left WITS he formed his own social climbing club, which gave him the chance to carry on climbing and also meet new people. Its numbers quickly grew and soon they had almost 40 members. We drilled the outside wall of our Germiston home and fixed it with climbing handholds and modified the carport with crudely welded pull-up bars. Every now and again we'd find ourselves rigging abseils from the roof of the house, off railway bridges in the neighbourhood, and even from the top of the local stadium lights. Nothing was off limits ... well, for us anyway. The security guards who patrolled the grounds thought differently, but in the end it all worked out well. We were not vandals, and I am a firm believer that innocence belongs to those who run fastest.

Twenty years on, some of those climbers from the WITS climbing club have gone on to become some of South Africa's leading mountaineers. As for my brother's club, it fizzled into non-existence when he moved across the country to Durban and later on to Australia. I inherited some of the ropes and gear and carried on climbing. Same circus – just different clowns.

Over the years that followed, I would experience my fair share of days in the crags and wild weekends away. Memories of long days scaling the various faces and returning to the campsite sunburnt and dehydrated are blurred by the nights that followed. I would revel in the various rock-climbing magazines, admiring super-athletes as they ascended massively exposed slabs, clinging to the rock by their bloodied fingertips. I would page through the route guides and examine description after description of the various routes, each climb graded according to its difficulty and named by the first person to complete the pitch. As a result, names such as Texas Chainsaw Massacre – the first pitch on which I was taught to "lead climb" – and Babies' Blood Gives Me Gas emerged. Climbing routes grew personalities and stories of their own, each with their own distinct and unique set of challenges.

One such tale was a classic "21" grade climb dubbed *The Greatest Doctor in the Universe*. This section of rock located on one of Waterval Boven's well-worn crags had a five-star rating and was perfectly suited to my style of climbing, with bold dynamic moves in the beginning, requiring confident and balanced moves up to an off-balance ledge no wider than the palm of my hand. From that precarious point upward, the handholds shrunk to tiny knobs and knuckles on the rock, requiring a cool head when attempting to clip the rope to the bolts on the face, which are often in places that were less than ideal. I would attempt this climb on many occasions over the span of three years, and no trip to Waterval Boven's Elandkrans Campsite was complete without a visit to "The Doctor".

I would eventually succeed on The Greatest Doctor in the Universe one muggy and overcast Saturday morning. After having warmed up on a climb at the other end of the crag, I tied the rope to the belay loop of my harness and fiddled around in my chalk bag, coating my calloused hands in the fine white powder.

This would absorb the sweat from my palms when things started to get gnarly. I craned my neck upward, visualising the sequence of moves, talking myself through the desperately bare crux just six or so metres above my head.

'Climb when ready,' my friend Warren said in his default tone of excited optimism.

'Climbing,' I nodded, confirming I was ready to go.

'Climb on!'

And up I started. Cautiously. Focused.

With both hands already in place on the first two handholds, I turned my head to Warren and with a hopeful smile I said, 'The doctor will see you now.' Having Warren on the other end of the rope did a lot to bolster my confidence. If I took a "winger" of a fall, he would catch me – just as he had done countless times before.

In my mind, that day marked the pinnacle of my life as a rock climber. At twenty-two, a large part of my identity and self-confidence was defined by how I felt while climbing. It gave my life meaning and ironically, it was when I was surrounded by high stone walls that I felt most free. Because although my upbringing was never stifled by overly strict parents or pressure to grow up to compete with the Joneses – if anything, pressure to succeed, or more accurately the pressure to *not fail*, was entirely self-imposed – I realise now that I suffered with what I recognise today as anxiety. Things like changing schools when my parents emigrated to Australia caused a massive knot in my stomach. Often I would end up in tears when my fear of not being able to cope with the unknown became too overwhelming for my eight-year-old mind.

Two years later our family returned to South Africa as my parents had realised that the land of milk and honey was not all it was cracked up to be. By chance we ended up buying the house across the road from where we used to live. But still, although I was never diagnosed with the condition, I continued to wrestle with anxiety. While in Australia, my mother had told me that I needed to be prepared for my return to South African education systems, and so

I spent afternoons repeating multiplication tables and practising my reading. It created a monster inside my head. And despite the fact that I was going back to the same friends and classmates I had before, I was hit with waves of nauseating dread at the thought of returning. Thankfully I went back to my old South African school and coped just fine. I was an above average scholar, I had a great circle of friends and excelled at drama and art.

My self-confidence developed along with my personality as I entered my teens and moved into high school. Scouting certainly helped; in the presence of positive role models, I could be myself and be good at it too. Taking part in the things I was good at bolstered my self-esteem, as the praise from others and the high standards I set for myself seemed to pay off.

But still my old nemesis anxiety would rear its head, just to make sure I never got too comfortable. The nights before returning from school holidays, the days before a test, and most Sunday evenings would give me a familiar hollow feeling in my stomach and a rattling sense of insecurity that I would not be able to handle what the new day held in store.

I was once told that it was "just nerves" and I would one day grow out of it … hopefully that will be any day now! I was prescribed my first antidepressant at age eighteen and although the names and doses have changed, they are still a part of my life as I enter my forties.

Years went by and life happened, as it does. People moved away, priorities changed and the role of rock climbing in my life would also evolve. But even at my best, I was still no brilliant climber by any stretch of the imagination. I was a social climber and eventually climbing was not about going harder or higher … it was just about going. Those weekends away were as good as a two-week holiday, filled with good times at the crag, around the campfire or even swinging from an 80-metre-high railway bridge. Returning to the normality of the working week was often made more difficult as aching muscles, calloused hands and my signature "racoon" tan lines left by my sunglasses, told the tale of another weekend "just hanging around with some friends".

That humid autumn day was the last time I climbed The Greatest Doctor in the Universe. But it would not be the last time I would hear the words "The doctor will see you now".

CHAPTER 2

THE DOCTOR WILL SEE YOU NOW

In my early twenties, student life was about throwing myself into my studies, running the First Germiston Scout Group and hitting the crags when time and money allowed.

My parents divorced the year after I finished high school and my mother and I moved away to a two-bedroom townhouse a few kilometres from my childhood home. It was not an easy time, emotionally or financially.

As far back as I can remember, my parents' marriage was always strained at best. My memories of happy moments with everyone smiling and enjoying each other's company are outweighed a hundred to one by the memories of arguments and unspoken tension. My father was made redundant in the early nineties for what turned out to be just over three years. His unemployment put the spotlight on my mother to be the breadwinner. The blow to my father's ego – coupled with the added pressure and his embarrassment – was always evident. With the weight of a family of five on my mother's shoulders, it was no picnic for her either and eventually she made the decision to walk away. Replacing a twenty-eight-year-old marriage with a clean slate was not a decision she took lightly.

Despite my mom having saved and planned for separation for months, things got tight from time to time. But we made do, especially as I took a weekend job waiting tables. In fact, I look back on those years with a sense of gratitude and a great pride.

I was fortunate enough to study a national diploma in Graphic Design at WITS Technikon. It was in that cold eerie building on Eloff Street, smack bang in the middle of Johannesburg, that I discovered a talent of which I had only just scratched the surface during high school.

Through the process of dismantling any preconceived notions of what I thought I knew about drawing and painting, I would be introduced to a world of art and design, new media, other young passionate designers ... and blue hair. I embraced a passion and talent I had never experienced anywhere else. It was here that I felt a sense of belonging and purpose, and that was reflected in my grades. Working through the night to meet deadlines became the norm, but I never resented it. When passion is involved, there is no such thing as sacrifice.

They were three eye-opening years, thanks to both the syllabus and the street life around our faculty building. As an aspiring designer and artist, I was exposed to a world without parameters. Johannesburg in the late 1990s had a pulse of its own with mass protests – 20,000 strong – and traditional medicine stalls stocked with remedies for everything from impotence to blindness, featuring shrivelled baboons' paws and ostrich heads which hung from the yellowed ceiling.

I would make my way down the streets and soak up the culture of the city, worlds apart from my sheltered suburban childhood, despite it only being less than 20 kilometres away geographically. For the first time in my life I was being encouraged to see and decide for myself, to take in all the surrounding avenues and alleyways had to give. In the classroom I found something I was good at and I was able to feed my self-confidence, in spite of the ever-present feelings of doubt and self-worthlessness.

I entered the working world full of fire and a conviction that, through impactful communication and aesthetics, I could change the world.

That notion was soon extinguished in the three months it took me to find my first "real" job working as a junior graphic designer for a small start-up with big ideas, led by a man who sold an ideal better than he did the software he was building. After six months of being employed there I arrived one Monday morning to find my computer's hard drive dismantled and someone else sitting in my chair. The Boss asked to chat with me in his office the same way a surgeon approaches an unsuspecting widow.

He then proceeded to tell me what I had already figured out. He said that the company was behind schedule and they could not afford to keep me on as they were downscaling considerably. I had received several clues that this was happening when my monthly pay cheques bounced on more than one occasion. The ones that had been clearing hadn't come without a sob story and the guy in charge doing some creative accounting. It was a bitter pill to swallow and logically I knew it had to end, but I still felt guilty and worthless as I sobbed my way home that morning. Most people would have fled to a pub to drown their sorrows or gone home to wallow in a pile of rented DVDs, Cheese Curls and self-pity. I didn't. Who knew how long it would be to the next pay cheque?

During my first tangle with unemployment, I managed to arrange an informal interview with a Creative Director, Alan Irvin, at one of the bigger ad agencies, Ogilvy and Mather. They weren't hiring, but he did take the time to give me several pointers on what to add to my portfolio. (Alan was married to my brother's business partner's sister, who happened to be the Prefect who purchased me at a "slave auction" at my high school initiation week in Grade 8. So he and I were close ... like distant cousins three times removed.)

Six months later I heard that he had since changed agencies and now held the position of Executive Creative Director, so I called him again; he took the time to view my amended portfolio and agreed to hire me as a Junior Art Director. I was incredibly grateful for both the opportunity and a chance to leave the interim job I had taken as a lecturer at a privately owned design school, with a meagre pay cheque that basically funded the contents of the petrol tank of my 1988 Golf Mk2.

Before I became acquainted with the advertising industry and its lingo, I was excited and intimidated by the title "director" and had no idea what to expect at my new place of work, Grey Worldwide Advertising. As it turns out, Junior Art Directors across the advertising industry are ranked on par with the delivery guy and the cleaning staff in the big scheme of things – except the cleaning staff could possibly earn more and have better working hours.

But I cannot complain. My first brief on my first day was for a television commercial, an opportunity many junior creatives only encounter after years of working weekends and mounting presentations for the "real staff". Over time Alan and I learnt that we share a very offbeat and often misunderstood sense of humour which made working there, for lack of a better word, educational.

I also made some great friends despite my unforgivable error of wearing Buffalos, the ugliest shoes to ever be considered fashionable, on my first day of the job.

I was relieved when I reached my sixth month at Grey. I was neither asked to leave nor had any of my salary cheques bounced, a new employment record for me. Six months turned into a year and I really started to find my feet. While working on a television campaign for the Mazda Drifter 4x4 vehicle, I stayed late one night to script an idea I was struggling to give life to, an idea that I saw as bright as day in my head. I could hear the monologue of the maniacal evangelist who rants to a crowd of oblivious consumers, preaching a message to them to destroy their televisions and escape the shackles of their couches. My vision included a bonfire crackling in the background as a few of his converted disciples threw Lay-Z-Boy recliners, DVD players and all the vices of their sedentary lives onto the towering inferno.

Sadly, the final product was a far cry from the post-apocalyptic revolution I had envisaged, but the sentiment was there, hidden behind the diluted PG-friendly revisions and the client's mandatory product shots. I remember the Head of Marketing sitting in the edit suite with a stopwatch, in order to make sure that the editor included exactly 50% of the commercial's thirty precious seconds to show the car. But the one thing I did manage to salvage from that slash-and-burn affair was the closing line of the protagonist's sermon, which was "My brothers and my sisters, come out and play!"

Ten years on, I can't help but smile at the direction my life has taken me, and the similarities that I share with that post-apocalyptic maniac. I may not have a cult of followers torching furniture, but the message I promote in keynote presentations, encouraging people to chase a fulfilling, fun and active life is still unchanged.

Alan asked who had written the script, to which I confessed. He liked the concept and how it had been written and before long I found myself handling more copywriting jobs. After a few tweaks from my partner (the actual writer assigned to the job) and a complete butchering by the director, the commercial made it onto television, but as a mere shadow of the original idea. The final product was a guy on the back of the Mazda Drifter 4x4 with a microphone and mobile speaker, the kind sidewalk buskers wheel around, ranting to shoppers about the evils of consumerism and the dangers of sedentary life. He looked more like a G.I. Joe figurine and it was filmed at the Hillfox Power Centre strip mall on the West Rand. It turned out more like an infomercial than the post-apocalyptic Mad Max riot scene I had originally envisaged. This watering down of my idea was one of the first cracks that would lead to me turning my back on advertising. My utopian ideal of changing the world through visual communication had fallen victim to the bottom line and its gang of key performance indicators.

One thing I am grateful for is that Grey Worldwide exposed me to many facets of the advertising industry, from radio production to television, from print to outdoor media, as well as constant involvement in the creative process from conceptualisation to client presentations. Eventually I found myself in a position where I was able to carry out both sides of the creative process, writing copy and art directing – a one-man band. And by June 2004, that one-man band was ready to go on tour.

My time at Grey was not a waste by any stretch of the imagination. I am still friends with some of the characters I met there and it is always a good laugh to think back to the mayhem that often went down during those "Grey days". Cricket games in the hallways that left more than one hole in the passage walls, racing Razor scooters around the building, wearing rollerblades into meetings and the fact that we were all actively involved in the destruction phase of the office renovations speaks volumes.

But it was time to take that brave step away from structured employment and closer to a career where I controlled the leave forms. It was during my time at Grey Worldwide that I would climb Kilimanjaro for the second time as well as take two month-long trips to climb Aconcagua in Argentina, leaving my bank balance and my annual leave status whimpering in the negative.

Freelancing would allow me to carry on doing what I knew, just following a separate set of rules. It made sense in my mind but there was still an element of doubt and I can vividly remember the knot in my stomach as I lay awake in the early hours on the night before I was to hand in my resignation letter. I imagined Alan exploding in a fit of rage, telling me how ungrateful I was for throwing this once In a lifetime opportunity in his face. Potentially I was about to make the worst mistake of my life, landing up unemployed and hungry in a gutter with no prospect of a future! Was I being stupid?

By this point I had a girlfriend, Megan, to consider too. *If you screw it up for you, you screw it up for Megan too*, I thought to myself. *And she doesn't deserve this!*

But my anxiety was in vain. Alan, who has remained a good friend of mine, accepted my notice and the more we chatted, the more we both realised that it was the right thing to do. Working as a freelance creative designer-writer was going to allow me to be more flexible as far as time was concerned. I would be responsible for my own income and the idea of fostering a direct relationship between effort and reward suited me perfectly. As is usually the case, my first major client was the company I had just resigned from, except on an hourly basis and on my terms.

Two years passed and business was doing fine. Had I shuffled my list of priorities, business could have been more profitable, but by 2006 Megan had become my fiancée and we were going to be married the following year, I had climbed Kilimanjaro four times, travelled to Russia to summit Mount Elbrus – the highest point on the European continent – and had undertaken various other expeditions too, including a trip to the Cordillera Blanca in Peru.

I had made the right choice. No longer was I throwing myself on my sword to sell dog food or artificial sweeteners. Instead, I was enjoying the road less travelled, the path that favoured adventure over diligence. I worked when I needed to and the rest of my time was devoted to what mattered most to me.

Megan was still studying at university, which I realise possibly contributed to the relaxed and carefree lifestyle we led. In April 2006, she and I went on holiday to Cape Town for a week-long holiday jam-packed with fun and adventure. We caught the Robbie Williams concert, experienced our first static-line skydive and climbed Jacob's Ladder, a massively exposed multi-pitch rock face up Table Mountain which ended in an epic descent down Platteklip Gorge in the dark, from which we escaped with nothing more than a grazed knee. It was truly a getaway that would do any bucket list proud.

Our holiday drew to an end and we came back to Johannesburg on a Sunday evening. The following night, Warren, two other friends and I went to the indoor climbing facility at WITS University. It was approximately 20 kilometres closer than the only other indoor climbing gym in Kya Sands – and best of all it was free. (In all honesty, the meaning of "free" is a figure of speech in this instance. The facility was only for members of the university's climbing club, but we were welcome to climb there whenever we liked ... provided nobody ever asked us for proof of membership.)

We had been planning a second trip to Mount Kenya at the end of that year to settle some unfinished business, having not summited on our previous attempt six years before. We spent most Monday evenings on the fabricated climbing wall in the Old Mutual Hall, preparing for the 700 metres of cliffs that stood between us and the summit of Africa's second highest mountain.

That Monday night was just like any other. After three hours of clambering up the chalk-caked ledges, cracks and outcrops of the brick wall, the evening was drawing to a close. I moved over to the wooden bouldering wall, an angled section of plywood boards fitted with a mixture of shaped, wooden and resin handholds. The bouldering wall was not very high, used mainly as a training facility aimed at improving technique and endurance. With no ropes needed, climbers use these walls to perfect difficult moves and sequences, un-roped, protected by thick landing mats. There were foam-rubber mats covered in thick nylon sleeves, just like those fat, cumbersome safety "high-jump" mats you messed around on that time you snuck into the school's sports hall. Just like any other Monday, we climbed hard and, as closing time approached, I used the remaining few minutes to climb the bouldering wall, traversing left and right, up and down just to finish my workout with that familiar yet satisfying ache in my forearms and hands which climbers refer to as "being pumped."

Before long my forearms were burning with lactic acid, and I decided that I was done for the night. And boy was I right. I was done for the night, and for the months that would follow.

Without sparing a thought, I simply turned my body and jumped from the wall and onto the landing mat, just as I had done hundreds of times before. Usually I would land on my feet, sometimes overbalancing to end up sitting, often with a white puff of chalk from the little bag attached to the back of my harness. I had done this as a kid many times before, usually from the top of the wardrobe, landing heroically on my bed before slinking my way to my brother's bed across the room and then out of the door, avoiding the treacherous river of lava that engulfed the floor of my room / secret cave.

But this time was different. I distinctly remember looking down at the mat as my hands left the holds on the wall; a wave of dread flooded my mind within the fraction of a second as the ground rushed up towards me. Below, like the jagged grin of a shark's smile, was a tear in the nylon cover that was meant to hold the mat together. Through the tear I could see the separate foam blocks that fitted together within the cover ... and I was headed directly for the slim gap between them.

The minutes and hours that followed after that fateful jump reside in my memory as flashes, staccato segments of time, separated by nauseating panic, despair and sheer agony.

I made contact with the mat, toes first. I felt my heels hit the mat too, but my toes continued downward and forced their way between the two yellowing grimy sponge blocks that were supposed to absorb my fall, not part around them like the Red Sea. My whole body jolted to a sudden ugly stop in an exaggerated foetal position, my torso hunched over my legs, my feet pointed like a ballerina. On impact the force contorted both of my feet inward, twisting them to face each other. I heard a crunch. Like a fresh mouthful of popcorn, the joints in my ankles gave way to the full weight of my body, dislocating both joints, fracturing several bones and rupturing every tendon from my shins down.

Fuck.

"Fuck" was honestly my reflex reaction. I knew this was serious and knew something was broken because I heard it break.

CHAPTER 3

WELCOME TO HADES

I open my eyes to a wave of panicked claustrophobia. My chin is on my chest, my back is hunched over and my knees feel as if they are right up against my ears. A crash course in the butterfly position from some high-impact yoga class.

The need to exhale makes me feel like my eyes are going to burst out of their sockets, so I throw myself onto my back, force the air from my chest and then refill my lungs. In doing so, I manage to free both of my feet from the flaw in the crash pad. In a moment of coherent logic before my brain gets wind of the shit-storm that is about to erupt below my knees, I realise that I need to get onto my back, get my feet in the air and tear my climbing shoes off.

Then, the pain. It is a surge of all-consuming agony.

I do think that there is a limit to which the human brain is capable of perceiving pain. A ceiling which exists, possibly as a self-preservation instinct, like a kill switch or surge protector to stop us from the sensory overload of trauma. Later I learn that Michael Masson, one of the crazier ones I worked with at Grey and who was there standing near the mat as I crash landed, looked at me lying on the mat like a dying cockroach and told me nonchalantly to "walk it off", but my contorted face indicated the severity of the situation and put an end to the joke. After that, the evening took a U-turn. To this day I still have no recollection of him saying anything to me, let alone making a wise crack.

Warren and the others throw their belongings into kit bags and I am picked up. Sitting on the arms of Warren and Michael in a fireman's chair rescue carry, I am taken across the gymnasium floor, up a flight of stairs, out of the glass doors of the building's main entrance, along the paved corridor that runs alongside the building, down another flight of concrete stairs and into the street where our cars are parked. The pain surges with the jerk of every step they take and my stomach turns at the thought of smacking one of my gangly limbs on a handrail or a door frame.

And then I am lying on the back seat of my car. The seats still smell strongly of the showroom. I close my eyes in an attempt to escape this nightmare, but with every nick in the road surface I am brought right back. Unable to navigate where we are, I realise we have made our way from the university to the Empire Road off-ramp and onto the M2 highway. We are going fast. Warren says he likes my new car and is surprised that it can go so fast despite its tiny 1400 French engine.

Now Warren's on the phone with my mom. 'One might be broken, the other I think is just sprained.' He's lying. He knows he's lying. My mom knows he's lying. And so do I.

It's an unwritten law when describing a fellow climber's injuries and predicaments to loved ones; euphemism is the name of the game until they are close enough to gauge the situation without the distortion of panic and imagination. My mom realises the severity of the situation. She arrives within twenty minutes of Warren's phone call at the Life Roseacres Hospital with a kitbag containing a toothbrush, a change of underwear, spare clothing and basic toiletries. My mother is a mother of three boys. Those who know all three of us often suggest she deserves a medal, possibly sainthood. For many years the standing joke was that my mom's car was capable of finding the hospital's parking on autopilot and there was a reserved bay near the emergency ward with her name on it. We'd been there for stitches, x-rays, plaster casts, tetanus injections, and more plaster casts. The nurses at the ER reception desks are among the handful of people who can pronounce our Eastern European surname, purely through exposure to it.

The car screeches to a halt under the fluorescent lights of the ER ambulance bay. I sit up and Warren opens the back door for me. Someone arrives with a wheelchair. I don't know who it is. I'm wondering how the hell I am going to get into the chair. I'm conflicted. I need to get into the hospital but there is a feeling of hopelessness as every thought of moving is too painful to think about, so nothing happens.

Arms. Legs. Some mine, others not. Somehow, I am now sitting in the chair and the cold chrome frame feels acidic against my skin as my nervous system enters the extreme phases of shock. In the emergency ward, the coldness of the monochrome corridors seems to stretch off into the distance in every direction. Fluorescent lights scorch my eyes.

Still cold. Forms. People. Nurses.

Finally, I am wheeled into the x-ray room. I feel a sense of relief in this dimly lit radiation chamber. I am being shifted around with my legs up at eye level on the table. The rest of me slumped in the wheelchair, useless, like tits on a bull. The radiologist is being polite and sympathetic, but I want to punch him in the face every time he turns my twisted feet to take the next shot. 'Okay, hold it there.' Every time I think it's over he returns again from the hole In the wall with another blackboard, ready to take yet another exposure.

Someone please kill me.

Back in the emergency room, I lose track of who is and who isn't there. Four of us went to the gym and then I fell. Did we all come through to the hospital?

I see Warren. Mikey (Michael Masson) has changed his tune and is trying to comfort me and reassure me, convincing absolutely nobody. The doctor on call emerges from nowhere, and without saying much, holds one of my x-rays to the light before sliding all of them onto the light box across the room. His BIC pen points out the various breaks in my twisted ankles. I am still sitting in the wheelchair, resting my elbows on the armrests and holding my legs under my knees to keep my feet in mid-air in a position that is least painful. The thought of putting my feet on the footrests turns my stomach. It always will.

The doctor is pretty calm. He explains it's pretty straightforward. 'This happens all the time. Most ankles are broken only one inch from the *ground,' he says, explaining how a simple twist in the wrong direction can cause a break. 'A bad stroke of luck, but no need for too much concern. Surgery tomorrow.' And with a forced smile he disappears from the examination room, leaving the nursing staff to take care of the details.*

At some point, everyone leaves the hospital. I'm in a hospital bed, both of my legs in bandages up to my knees, resembling off-white tree stumps. My toes protrude out from the dressings, bright red from the dyed leather of my climbing shoes. The doctor has put me in slabs, plaster of Paris bandages layered from the backs of my knees, down my legs and under my feet. They harden into custom-fitted splints to keep things in place until I go under the knife tomorrow.

In the darkness of the hospital sits my mother, resting her elbow on my bed with head in her hand. We speak for a while, the usual jokes about another visit to the ER, the usual awkward mixture of apologetic appreciation and euphemism as we both try to downplay the situation. As the drugs they pumped into me start to take effect, the anxiety slowly ebbs away from me. But the knot in my stomach tightens like a vice caused by the dull roar radiating from the lower half of my body. My mom leaves, promising to return in the morning. I am alone. Just me and the insurmountable feeling of dread. I have no idea what this means or what the future holds, but all signs are pointing to a complete fuck up.

On the TV there's an advert playing for Telkom, South Africa's telecoms provider. The soundtrack features a woman singing 'I just know your life's gonna change ...' That woman's voice repeats through my head again and again as I drift in and out of a shallow sleep.

I had no idea to what extent my life was about to change or be turned upside down, but change it did.

Welcome to Hades. Leave your life as you knew it at the door.

CHAPTER 4

REQUIEM FOR A DREAMER

That night was arduous and I got very little sleep. I jolted awake with every movement, which shot needles of pain up my legs. The delusional old man wailing down the hall in search of his late wife didn't help much with soothing my anxiety. He had escaped from his bed and staggered up the corridor outside my room, his pain and anguish all too real. As he sobbed, heartbroken, the noise cut through my pethidine haze and I woke up in fright, feeling disorientated and in a lot of pain. My confusion soon turned into aggression towards the geriatric who had brought me back to consciousness and this new, horizontal world. Eventually two nurses arrived to console him and escort him back to his bed.

Once things returned to normal, I lay awake for a while sobbing – not because of the pain, but out of apprehension and fear of the future that lay ahead of me. It wasn't the future I had asked for.

So many questions raced laps around my mind. *How bad are the breaks? How long will it take to recover? Will I recover? What about climbing? What about work? I have a troop meeting to run on Thursday night and those scouts need me to be there. How will I be able to run the scout troop? If I can't work, how am I going to pay for the Renault?*

My entire life was now literally balancing on a razor-sharp knife edge.

At some point I called the nurse and asked for another injection to ease the pain. Finally, I sank into the bed and slept for a couple of hours.

My mother arrived later that morning and spent the entire day at the hospital. We waited patiently as the other patients in the ward were wheeled off and returned like ships in a harbour, each vessel returning with a cargo of fresh bandages, blood streaked tubes, drains and drip stands. My mother and I would speculate the cause of each person's injury judging by their dressings and general appearance, and guesses ranged from falling off a ladder to motorcycle accidents. Eventually it was my turn for surgery and I too was wheeled down the passage leading to the operating theatre, my head thick with painkillers and the Dormacum that I was given to calm and prepare me for my little nap.

My surgery only happened late that afternoon. The attending surgeon put me at the bottom of the day's schedule, not knowing how long my procedure would take.

My impatience quickly turned to fear as the orderly wheeled me away. My heart was thundering in my throat; I felt like a toddler on the first day of nursery school. It was an unwelcome taste of not being in control and I didn't like it. Roof panels and fluorescent lights slid in and out of my view, making me nauseous and disorientated as we sailed headfirst into the operating theatre.

Several staff grabbed the sheet I was lying on and hoisted me onto an icy cold table. There were four or five people busy with trays of what resembled barbeque tongs and an array of cutlery. The anaesthetist appeared next to me from nowhere and placed a plastic mask over my nose and mouth. That sour smell of nitrous oxide was there at each surgery that was to follow. A nurse strapped my arm out to the side, just like on every death row movie I'd ever seen. It was only then that a concentrated fear washed over me as I realised that I was about to resign myself completely to these faceless henchmen who would have free rein over my body.

I looked across at the line leading to the drip in my hand and watched the milky white liquid descend down the tube. The anaesthetist told me to count from one to ten, and I felt surprised that it wasn't the other way around. In every reference to anaesthetics and surgery I knew, the doctor always instructed patients to count backwards from ten.

I began my reverse countdown. One ... two ...

CHAPTER 5

UNDER THE KNIFE

It was a massive effort to open my eyes to a blurry new world, after what felt like a blink in time but was actually a couple of hours. I was covered in fresh bandages from my knees down. My feet didn't even look like feet any more; they were more like logs. A stranger's legs in a stranger's life.

While I took leave of my body, the surgeon opened my ankles and placed two screws in both my right and left inner ankles (bilateral medial malleolus fractures) attaching the broken segments of bone together, and a plate with five screws on the outer ankle of my left foot (lateral malleolus fracture) to secure the end of the fibula back to the main body of the bone. The site was then closed up with thirty-two steel staples.

Megan was working her community service year in Pretoria, about fifty kilometres from Johannesburg, where she stayed in a flat during the week. That evening was her graduation and I would inevitably miss it, for which I felt incredibly sorry. At some point during my surgery, her mother phoned my mother to say that she would fetch me later that day and drive me to the graduation ceremony. The quixotic notion of me spending hours in a crowded auditorium shortly after surgery was nothing short of impossible.

In their defence, they had completely underestimated the extent of my injuries. And so had I.

The two days after my surgery were spent flat on my back in my hospital bed. My feet were wrapped in thick crepe bandages, making it impossible to imagine what awaited me under the dressings. It would be ten days before I would get a glimpse of the crash scene. It was only at my first check-up after surgery that I was able to see what had become of my feet. For the first time did the true severity of the injury show itself. Until then, my only reference to the injury was how it felt and what I could, or could not make out from the x-rays.

For the first time I could see "a real injury" as the surgeon peeled back the blood-encrusted cotton wool encasing both my feet. I was stunned and disgusted by the amount of blood that seeped into the dressing. Across the skin covering each of my three incisions were steel-legged centipedes the length of my hand. The blueish-black bruising appeared in blotches around the base of my heels and between my toes and had begun creeping up the back of my calves – eventually turning them a mottle of green, yellow and purple. My toes had become so swollen that they reminded me of the scene from the movie *Patch Adams*, where he blows up a rubber glove to make farm animals for the kids in a hospital ward.

I was wearing faded green cargo pants that day, as winter had arrived and those were the only pants I could manipulate over the casts. I was also wearing a navy-blue T-shirt I had designed for the outdoor clothing manufacturer, First Ascent, years before. Across the chest was a photo of the north face of Everest, with white lettering that read, 'This subscriber is not available at present.'

I was a still a climber at heart – merely warming the bench for a while, but a climber nonetheless. For the time being, at least.

Staying with my mom in her first-floor townhouse proved to be a nightmare. The wheelchair from the hospital was a steel behemoth that barely fitted in the back of my mother's tiny Renault Clio and the cumbersome journey up the stairs left me feeling incredibly guilty and worthless as my mother manhandled the chair whenever needed. When I first arrived home from the hospital, our neighbour's son happened to be there. Johan is a six-foot-plenty sumo wrestler with national colours, capable of head-butting cows into corned beef tins. Before I knew it I was hoisted over his shoulder like a sack of potatoes and carried up the flight of stairs and into the house, where he planted me onto the couch. I would stay there for the remainder of the day. The humungous hero then turned and waved goodbye and disappeared. Outside the door I could hear my mom talking to the various neighbours from the townhouses in the complex. The novelty of my accident was still new and their conversation was light and funny.

'Kids will be kids,' said one person.

'You can't keep them in cotton wool,' replied another.

Whenever my mom packed my wheelchair into the back of her car, I would sit on the top step and move each foot to the step below before lifting myself on my hands and lowering myself onto the next step down. There are fifteen steps from the front door to the car park. I remember them all.

Foot. Foot, bum, foot, foot, bum ...

The house was tricky to navigate as a new wheelchair user and there were equal amounts of knuckle skin and plaster lost as I learnt to negotiate the corners between the lounge, bedroom and tiny bathroom. The bathroom was too narrow to get into, so visits were kept to a minimum and I used a pee bottle most of the time. My upper body strength improved fast as I learnt to hoist myself out of the chair and into the bath. You learn a lot of things fast.

My first sponge bath since the age of four was a lesson in patience and humility. I managed to get myself into the bath while keeping my feet up above the water line. The exit manoeuvre was not as successful. I lifted myself using my forearms against the side of the bath and noticed a sharp stinging pain just under my elbow. I lifted my arm to discover a Gillette Mach 3 razor and three matching slices in my arm, causing blood to trickle down and turn the bath water orange. The first aid kit was always close by.

After about two weeks of suffering with the Ford Bel Air of wheelchairs, a family friend phoned and offered to sell me a chair that had belonged to their late father. It was aluminium and going at a fraction of the actual cost, so my mom and I flew over there as fast as we could (which was not as fast as you'd imagine).

Foot. Foot, bum, foot, foot, bum ... The new chair was half the weight of the rental and before long I had stripped off the arm rests, narrowed the axle width and replaced the foot rests with a piece of climbing cord, effectively reducing the overall weight and length dramatically. The "new" chair was royal blue and had the word "Racer" screen-printed on the back of the nylon backrest. It was only a matter of hours before I had learnt to ride on the back wheels, rocking gently as I balanced with my giant plastic feet in the air. I actually became really good at it and used to challenge myself to get from one room of the townhouse to the next without touching down. It wasn't without the odd accident and I occasionally found I had over-balanced and found myself flat on my back. Sometimes I'd laugh and wrangle my way back into the seat, other times I would just lie there like a tortoise on its shell.

And sometimes, on hard days, I would just lie there, curse my life and cry.

I have suffered with depression and occasional anxiety for most of my life. I was officially diagnosed after high school and I have been on medication for the majority of the time since. It is something I have come to terms with and with medication it is a manageable condition. I used to hide the fact that I suffered from depression, to the extent that I spent the better part of a year hiding my medication from my girlfriend at the time, taking it each day on the sly, because apparently, I didn't need it. According to her, depression was all in my head, and the argument it caused made it easier for me to sneak my daily tablets like an alcoholic raiding their secret stash.

I used to hate the fact that I needed the medication to be "normal", like there is something missing or wrong with me. I have since realised that there is something wrong with me, but it is one of a million ailments that affect people everywhere. I can rationalise it and say that if I had a dysfunctional heart, I'd take medication for that too. I have abandoned the shame and stigma around depression. It is what it is.

As the novelty and usual jokes surrounding my accident wore thin, so did my tolerance for the situation I had been cast into and the bum hand I had been dealt. *This was not the life I had in mind*. My dreams of seeing the world from mountaintops were no longer within my reach, just like the items on the top two shelves in the fridge.

Robby "That Guy Who Climbs Mountains" had become Robby "That Guy in the Wheelchair".

Guess which name I preferred.

The days alone at home became longer. I'd wait for my mother to get home after work the same way a dog awaits its owner – minus the jumping on couches and scratching at the door. Visits from my fiancée, Megan, were mostly on weekends. The periods of time in between were spent watching television and working on a few art projects I took on in an attempt to lift my mood and distract me from the queue of Groundhog days that had become my life. One such project that comes to mind was a portrait of a Zanzibari woman I had photographed a few years before in my more adventurous days. She was walking in a line of women through the village of Nungwe at the northern tip of the island. I replicated the portrait on a piece of board that measured a metre and a half in height and almost as wide. I created the picture by tearing and sticking thousands of coloured pieces of paper from magazines, each piece no bigger than a fingernail. Why the hell not? All it cost me was time, of which I had oodles.

The occasional visit from friends and family buoyed my spirits, but I spent most of my time with my feet in the air while I perfected the concave in my mother's couch cushions. I tried to muster some freelance design or copywriting work that I could do from home, but there were more bills than there was money coming in. Keep in mind that this all happened in the days of dial-up before the notion of working from anywhere other than the office was conceived. My mother lent me money as far and as often as she could, and between the personal loans and stealing from Peter to pay Paul I was running out of options.

This was far from ideal considering that there was a wedding planned for February and one of the names on the cake was mine.

After the initial surgery I was instructed to avoid placing any weight on my ankles. This meant that wherever possible, both my feet were elevated or at worst resting on the footrests of my wheelchair. After eight weeks I was allowed to start bearing weight for short periods of time using crutches. This proved to be easier said than done and when the time came, any efforts at rehabilitation were incredibly painful. Something just felt wrong in my gut. Eventually after several weeks and very little progress, the doctors decided that they would operate again to remove the metal plate and nine screws from the original repair, in hopes that they were the cause of my pain and inability to recover, which now in hindsight makes very little logical sense.

Weeks went by and I was still suffering considerably. Eventually doctors took the decision to perform a three-dimensional scan of both my ankle joints. The R6,500 price tag was thankfully covered by medical insurance and the scan revealed further damage that had not been detected in the first two procedures. In addition to the tibia and fibula bones, the talus bones in both ankles were broken and showed signs of deterioration. Because the initial x-rays were typical of a routine ankle fracture, there was no indication of the breaks in the talus bones. My injury was treated like the other ankle fractures that limp their way into the emergency room on a weekly basis, so the other fractures went undiscovered at first, hence the inexplicable pain and inability to rehabilitate months after the accident.

A third surgery was scheduled and from all accounts it was going to be a major undertaking. On both my left and right feet, the surgeon would have to saw off a part of my tibial malleolus (the bone that sticks out on your inner ankle) and separate my foot from my tibia and fibula to be able to access and repair my talus bone. Once that was done, they could screw the sawn-off piece back into place. The separation of foot from leg required a bespoke clamp for which they would drill holes into my heel bones and shins to anchor each arm before opening the clamp which would create a gap big enough to access the affected bones. The procedure included applying a paste containing human bone tissue, which essentially was a bone graft using a putty knife and trowel.

Among the other forms and waivers I signed that morning was a declaration to accept human tissue – quite an unsettling thing to do just hours before going under.

On the day of the operation I landed up waiting several hours in my ward because the necessary clamp had not been delivered to the hospital yet. I felt like the owner of a French car, stranded and immobile, waiting for the necessary spare parts to get to my mechanic. During my wait I had an opportunity to ask the anaesthetist to take photographs of the procedure, a morbid curiosity which was quelled very quickly when I eventually saw the snapshots from the operating table. It was more a case of being frightened than being disgusted at the blood and tendons, stretched open with cold, chrome claws. It was surprisingly unnerving to see that far into my own body and once again I was reminded of how vulnerable being operated on, while defenceless and unconscious, made me. They would cut me open, fiddle around, turn, twist and tweeze me, staple me up when they were done and leave me helpless and in agony … and all with my permission.

Those gruesome pictures of my exposed joints, gaping under the steel clamps, will not be included in the appendix.

CHAPTER 6

A BITTER PILL

Approximately eight months after my accident, I was still wheelchair-bound in two plastic "moon-boot" air casts and unable to bear weight on either foot. The ever-mounting anxiety about my financial situation and the impending wedding was causing me to unravel. I was sleeping less and less, passing the hours in cold sweats and panic.

Eventually it was time to face the inevitable and I called my fiancée. I remember the date well. It was 3rd November 2006, exactly three years since we started dating. My intention was to invite her to my mother's home and we would order pizzas (the only thing that wouldn't exceed my credit card limit) and I asked if her parents would join us to discuss the growing concerns about my dire financial status and how it affected the wedding happening in February, just three months away.

I will never be able to fully recollect the details of that evening or the argument that ensued. But I will say that I am sorry for what happened that night. Things were said, lines were crossed and people were hurt. The blame and consequence of what transpired will be carried by all involved, and I regret that it happened. What was said, or who said it, is of no relevance now, but what I intended to be a constructive formulation of a back-up plan to accommodate my predicament turned into a screaming match between our two families. In the midst of that heated argument, I distinctly remember zoning out and thinking that this was not what was supposed to be happening. It was almost like an out-of-body experience, like I was watching from the sidelines.

And then something happened. Something I am not entirely clear on.

Before I knew it, all three of them were leaving. It was over, and any bridges that could have been burnt were a blazing inferno. In my eyes the relationship had been damaged beyond repair, the wedding was not going to happen and all that remained was for me to settle my share of what had already been paid for.

After they left I sat in the lounge, where just an hour ago there was a chaos of words and tears, my mother trying to console me and help me try to find an iota of sense in what had just gone down. Along with my sense of comfort, dignity and self-worth, my faith in a God had dwindled. I wrestled with the depression that came with a life I had not chosen, blurred through the lens of constant pain medication.

I lifted my head, my eyes swollen and blurred. 'Where was your God tonight, Mom?' I demanded, sounding more hopeless than angry – my words felt as if they were coming from the back of my nose.

'I think He was right next to you, my boy.' My mother's words offered me some comfort and consolation, which sadly was short-lived. We sat speaking until after midnight, in a home that now felt starker and more desolate than ever. The white tiles, walls and ceiling echoed the hollow feeling that flooded my being.

My mother eventually went to bed after completing the usual routine of checking that I had an empty pee bottle for the night, enough pain killers and anything else I might have needed. Before leaving for bed she hugged me once more and told me to try to get some rest. I watched her as she left the lounge and turned the corner into her bedroom. My gaze then strayed to the empty couch beside me, the incompressible screaming still ringing in my ears, before moving over to the glass coffee table. On the table was the remote for the TV and a white plastic container, with navy-blue lettering partially covered by the pharmacy sticker.

I don't remember what was on the TV that night, only how my head throbbed and how hard it was to cry in silence. Any attempt to sleep would prove to be futile, my head was still swimming with thoughts about the catastrophe that had just torn through my life and the frustration of not being able to remember large portions of the argument. I think my inability to recall what had happened was largely due to the potent mixture of emotions – extreme distress, anger, disbelief, and dread, all chased down with a healthy shot of adrenaline, must have sent my brain into overdrive. And I don't suppose the painkillers I had chugged down two hours before aided the situation either.

November 3rd was supposed to be a date to be celebrated, but it had become something completely different.

In the weeks leading up to that night I had entered a downward spiral. The future I envisaged had been destroyed and with it my sense of hope, my belief in making a recovery and my overall state of mind had begun to deteriorate. Depression, frustration, self-hatred and a fear of never recovering had taken hold, to the point where I began entertaining the thought of taking my own life. I was tired by the constant battle of everyday life being difficult and painful. My existence was a burden to those who loved and cared for me and my never-ending reliance on others weighed heavily on me. The distant hope of recovery was fading to a point where I felt I didn't want to heal. I wanted it to be over. It was time to admit to the fact that I had reached rock bottom. I could sink no lower.

A little after 1 am I sat silent in my wheelchair; the only noise was from the periodic trains coming and going from the station across the road. *This is it*. No money, no relationship, no wedding. I had nothing more for life to take. Once more my eyes drifted to the container of Synap Forte tablets.

Our human survival instinct forces us to do everything within our power to make it to the next day. Being suicidal is a state of mind which has the ability to override the instinct that protects us from harm and replaces it with the relief and promise of not having to face another day. It defies all rationality and logic and goes against the grain of every notion of self-preservation or healing.

So there I sat. I had resigned myself to the idea that I wasn't ever going to heal. I didn't want to. The idea of recovering fully was now a far-off dream.

That night in my wheelchair I struck a deal with myself, a deal that would make my decision as clear as black or white, with no room for negotiation or backing out. A deal is a deal.

Synap Forte was a morphine-based drug used to manage high levels of pain and has since been removed from shelves because of its addictive properties. The blue and white adhesive label read "Two tablets every four hours for pain." I was gulping three or four at once, four times a day on difficult days.

If there are more than seventy tablets in this bottle, I will take them all, I thought. That was the deal. I knew about thirty-five tablets would be enough to kill me. From what I had researched on the internet, a dose that size could be lethal. It was enough to repress my breathing and slow my heart down enough to put me in a coma. Thereafter, my kidneys would shut down and it would be done. And so I chose double that amount to make absolutely sure that I would do the job properly.

The only rational thought I could muster was that any fewer number of tablets might not do the job and I didn't want to leave a vegetable on a life support machine for my mother to live with. I was not prepared to burden her with the decision and doubt of turning off the machines. This was not for her to carry. That, and the fact that South African health insurance will not pay for failed suicide attempts. Fucking this up would have far reaching costs and consequences and I did not have it in me to risk inflicting that on the ones left to clean up my mess.

Now, don't think for a second that this was an act of irrational stupidity. In the days that preceded this moment I had wrestled with the impending consequences of my mounting debt and failure, lying awake in cold sweats, night after night, each one more intense than the last. Every day that crept past was thrusting me closer to being married but also to being crippled financially, physically and emotionally. The thought of starting a marriage as a stone around my now ex-fiancée's neck, unable to provide, was literally killing me. Nobody knew to what extent I was in debt, having not earned anything close to my expenses in seven months and after having bought a new car just weeks before my accident. This was not a decision made in the heat of the moment. These things seldom are.

For a long time now I had wanted the world to stop so that I could climb off.

CHAPTER 7

WHAT NOW?

The tablets fall easily into the palm of my hand, filling it quickly and coating it in a fine white powder. As I breathe in, some of the powder enters my nostrils, leaving a bitter but comforting taste in the back of my dry mouth. I start to count.

One, two, three ...

Fifty-three, fifty-four, fifty-five, fifty-six ...

Fifty-seven.

The bottle is empty and there are only fifty-seven tablets on the table in front of me.

Fuck.

What now?

I feel angry. Life is mocking me by robbing me of the last morsel of control I am trying to assert upon my life.

I can't hang myself. As a climber and Springbok Scout, I know every knot under the sun including the hangman's noose – all thirteen coils of it. But I've given my climbing ropes to my friends who were actually able to use them. I can't jump in the car and buy more tablets at the pharmacy and I remember once being told that you cannot drink enough bleach to poison yourself fatally before your body's natural reaction causes vomiting, leaving you in a lot of pain and probably with a colostomy bag for the rest of your life. And I don't have access to a gun or a razor blade.

I hate the life I am stuck in, but even more so I hate the fact that I am powerless to change it or even put an end to it. It really couldn't get any worse.

Imagine the realisation that you are such a failure that you can't even kill yourself.

I sit staring at nothing for who knows how long before I feel a string of drool drop down my chin, leaving a wet circle on my t-shirt and jerking me back to reality. I wipe the spittle from my mouth and onto the leg of my shorts. Using my dry hand, I sweep all the little round pills back into their container and brush the last powdery evidence away so as not to leave a trace of how pathetic I am. I then wheel my chair to the edge of the couch, lock the brake and slink onto the couch and into a depression I have been perfecting since April. With my left hand I reach up and slap the light switch off.

I am lying here alone. Just me and this life I haven't asked for and have no power to escape from.

CHAPTER 8

THIS

I awoke to the brightness of the morning sunshine streaming into the lounge. I was immediately sucked back into a continuation of the previous night's nightmare. Scenes from the fight were still fresh in my head, forcing the realisation that this was indeed my reality. What was done could not be undone.

Nobody, including my mother, was aware of what had happened in the early hours of that morning, after everything had turned to shit. It was only when I started including the story in my presentations that people become aware of what had almost gone down that evening. Some people who were very close to me at the time will only learn about this if they ever read this book.

I cannot call it a suicide attempt because it was more of a turning point. An attempt would have involved me swallowing the tablets. That night was the catalyst which forced me to begin to create a new way forward. This path was not headed anywhere good.

Over the days and weeks that followed I would come to terms with my lack of choices and found myself facing another pivotal decision in my life. How was I going to handle *this*? This was not where I chose to be. This was painful and tiresome. *This* was a place governed by anger and self-pity. *This* was not a way to live. *This* was a way to die. And *this* needed to change.

I needed a new mantra. Over time I had told myself so often that I didn't want to heal that I had started to believe it, and our beliefs have the ability to shape who we are. In the weeks that followed I was taught several hard lessons which enabled me to start changing what *this* meant. I was surrounded by people who never once considered not loving me or believing in me, even when I had stopped – and in doing so had taught me that maybe this wasn't going to change any time soon, but the way I decided to tackle it could.

A few days after the fight happened, my mom contacted my brother Mark who lived in Durban North, approximately 600 km from our home on the East Rand of Johannesburg. He and his wife had relocated there a few years previously and my mom suggested I go and spend a week or two with them for "a change of scenery". Their home was on the ground floor so I could wheel myself out into the garden, enjoy some company during the day and just take a break from the white walls I had been confined to for what was starting to feel like an eternity. It was a welcome change for me and I appreciated the fresh coastal air as well as the distance from the memories of the last few days. I was also glad to be able to give my mom a bit of a break from nursing duty, but she would never have seen it as that. My mother is a caregiver by nature, deriving a lot of fulfilment and self-worth from everything she did for me, disguised and downplayed as motherly love. I am grateful for her undying commitment to my wellbeing and shall be until the day I die.

The process of flying to Durban took as long, if not longer, than it does to drive there by car. I was checked in as an assisted passenger and I was transferred to an airport chair while my "wheels" where checked in with my luggage. Assisted passengers are the last passengers to be loaded onto the plane and also the last to leave, and only once the last passenger has left does the vehicle equipped with a hydraulic lift arrive so you can be wheeled directly from the plane into the back of the truck which takes you to the terminal building. During the time it took for the truck to arrive, I managed to convince the air hostess to give me the seat belt used to demonstrate the safety drill. A little charm and two broken ankles go a long way in convincing someone to break the law. I wore that nylon belt complete with its massive aluminium buckle in my jeans for years afterwards.

Despite the massive effort to get there, the time in Durban was really good for me. With my brother and his wife's involvement in the church, their house and social calendars were always full. It was so good for me to be around new people and places that didn't remind me in the slightest of the life I had left behind. I slept on a sleeper couch downstairs in my brother's lounge and had one shelf in the bathroom for my belongings, but it was a change, which is as good as a holiday, a holiday from a broken life and a broken heart.

I had started using crutches occasionally for a few minutes a day which, despite being incredibly painful, did a lot for my spirits and motivation to recover.

One morning I went onto the internet and downloaded a photo of Mount Everest taken from the Tibetan side, high and intimidating, its slopes covered in ice and snow. I opened the cupboard door and stuck the printed photo on the door at what most people would describe as waist height. For me the page was at eye level. In a wheelchair I wasn't much more than a metre in height, so the picture was in the perfect position for me to see every day. The photo became an encouragement to get up each morning, brush my teeth and put on clean clothes. It was a reason to endure the physiotherapy and a reminder that each day was one closer to the life I wanted for myself, the life I believed was possible before all of *this* had happened.

In those first few weeks in Durban I replied to an advert for a Creative Director position in a small "well-established" Durban-based advertising agency. The interview took place on a Friday afternoon quite close to Christmas. I met the two owners and they explained the scope of work and that I would head up a team of sixteen creative designers for a range of clients namely Suncoast Casino, a pizza franchise, and the Natal Sharks Rugby team. Despite the company being closed and the rest of the staff being on leave, the place looked great and I took the job on the spot.

I returned to Johannesburg just after Christmas to pack up my life. I placed my past into boxes, sealing up the hurt and bad memories, ignorantly believing that I could move away from everything that had happened. In the first week of January I was able to make the drive to Durban on my own. On the day I left, I said an emotional goodbye to my mother before she left for work. I gathered my last few belongings and wrote her a note to thank her for everything she had been and done for me. In the last few sentences I started to fall apart, my hand smudging the ink as the flood of bitter tears splashed onto the page. Leaving my mother was incredibly hard and several of my rest stops along the way to my new home were not just to stretch my legs but more to sit and sob in fits of guilt and self-doubt. The thought of how empty her house would be now was wracking me with an indescribable pain. She could have her home back with all of her furniture returned to its normal position. No chunks of plaster missing from my bad driving, no more tyre marks or scrapes on the walls. Just her and Petzl, my adopted sausage dog remained in an otherwise empty home. Given the choice, I know she would have taken the damaged plaster and paint over the emptiness a hundred times over.

But it was the new start I needed at the time, a way to leave the pain and sadness behind me and feel the sun on my face for the first time in way too long.

My answer to that question "How am I going to handle *this*?" had changed.

This was now a challenge. *This* is what I was now working towards. This is what I needed to go through. *This* wasn't going to be easy.

This is going to be worth it.

CHAPTER 9

OGILVY

Relocation to my new life was happening. I settled into my new room in my brother's house. It was upstairs and I could now manage to access it, an achievement in itself. My new roommate was great. His taste in decor was a little immature but it was home for now. It was just a mattress on the floor of my six-month-old nephew Will's nursery, but it felt right. At night I would sneak in and slither into bed like a ninja so as to not disturb him, and each morning I woke up to him standing at the edge of his cot gurgling and singing to me while Mozart played from the mobile that hung above his little bed.

My career path, however, was not as amicable as my living arrangement and I realised within a few days that I had been duped. The idyllic agency I had been appointed to lead turned out to be three or four staff under the tyrannical control of the owner and his partner. Before long I learnt that this sweatshop had a reputation for its shocking working conditions, dishonesty and turning over staff the way you flip steaks on a hot grill.

Once again I was wrestling with the self-doubt of having made another mistake. I had uprooted my life in hope of finding a clean slate and now I was dreading each morning, surfing a constant wave of anxiety and having my self-confidence blatantly trampled on. But something good did come from working there. By the time I handed in my resignation just fourteen working days later, I had formed several new friendships with people with whom I shared the common interest – hating that shit pit. As I moved companies, I met several more people, all of whom turned their noses up in joint distaste for the agency I had just come from. There was even a Facebook group consisting of all the "survivors" of said shit pit, one of whom was also the agency owner's half-brother.

Before leaving I managed to have a conversation with Martine, the incredibly talented and exceptionally bubbly DTP operator who also did the job of coordinating the studio workload. I told her that she was not condemned to stay in that place where she was being completely taken advantage of and ill-treated. I encouraged her to look around and find something more rewarding where she could use her people skills and not feel like a beaten dog every day.

I left that company for a position as a senior copywriter in another agency which would also only last about six months. Fitting in was proving difficult and I struggled to find a sense of belonging there. My habit of keeping people at arm's length had already begun. I would sit in the open-plan office and listen to the people around me discussing the many parties and exactly "how big" they had gone or their excitement for the next night out on the horizon. Part of me sat waiting, half expecting someone to invite me to join them, and the other part of me was already formulating an excuse in case I ever was asked.

One morning I received a phone call from Martine, who told me there was a position at the agency she had moved to. They were looking for a senior copywriter and she arranged for me to meet the Creative Director that Friday afternoon.

After one of the most interesting interviews of my career, involving downing a beer, a shot of tequila and several advances from my soon-to-be-boss, he eventually said to me 'You're not my type, I wouldn't fuck you. But you've got the job if you want it.'

And that is how I found myself at Ogilvy Durban.

CHAPTER 10

A SEED IS PLANTED

During the time I spent in Durban, my friends John Black and Gilad Stern had begun researching various operators with the intention of joining a commercial expedition to climb Mount Everest.

John, my closest friend, had been living in Cape Town for several years, having followed his career there. He was introduced to Gilad by a mutual friend and through their common interest in climbing, they had become good friends. Gilad and I became friends on an unsuccessful expedition to climb Aconcagua, the highest peak on the South American continent, in 2002.

After investigating several international expedition operators, the two of them had settled on Himex (Himalayan Experience), a reputable guiding company run by Russell Brice, an experienced and lauded Everest veteran from New Zealand. It was Brice's regard for safety and his flawless record of never having lost a client on the world's highest peak – a feat not many operators can claim – that convinced them. The decision to go with a Himex expedition is not based on price. The cost of joining any international team to climb an 8,000 m peak is expensive, with price tags dangling in the tens of thousands of American Dollars. This particular package was going to put anyone wishing to attempt Mount Everest that year out of pocket to the tune of $48,000. This fee excluded flights to and from Kathmandu, any climbing equipment or clothing, any expenses of a personal nature or travel insurance. Add in the loss of income for the duration of the seventy-four-day trip and the total sum added up to close to $60 000.

As a South African earning Rands, this amount of money was absolutely unfathomable to me and pretty much everyone I know, especially when you consider that it was the equivalent of a three-bedroomed house or a luxury car at the time, for a climbing holiday with zero guarantee of success and a one in ten chance of losing digits to frostbite or worse, death. In 2008, it would have taken me five years to save that amount, provided I lived under a bridge and didn't spend a single cent ... ever.

As I am writing this passage, it becomes even more evident how ridiculous it sounded when put down on paper. It is no wonder I received the responses I did when explaining my expedition to people at keynote presentations or strangers I met at social gatherings, reactions ranging from shock to surprise or even of utter disgust.

Three years prior to this, as my passion for high-altitude mountaineering began to grow, I had found myself scouring climbing magazines, tearing up endless pages from sketch books in an effort to find or create a design of a mountain for a tattoo I so badly wanted. I eventually did happen upon an advert in one tattered magazine and I started the process to refine the design before it was to be driven into my skin. The range of peaks stretches across my back from shoulder to shoulder, a symbol of the mountains where I felt my strongest and most at peace. The mountains were a sanctuary where, amidst the dust and gales, life had a simplicity, one which I felt was gone forever. People would ask me which mountain peaks were represented in the tattoo and I would tell them that it was just a drawing, an icon of all mountains, but truth be told, the central peak that crests over the bony protrusion at the base my neck is Her. The most painful one to tattoo over my spine (which caused me to black out repeatedly during the session) is none other than Lady Everest.

Back in 2005 the tattoo was an expression of my spirit and a promise to myself to carry on climbing. It was not about going higher, it was about going.

When I look back on my life story, it makes me smile to think that even back then I believed that when a dream is put down on paper – or my case skin – it is given life. When the dream is committed to ink it ceases to be a dream and becomes real. It becomes a goal, an emancipated objective, something which I would be accountable for.

Both John and Gilad had decided that they would join Russell Brice and Himex on an expedition to attempt to summit Mount Everest via the northern side (Tibet) scheduled to start in the April of 2008. The rationale behind their decision to join Himex above other cheaper operators lay in Russell Brice's perfect safety record and also the facilities and amenities Himex offered climbers in Base Camp. South Africa's weaker currency makes an expedition of this magnitude near impossible for the vast majority of people, and if they were to get a shot at this hill, they had to put all of their eggs into one basket and do it correctly. Brice prides himself on providing his clients with as many creature comforts as possible, which included a massive dome-shaped communal tent complete with a widescreen TV and reclining lounge chairs, individual sleeping tents, a gas heated shower (tent) and top-notch dining. If clients are able to relax and stay healthy in Base Camp, it would translate to better results higher on the mountain. With a price tag of nearly a million bucks, one would certainly fucking hope so, because a second chance was not even an option.

From the moment John first mentioned his intentions to take on Everest in earnest, I experienced a wild mixture of hope, despair, delusional excitement and a morbid jealousy. On the one hand, I was so elated to hear my best friend was going to climb the mountain we had both dreamt of for years, and on the other, I was gutted to hear my best friend was going to climb the mountain we had both dreamt of for years. It was happening in eleven months' time. Mount Everest had held my affection for a very long time and now it had become something more than a boyhood dream.

For the next three days I would lie awake well into the wee hours of the morning, wrestling with the excitement that this opportunity presented and also the hopeless despondency of the massive cost. I was certain that if I ever had any chance at climbing this mountain, this was it. Being with John and Gilad would bolster my confidence and help ease the eleven weeks away from home.

My decision did not come easily, but after many hours considering what lay ahead, I made up my mind to follow the inside voice (and that photo of Everest stuck to the inside of my cupboard door) that had been beckoning me to the mountains since I was a boy. And so I approached my two potential teammates and told them I wanted to join. They were more than happy to have me along, provided I found the finances. Brilliant news!

This was potentially yet another poor decision. I was not even close to being considered "fit for duty" as far as high-altitude mountaineering is concerned; in fact I was barely functional. I could stand for a couple of hours at best before the ache in my lower legs forced me to sit down. Somewhere deep down inside me was a tiny bit of self-belief that urged me to accept this challenge, but faith in my ankles was non-existent at best.

On paper it didn't make sense. In fact it was downright laughable, and I knew that the idea would not be endorsed by any of the doctors, surgeons or physiotherapists that had treated me. But a good friend and mentor once told me "trust yourself", and so that is what I did.

Over the next few days my excitement soared as my productivity at work entered a nosedive. The research and planning had begun and a course of action was starting to emerge.

A few weeks before this opportunity had come to light, my mom had decided to relocate to Durban to be closer to two of her three sons. She moved in with me, sharing my bachelor flat the size of a double garage. As cramped as it was at first, it was so rewarding for me to be able to take her in and be the guardian for a change – a drop of payback in the ocean of care she had given me.

On the day I decided to announce my intention to my family, I rehearsed the scenario in my head as I drove home, imagining both possible reactions. Either they would jump up and down and slap me on the back, or I would be met with an assault of all the reasons why I shouldn't do it.

As luck would have it, my mother was home from work and my brother Mark and his wife were at my front door. This must have been fate! They had all gathered to hear my great news and to celebrate my decision. Things were going my way!

We exchanged small talk and suddenly there was a pregnant pause. I took in a breath to start my sentence, but just then my brother turned to my mother and said, 'We've got something to show you.' Mom's face creased slightly, intrigued but also concerned. Reaching into his back pocket, Mark passed her a small piece of paper that was black on one side, white on the other. 'It's a new family photo!' he exclaimed proudly, and a glowing smile spread across my mother's face. There was a little girl on the way, my brother's second child and my mother's only granddaughter!

Of course I was overjoyed; the news of a new addition to the family is one of the most cherished moments ever. My news could wait, and that it did. This was their moment; mine would come.

I eventually did break the news to family and friends, but as expected I was met with a mixture of reactions, from concern to fear for my life as well as pure disbelief. For most people, as for me, the idea of Everest seemed abstract, too large and intangible. I may as well have been one of the Wright Brothers telling people we were building a flying machine.

CHAPTER 11

FINDING HOPE

Over the next few weeks everything would change. Now my days were filled with excitement and purpose. With my spirit lifted and my energy renewed, the journey to Everest had already started. It was not long after committing myself to this venture that I came upon the fundraising idea that would hopefully honour the cheque that the little voice in my head had written. And the Climb of Hope was born.

I always credit my "advertising brain" for coming up with the concept. In order to find sponsors, the fundraising model would have to be newsworthy, specific in its intent and purpose and would have to benefit more people than just me. For those aspiring adventurers that approach me after presentations and ask me for the "silver bullet" of sponsorship solutions, know this. THERE ISN'T ONE. Finding financial backing to embark on even the most outstanding of objectives is damn near impossible. You are asking companies and individuals who have never heard of you (the chicken and egg conundrum) to give you their hard-earned money to essentially go on an all-expenses paid holiday that could very possibly result in your demise, leaving you face down in the snow with their branding plastered all over your corpse. Throw in the facts that mountaineering and most adventure sports are not mainstream, hold little intrigue for the majority of the market and return on investment is often less than – or equal to – naught. "But we'll take your logo to the top" may have held some water a long time ago, but won't get you very far in terms of increasing your sponsors' bottom line.

I will, however, tell you that it is easier to ask one thousand different people for a dollar than it is to ask one person for a thousand dollars. If the concept is worthy of people's support, it will get it. Your cause needs to be something close to both you and the people you are approaching. Climbing Kilimanjaro to pay for school shoes for children halfway across the planet may be a worthy cause, but if there is little or no context then people can smell a rat easily, especially when asked to part with their hard-earned cash. If people can feel an authentic connection to the cause and purpose of your objective, then with enough hard work, sweat and even more tears, then and only then will you have a chance of success.

For me, choosing a cause was an absolute no-brainer. I chose cancer, a disease that figuratively resides on my doorstep and has affected many people within my circle of family and friends. Both my parents have had cancer. My mother survived breast cancer, and at fifteen years old I was given a front row seat to witness the courageous battle to recovery, a lesson I would be grateful for many times over in my life. Some time after my expedition to Everest my father was diagnosed with colorectal cancer, which led to his passing away shortly after. Three of my grandparents died of cancer-related causes. Two of my mother's best friends, my Scout leader and good friend Vic Hanger, my best friend John's immediate family ... the list goes on, and I could fill a page with very little effort of people who have encountered this disease in one form or another.

One person in particular was Hans Ritky, an Assistant Troop Scouter whom I met in my early teens. He died of Non-Hodgkin lymphoma at the age of thirty-three after a relatively short illness. Hans was my role model, mentor, friend and confidant. He was the kind of man I hoped I would one day grow up to be. To say I idolised him is an understatement, and as you can imagine his death affected me terribly. I had not only lost a very close friend but also the man I measured myself against. His death in the third year of my studies almost derailed me entirely.

On the day he died, I was tormented with the disbelief that Death had won, despite Hans' overwhelming positivity and his strength to wipe the tears of those who had gathered at his bedside. My disbelief was followed by the burgeoning feeling of *what now*? My compass was gone and forging a new path on my own was one of the most intimidating but necessary things I have ever had to do. One lesson Hans taught me that I will never forget was from a conversation we had when I'd been assigned the role of Troop Scouter, essentially heading up the troop of young men. Hans waited for me to finish voicing my doubts, of which there were many, and then he calmly smiled at me and said, 'It is not a case of "can Robby"? but more a case of "Robby can".'

Twenty years have passed since that conversation. Turns out that there was more than some truth in his words.

I did not have to look very far to see that cancer was the cause to which I would dedicate my one shot at Everest. I was to climb a mountain for those facing their own obstacles every single day of their lives, a fearful disease that dwarfs Everest time and time again.

I named my campaign "The Climb of Hope – Climb high for those who can't."

The fundraising idea was simple. Most of the summit photographs you'll ever see have windswept people in iced-up goggles and down suits clutching a small flag, often no bigger than a notebook, in their hands as they lean forward, holding their banner up for as long as it takes to get "the shot". At altitude (I would learn this the hard way) every kilogram feels like ten, every bit of space in your backpack is sacred and should be used wisely.

The Climb of Hope banner measured a monstrous 3.6 metres wide and 1.2 metres high and once it was printed, hemmed and finished it would clock the scales at over half a kilogram. I would take the world's largest summit banner to the top of Everest and for just R500, anybody could be a part of the journey. The banner was divided up into blocks, each one slightly bigger than a business card. By purchasing a block, anyone could advertise a company logo, feature a photo of a loved one or someone lost to cancer, or even print a marriage proposal on the giant summit flag, and I would take it to the top of the world for them. If I sold every block on the flag, I would raise enough money to cover my expedition expenses and the remainder would be donated to a cancer-related charitable cause.

I opened a bank account and designed the logo, letterhead, and business card, as well as several other campaign elements (all during office hours) and the dream was given life. I was on a mission to sell blocks to anyone who was interested. In fact, you didn't even need to be interested, you just needed to look my way and I was on to you like a salesman in a mall passage. When I wasn't pedalling my wares to every person I knew, as well as those I didn't, I began the unforgiving task of approaching sponsors for the necessary clothing and technical equipment, camera equipment and all the smaller details that became apparent as the expedition planning evolved.

To my surprise, the responses I received were largely positive and I will always be grateful to the people who went the extra mile for me and the Climb of Hope project. First Ascent, one of South Africa's leading outdoor apparel manufacturers based in Cape Town, replied with an offer to clothe me, which included everything from thermal underwear to the lifesaving down suit I would wear for the entire summit push. Drifters Adventure Centre sponsored me by providing my climbing boots – which in 2007 cost R9,500 – as well as a majority of the technical equipment such my harness and all the climbing hardware such as karabiners, ascender devices and belay devices that would keep me attached to the mountain. Canon South Africa sent me a digital camera; a video camera complete with a photographer's backpack. Dischem Pharmacies gave me a R5,000 voucher which would cover all of my medication, first aid supplies and toiletries. There were many other sponsors who took care of my every need and more, which went a long way in cementing my faith that good people and brands do exist.

Looking back at the bigger picture, there was one sponsor whose contribution made the trip possible. Roche Pharmaceuticals approached me after one fateful radio interview and the expedition gained an entire new life of its own. What had started out as an opportunity to announce the fundraising idea to get me to Everest became the turning point in my expedition journey. The talk show host was David O'Sullivan, an armchair adventurer who had an interest in high-altitude mountaineering, and his questions led me through the who, what and why of what my ambitious plan.

A week after the interview my mobile phone rang, and I remember running to the back of the building to find somewhere quiet, away from the madness of the studio. The woman on the other end of the line said in a very gentle but professional manner that she had heard me on the radio and she was hoping I would be willing to work with them. I was gobsmacked! Me, willing to work with them?! At that stage I would have been willing to donate a kidney for any assistance. This had to be a miracle!

And that's how I met Tanya Bennetts. Tanya represented Roche at the time and their contribution was in the form of public relations and marketing assistance to promote the expedition and also to raise awareness for Hodgkin's and Non-Hodgkin lymphoma, the very same disease that had killed Hans seven years earlier. This seemed too good to be true and I emerged from the printer room after the phone call as white as a sheet but smiling from ear to ear. This was the first of several miracles to happen. Every time the phone rang I beamed with excitement. Calls from strange numbers were welcomed with a very enthusiastic and polite greeting.

On the following Monday I received another phone call that would prove to be pivotal in the success of my expedition. It was a man with a slight Afrikaans accent who mentioned that he too had heard my interview on the radio in his car that Friday and the conversation went on from there. In all honesty, the sale of blocks on the banner had been incredibly slow. The bank account had about 0.001% of what we were aiming for.

The man on the other end of the phone then asked very casually, as if we were discussing last night's episode of *Grey's anatomy*, 'How much are your total expenses? What are your hard costs?' I replied in my best "formal and professional, yet not pompous or arrogant" voice, 'The expedition is going to cost around 48,000 US dollars.' The phone fell silent for what seemed an eternity while my mind raced through the hundreds of possible responses. And then in a calm and friendly voice the mystery man on the other side said, 'Okay that seems fine, I'm sure we can work with that.' Or at least that is what I think he said as I felt the blood drain from my face and a surge of breakfast charge for the back of my throat.

Over the next few minutes Mr Ulrich Fobian, a marketing director for one of South Africa's biggest corporate banks, explained how he had left work early that Friday afternoon to take his family on a holiday to the Kruger National Park and by chance had heard me talking about the Climb of Hope project and my ambitions to summit the highest mountain on Earth. Coincidently, the company he worked for was setting out on a four-year campaign to become the best business bank in South Africa and the campaign's theme was Everest, with each benchmark named according to the camps on the mountain.

And just like that I was on my way to being a sponsored climber.

In the weeks that followed, a proposal was compiled outlining all the relevant details of the trip and a breakdown of the costs. As a formality, I was also invited to meet one of the bank's senior directors for breakfast at the Durban Hyatt Hotel to discuss my coming on board with the bank. On the morning of the meeting I wore my chinos as opposed to my usual jeans and, not owning any shoe polish, I wiped down my black leather shoes with the facecloth hanging in my shower. Feeling a lot like Bart Simpson on his way to church, I made my way to the fancy hotel for breakfast with Ingrid Johnston, one of the top directors for Nedbank's Corporate Banking Division.

In complete contrast to what I had expected, Ingrid was very relaxed and friendly. In fact, I wasn't ever sure what to expect as each exposure, meeting and proposal document was the first of its kind in my limited experience, as far as putting together world-class expeditions was concerned. But at the end of the meeting we had a good idea of what would be expected of me and *vice versa*. This expedition would take me on a journey of new experiences and expose me to new people and fascinating cultures, and all before I even set a foot on the mountain.

Among the chaos of it all I managed to get the Creative Director and Managing Director of Ogilvy Durban to agree to keep my position for me during my absence. It meant three months' unpaid leave, but at least I would have something to come back to. 'That's if I come back alive,' I said jokily, halfway out of the MD's office door. My punchline was met with a blank stare.

In the months that followed, the mountain would envelop my entire life, dominate every conversation and attract the interest of everyone I had contact with. On the day that the courier delivered the boxes containing all my clothing from First Ascent, every person in the studio building where I was working gravitated towards my desk as I opened each box to go through the contents like a child on Christmas morning. As the weeks progressed, more sponsored gear and equipment would arrive and people would often direct the delivery guys to my desk by default.

If you've ever seen the movie *Into the Wild* starring Emile Hirsch, you will be able to imagine the kind of focus and obsession I had for this mountain. Just as Christopher McCandless (Hirsch's character, aka Alexander Supertramp) answers almost every question regarding his future plans with one word – 'Alaska!' – so did I, except *my* "Alaska" and my sole purpose for existing was 'Mount Everest!'

The chicken-egg situation that was fast becoming my life only became evident to me later when I was able to reflect on it with the benefit of hindsight. I found it hard to make friends or to meet women in social situations, so I spent most of my evenings at the Virgin Active gym at Gateway Shopping Centre in Umhlanga, racking up laps in the pool or sweating my ass off on a spinning bike. I kept mostly to myself in order to prioritise my training, which made it hard to form meaningful relationships, so I kept mostly to myself in order to prioritise my training, which made it hard to form meaningful … you get the picture.

On the nights I did stay late at the office, designing flyers, using the internet, colour printer and free coffee, I would arrive home at eight or nine o'clock and still go for a run around the neighbourhood for an hour or so. I got to know Bonnie the Production Manager quite well as we would both work late and share the locking up duties of the various doors and set the alarm. Ironically, Bonnie would later join the list of people I was climbing for as she succumbed to a brain tumour several years later.

Running was a necessary evil which was awkward and slow, but it provided the endurance training I needed for the goal ahead. Except this was endurance of pain and fatigue, not cardiovascular endurance. Some weekends I would get on my bicycle and head up the motorway to the holiday town of Ballito and back. It was a good workout for my legs as it resulted in less impact on my ankles and less inflammation. It would take me several days to recover from the swelling and awkward limping and it often disrupted my training routine.

Meanwhile, in Cape Town, John and Gilad were hiking up Table Mountain, often at night or early in the morning before work. We were all learning to juggle day jobs, relationships, training and a mistress: Chomolungma, the Goddess Mother of the Earth – Mount Everest by her Tibetan name.

There were days when I did not feel like training, when stiffness and soreness marred my motivation. I had to remind myself with something my first copywriter from Grey Worldwide used to say. 'No quarters given. None asked.'

This basically means that no mercy would be shown me and none asked for either. Just like anything in life, including large mountains, preparation holds the key to success. You will either put in the hours, sweat and tears when the time comes, or you won't.

The mountain will never ask if you have a valid excuse.

CHAPTER 12

EVEREST IS CLOSED

I was woken up by my cell phone alarm just like every other morning, except today was going to be different. It was mid-March in 2008 and it was a matter of days left before John, Gilad and I would be boarding the plane to Kathmandu and eventually the Base Camp of Everest. I looked at the screen to see it was John calling. We had been in touch a lot in the weeks leading up to the expedition and emails and phone calls at all hours were to be expected. But with less than a week to go before we were to fly out, our expedition plans would be changed by circumstances that were truly out of our control.

'Check out the news. It's a fuck up!' said John in his unique brand of seriousness. He and Gilad had been awake since four o'clock that morning on a training hike up Lion's Head in an effort to get used to their high-altitude mountaineering boots. (They found out very quickly that those boots cannot be "worn in" – it is more a case of you learning how to walk again in these monstrosities which look more at home on the moon than on a mountain).

I opened my laptop, which was still at the foot of my bed from the night before. I didn't own a television set so I would often fall asleep to whatever series or movie I had pirated from the server at work. I connected to the internet manually and the page loaded as fast as my 3G modem card could process it. There it stood in bold black letters on a white background. **EVEREST IS CLOSED**. What added to my confusion was that the article featured a photo of the 1968 Olympic podium with John Carlos and Tommie Smith raising the Black Power salute in black gloves in one of the most memorable political statements in Olympic history. I was lost; the photograph didn't match the headline. But as I read the breaking news my heart sank.

The 2008 Olympics were being hosted in Beijing, China. As part of the build-up, China planned to take the Olympic torch to the summit of Mount Everest in a display of greatness and influence to the world. The grandiose plans resulted in a media blackout and a complete ban of any travel in and out of Tibet, effectively shutting out any expeditions attempting the mountain from the northern side. My immediate reaction was one of disbelief; I was already dialling John's number.

While the torch was making its way around the world, people were protesting and parading "Free Tibet" banners. Several monks had committed acts of self-immolation in an effort to draw the world's attention to the political injustice suffered by the Tibetan nation under the oppression of Chinese rule.

Our trip – our chance of a lifetime – was cancelled, just six days before the departure date. My equipment had been tried, tested, packed and repacked at least five times. The only things left on my to-do list were to take delivery of my foreign exchange and pack my toothbrush. My duffel bags were literally packed and waiting against the wall of my studio flat, ready to be taken to the airport. The entirety of the last year had been geared around this expedition. Every waking moment, every decision was made in accordance with the imminent expedition.

And now it was gone.

CHAPTER 13

MISCARRIAGE

Within a few weeks of the cancellation of the 2008 expedition, I made an appointment to start seeing a psychologist in an effort to try to come to terms with the depression and irrepressible feeling of loss and my sense of purposelessness. Together we discussed the various aspects of my life and in particular, how the postponement of my Everest climb had affected my state of mind.

I was mid-sentence in a futile attempt to bullshit myself into trying to find the silver lining hidden within this convoluted and highly politicised fiasco when I was interrupted by the man sitting opposite me in John Lennon spectacles and a black-collared shirt. 'It's like you have experienced a miscarriage,' he stated calmly. I was stunned into silence for a few seconds as his words had to sink in.

It was *exactly* like a miscarriage.

I had been dreaming of this opportunity for a very long time and counting down the days until it was due to arrive. The name was picked, and clothes and toys had been chosen with care and even the nursery had been painted. My every thought and emotion revolved around the big day and then all of a sudden, without any warning or fault of my own, it had been taken away. Due to an unforeseen complication there was no more baby, just the bitter heartbreak of having to come home to a house full of reminders that something special was not there. Instead of stuffed bunnies and tiny cotton vests, I came home to a pile of fleece jackets, a down suit, and a Tupperware box full of medication, first aid supplies and a pile of karabiners, slings and climbing hardware.

It would take several weeks for the shock and despondency to wear off. Once again it became a conscious decision I had to make if I wanted to rectify my attitude and frame of mind in order to continue towards my goal, despite the posts having been moved. We are all familiar with the saying "It is possible to eat an elephant. Take one bite at a time and never stop chewing." I was experiencing a serious case of the hiccups that you don't get told about until you are several bites into it.

There are many things I still had to be grateful for. My main sponsor Nedbank, who were covering my expedition costs and expenses for the thirteen weeks I was away, were incredibly understanding of the situation, having realised the severity of what was going down on the other side of the world. In fact, all of the companies and individuals bar one were willing to carry their support over to the following year. The fundraising resumed and I continued to promote the sale of space on the Climb of Hope banner, which was now nicknamed The Banner of Miracles.

Looking back now, there was indeed a silver lining to my situation. The expedition had been postponed but it wasn't cancelled, and Everest would still be waiting for me the following March – but this time with a summit attempt from the south. Russell Brice offered to hold our expedition fee until the following season, absorbing any costs the postponement incurred. All I had to do was make a conscious decision to see it as a gift of time. I had another eleven and a half months to train and prepare, but also eleven additional months of recovery time for my still fragile and inconsistent ankles. But eleven months is a long time to wait considering the advanced stage of both my physical and mental preparation and I started to feel as if my time in Durban was drawing to a close. Since relocating to the coast, it was apparent to me that I had made little progress in terms of establishing a real life there. I believe my decision to move there in the first place was an escape, in the hopes of a clean slate far from the reminders of my "old life" and the painful memories of the relationship I had ended.

"The mountain" had become an obsession, replacing my need for close friends. I often dodged my way out of social engagements and offers from colleagues to step out of my comfort zone. I knew my expedition to Everest would be a pivotal landmark in the story of my life and I treated it as such. Besides, I had become very accustomed to my own company.

The final decision to move back to Johannesburg happened in the middle of a paddock in the KwaZulu-Natal Midlands. I accepted an invitation to a work friend's birthday at her family farm in Nottingham Road. Normally I would have wormed my way out of any kind of occasion like this, but this happened to be the person I had developed feelings for over the last few months. She was an amazing, adventurous and independent woman and I got on very well with her. As the only two writers at the agency, we would land up working together a fair bit and eventually we decided to commute to work together in an effort to save petrol as we lived a few blocks apart in the suburb of Durban North.

There are few things in the world more disheartening than when the person you consider to be the closest thing to "a second chance at love" has a long-standing boyfriend. It is even more disheartening when you meet the guy and he is an incredible person who is nothing short of being the perfect man for the job. Any fantasies of swooping her from the clutches of the wretched villain to gallop off into the sunset together were as dashed as they were delusional.

The party was small but by no means lacking an amazing atmosphere. An hour or two after midnight my mood began to turn. The familiar feeling of loneliness and alienation was never far away and had it begun to well up inside of me. I separated myself from the noisy crowd to wander off into a nearby field for some sombre introspection. I was by no means paralytic; rather I was tipsy or, for lack of a better word, mellow, bordering on melancholic. Coming to this party had made it clear that I lacked any sense of belonging. I had reached the realisation that Durban was not my home and any last sliver of romantic hope had been completely annihilated.

There, lying on the grass and staring up at the clear sky, my back soaked from the dew, I screamed at God in a voice that was more hopeless and frustrated than angry. 'What do you want from me?!' I demanded, almost expecting to hear some kind of response. But nothing came. My words evaporated into the dark summer night, absorbed by the wild grass and tidy rows of trees.

I rose to my feet and headed directly for the farmhouse, grabbing my car keys and overnight bag. I asked someone to give my apologies for leaving and drove the ninety kilometres home. I had been invited to stay over that night as there was no shortage of guest rooms, but I was overwhelmed with a self-imposed need to escape from where I felt I didn't belong. The empty highway wound its way back down the hill into the city and I eventually arrived home, walked up the creaking wooden stairs that led to my bachelor pad, and collapsed onto my bed to the usual serenade of the frogs in the lush overgrowth of the overgrown garden downstairs.

The following Monday morning, I apologised for leaving the party. And then walked across the courtyard to the Managing Director's office and gave three months' notice of my resignation. I also notified the people from whom I was renting my flat that I would be leaving. In the last few months John had also returned to Johannesburg from Cape Town, and during a phone call he had offered me one of the five bedrooms in his new house in Constantia Kloof on the West Rand. I would move back to Johannesburg three weeks before flying out to Nepal.

Everest was the perfect way to end one chapter and begin another.

CHAPTER 14

THE REAL MCCOY... AND ME

Our flight from Doha arrived around four o'clock. Gilad, John and I walked off the plane and directly into the humid chaos of the Nepalese spring. We filed through the airport, purchased our 90-day visas and then descended the stairs to the barren cement hall housing a banged-up baggage carousel. My bags were among the last to come through on the rickety conveyor belt and when they eventually arrived, I breathed a massive sigh of relief. We stood shoulder to shoulder with about sixty other tourists, climbers and trekkers, each one eyeballing the other, gauging one another and their intentions. Wrestling our three gear bags, plastic camera cases and hand luggage onto the aluminium trolleys, we headed for the door.

We soon learnt that mayhem is a way of life on the 40-minute drive from the airport to the hotel, which took us through a dust-covered frenzy of streets and alleyways. Our minibus stopped only to give way to motorists and scooters pushing in from all directions and the occasional cow resting on the tarmac in the middle of peak-hour traffic. So pretty much whoever wanted to push in, did. The bustling madness of the main city streets gave way to a quiet cemented alley which took us in a matter of seconds away from the orchestra of traffic, police whistles and car horns. In front of us stood the cleanest, most modern building we had seen all day, the

Radisson Kathmandu. Unfortunately, we were in the smaller, much less-modern hotel across the car park.

At the Tibet Hotel we were immediately hurried to the meeting room on the top floor. We snuck into the back of the room. We were the last to arrive, interrupting the first 2009 Himex Everest expedition briefing which was already underway. Just my luck. The only chair left in the room was next to a gigantic guy I nicknamed Vladimir the Bonecrusher, a six-foot-seven-inch hulking brute of a man. His number-one-all-over haircut, solid jaw and serious frown told me that this guy meant business. He was well into his fifties, the real McCoy, but I found myself dwarfed next to him. His eyes were fixed ahead of him, his brow creased in a deep concentration that made it impossible to steal even a smile, never mind a handshake.

With the scent of a new country fresh in my nostrils and all the excitement of our first commercial Himalayan expedition, I was soon distracted. I found myself scanning the room, recognising faces from the Discovery documentary, *Everest: Beyond the Limit*, which I had studied and scrutinised in the months preceding the trip: Monica the Spanish doctor, David Tate the British businessman who attempted the double traverse in the second season of the series and, of course, Russell Brice. *The* Russell Brice.

From what I had seen on television and in our limited correspondence, it was easy to see that Russell was a meticulous and soft-spoken man with a head for organisation and logistics and a very low tolerance for bullshit. In the months that followed I would learn as much as I could about the grey-haired New Zealander. Well, as much as he would let me.

Russell addressed us from the front of the room and I had to sit up and crane my neck to see him in between the broad shoulders and closely buzzed heads of my new teammates. He looked a lot taller on television. Russell went through the itinerary of the next few days and spoke briefly about hotel arrangements. He then issued us all with two rolls of toilet paper and a few bottles of hand sanitiser. Not exactly what I was expecting for an expedition briefing to the highest mountain in the world! But it was all part of Russell's intricate plan. From Day One, the rule was that nobody was to enter any of the dining tents without washing and sanitising their hands, a tiny detail that prevented the spreading of "bugs" which are known for tearing through climbing teams and putting an unplanned end to many people's trips. The toilet paper was to last the duration of the ten-day trek to Base Camp. Once again, if everyone has their own, the risk of transferring germs from one person to the next is reduced. Just another check on Russell's list.

There I sat in the room among real "hardcore" mountaineers, several of them Everest veterans, some of them Seven Summit chasers, most of them older and more experienced than me, just a guy from Germiston with all the gear and no idea. Just me...and these dodgy ankles.

I am the chink in the armour. I am the Achilles heel.

CHAPTER 15

LEAVING THE REAL WORLD BEHIND

The next morning began abruptly with the sound of a pair of New Zealanders banging on our hotel room door. Neither John nor I had adjusted our watches to Nepal time and we were still sound asleep when we should have been downstairs in reception with our barrels packed and ready. It wasn't the start we intended, but in the blink of an eye and two strokes of a toothbrush we were downstairs, the wrinkles from my pillow still pressed into my face.

We travelled to Kathmandu's domestic airport through the same bustling streets we had driven on less than twenty-four hours before. At 5:30 am it became apparent that what I thought was "rush hour" the day before was just "traffic". The domestic terminal, which I must say has very little domesticated about it, resembles a cattle shed, partly due to its appearance but more so because of how people are herded through there like livestock. The light blue walls and fluorescent lights exaggerate the starkness of the entrance hall, but the floor is mostly hidden by people, expedition members' duffel bags, and burlap sacks containing everything from tents to gas bottles. We were headed for Lukla, the village on the other side of the valley, just a fifty-minute flight away. In years to come, I would become very familiar with this airport, learning that Kathmandu air travel is anything but consistent.

Palms must have been crossed with silver because we were ushered through the terminal and onto our planes with relatively no hassle whatsoever. We were piled into the plane and I remember trying to soothe my mounting nerves by concentrating on the free back massage I was receiving from my rattling seat. I sat cross-armed with my eyes fixed out the front window; it was too noisy to even think about trying to make friends. Besides, the atmosphere was tense in general. We all knew we were flying into the .most dangerous airport in the world – Tensing-Hillary airport in Lukla. The runway is 457 metres long and 20 metres wide at an inclination of 12 degrees. Any landing you walk away from is considered a success.

But land we did before making our way into the first of many wooden lodges for some lemon tea and to stay warm while our loads were shared among the trains of yaks and Sherpa porters that would be ferrying our luggage to Base Camp.

About three hours into the hike on the second day of the trek was our first sighting of Mount Everest. The path from Phakding, where we had spent our first night of the trek, crosses the Dudh Kosi River (meaning "river of milk" due to its milky white water, which is glacial run-off) via several steel cable bridges and then snakes alongside the river bank, before turning left across the final suspension bridge. There are mountainsides on either side of the river. The dusty highway steepens drastically, zigging and zagging, gaining a notable amount of altitude before reaching the village of Namche Bazar. Through a clearing between the pine trees, approximately two hours before reaching the village of Namche, stands Mount Everest, Chomolungma in all of her glory. This was the first time I would see her in real life. Not in one of the many books I had read, not on the postcard racks of the manic streets of Kathmandu, but there in front of me. It is so hard to describe the sheer magnitude of the mountain in a way that would do both the mountain and my reaction any justice.

As excited as we all were, grabbing each other by the arm, posing for photographs in the brief gaps between the forming clouds, I will never forget how quickly my excitement was dissolved by one thought. It was the biggest thing I had, or ever would see, in my entire life and we were viewing it from forty-five kilometres away. Getting to the bottom of this mountain was proving to be a challenge in itself. Getting to the top was going to be a whole other thing altogether.

After a short break we got back to the task at hand: getting to Namche Bazar, the biggest village in the valley and our rest stop for the night. It is here that I also bumped into Ed Viesturs at the Everest Bakery, the first American to climb all of the 8000-ers (the fourteen mountains higher than 8,000 metres above sea level), and to do so without the use of supplementary oxygen. As awkward as it was, I asked him to pose in a photograph with me before he nonchalantly settled at a table for a cup of coffee. There we were. Rubbing shoulders with mountaineering legends, sipping hot coffee and enjoying apple crumble in the Himalayas, en route to the biggest mountain in the world. That was the moment it became clear that shit had indeed just got real.

I can't attribute my partial memory loss of the trek to Everest's Base Camp to the effects of altitude, but rather the fact that I was entirely focused on the task of climbing the peak. The days leading to the base of the mountain were merely a formality. I was solely concerned with the climb that began where the Khumbu Valley turned upward into the icefall. In all honesty, I'll admit that I was also overcome with the inane habit of comparing myself to the other trekkers and climbers in our group, constantly observing everyone, evaluating their experience, age, fitness levels and physicality, not for the purpose of judging them, but more for judging myself.

It was as though there was an ever-changing leader board of names in my head. I realise now it was an evaluation of my own skills, fitness level and experience based on a lack of self-confidence and the belief that I was out of my league, moving among men and women more deserving than myself.

More so now than ever before, I was in the clutches of an overbearing sense of inferiority.

I am the chink in the armour. I am the Achilles heel.

CHAPTER 16

HOME ON THE RANGE

As a hiking destination, Everest Base Camp leaves a lot to be desired. Anyone who has trekked that route will tell you that the most spectacular views of Everest and the surrounding landscape are from the summit of a small peak named Kala Patar, close to the village of Gorak Shep, or from the Chola Pass near the village of Gokyo. The final destination for those trekking to Base Camp is not the highlight of the trip, but more a photo opportunity next to a pile of stones and a wind-worn banner announcing Everest Base Camp. Base Camp is a city of tents perched on whatever level ground is available at the bottom of the Khumbu icefall.

Traditionally, expeditions would erect their camps close to the icefall so it was easy to access the start of the climb. Team after team arrive at the beginning of each season and before long, it starts to look more like a music festival except with ice and stone and not beer cans and vomit.

Over time, camps have migrated further and further away from the fall due to recent avalanches from the Western Shoulder of Everest, which have demolished camps and wreaked havoc, covering the area in a thick layer of ice and powder snow with very little warning.

The position of the Himex camp was yet another well thought out ace up Russell Brice's sleeve. We arrived at our new home only to notice we were at least 800 metres away from all the other teams' tents and the general reaction was one of confusion. I, for one, was concerned that we might miss out on the experience of "Base Camp life" that I had read about in the many Everest-related books that have filled my bookshelf back home. But our gripes were all put to rest very quickly when it was explained to us that our position, despite being about a half an hour longer to reach Crampon Point at the start of the icefall, was far away enough so that we could minimise the spreading of diseases and infection. When the moraine metropolis was at its fullest, it was home to close to 500 people in a relatively confined space and, due to the nature of the terrain, it becomes impossible to separate ablution tents from sleeping quarters from kitchen tents. As expected, it is not uncommon for stomach bugs and such to do the rounds at least once in the duration of your stay.

In addition to the safe distance we kept, there was a sign made from a Himex flag that hung at the entrance to our camp. Hand-written in permanent marker were the words, "Sorry! By invitation only."

"Trekkers", as they were referred to, were known for dropping in to say hello and take a look around the various camps, the way tourists observe living exhibits in a theme park. And more often than not they came bearing gifts like the flu and throat infections. On a two-week trip like the trek to Everest Base Camp, coming down with any number of sicknesses would be inconvenient but bearable. It would require a little more from the affected person but with some medication, you would make it. The game changes significantly when factors like the body's reduced ability to heal at altitude, massive exertion levels, living in a tent in a cold and dusty environment, the exorbitant price tag, and a case of the sniffles becomes a serious problem.

Our new home was a series of levelled platforms that, when placed together, were no bigger than two tennis courts in area. Our Sherpa team had been there for two weeks prior to our arrival, moving boulders and shovelling ice and scree, flattening and filling the landscape in order to accommodate the stores tents, sleeping tents, dining tents and the colossal white dome tent, fondly nicknamed the "Tiger Dome" after the giant woven tiger carpet that occupied the centre of the interior. The Tiger Dome would be our communal shelter from the elements where we could pass the hours on days when we weren't on acclimatisation trips or between meals or sleeping. Complete with an espresso machine, reclining chairs and gas heaters, this tent also doubled up as the cinema and dance hall from time to time. It would also host a games night I put together with some help from some of the team members.

Together we would create our own Trivial Pursuit quiz challenge and a makeshift game of 30 Seconds, secretly loaded with some really dodgy topics that made even the hardiest mountain men blush. Watching Kirsty the Geordie camera operator trying to explain the infamous internet shock video involving two girls and a plastic cup – using only references and hand gestures – had us in stitches and established several boundaries and the tone of the trip. The night was an absolute hit and I have hinted several times to Russell to employ me as his entertainment officer on future trips. The answer is always no.

On the northern edge of our camp were two rows of yellow and red sleeping tents, pitched to military precision, that would house the team members, guides and team doctor for the duration of our stay. John, Gilad and I chose three tents next to each other and all three of us went about modifying the back vestibules by digging a trench to store the gear we didn't use often. The furrow measured about three feet wide by one foot across and almost as deep. The ground was a mix of stone and solid ice and our unacclimated efforts at landscaping using our climbing axes would take a good part of the morning.

In the days and weeks that followed, I would continue my home renovations to include a clothes line, a hole which allowed me to sit with my feet in while I put my boots on, and even a paved front patio overlooking the activity of the camp. Russell occupied one of the larger stores tents. Within the three internal compartments were the "internet café" – a small camp table with a laptop and modem – the doctor's office (where Monica Piris kept a well-stocked mobile field hospital complete with all the medication, resuscitation equipment and even a bathroom scale) and Russell's home for the sixteen weeks he would spend in the moraine each year, living on a glacier. I never ventured anywhere near his quarters, but I once saw the corner of a camp stretcher with his sleeping bag laid out neatly on top of it during one of my routine check-ups with the doctor.

Mealtimes were often the highlight of each passing day. Breakfast would usually be announced by the clanging of a ladle and pot by one of the kitchen staff. The team members who found lying down for more than ten hours at a time too uncomfortable, as well as those who had filled their pee bottles during the night, would already be awake, gathering in clusters outside the mess tents and enjoying the view of the icefall and Everest's Western Shoulder as they slowly defrosted in the morning sun. For others (well, just me) the clanging would be a final warning to pull on something warm and stagger down to breakfast, arriving as the last few people were finding a seat, sleep still crusted in the corners of my eyes. On the odd occasion the warmth and comfort of my down sleeping bag and foam mattress proved overpowering and I would surface a while later to the jeers and wisecracks of my new-found friends. I figured it was unnecessary to rush when we had the entire day to take in the calories we needed. If I'm honest, the first few steps of the morning are very difficult and painful for me, and I would try to put off the awkward stumble from my tent for as long as possible.

I am proud to say that I never missed a single lunch or dinner. They were the social events of the day and the atmosphere was, more often than not, electric. With climbers from across the globe from Alaska to Japan and everything in between, the nights were loud celebrations, pots being passed back and forth as we sat shoulder to shoulder in one big happy family of puffy jackets and beanies.

One particular meal I shall never forget had the entire team in hysterics. Within our team were several Japanese climbers who, mostly due to diet and the language barriers, kept to themselves.

They had two Japanese guides who looked after them, one of whom was the amazingly strong and talented, yet slightly insane, Hiroyuki "Hiro" Kuraoka. To give you a better idea of Hiro's character, one of his most recent Facebook status updates was a photo of him on the summit of Aconcagua in the Andes with the team he had guided there, posing in a Darth Vader mask at 6,896 metres. He is incredibly good in the mountains and a talented photographer, but, as I said, he's utterly nuts.

Hiro burst into the tent, intent on speaking to Monica who was sitting opposite me. Without a smidgeon of discretion and without lowering his voice, he asked Monica if she could come and see one of the Japanese climbers for a consultation.

The doctor, obviously concerned and trying to gauge the urgency of the ailment, asked 'Is everything okay? Is it serious or can it wait until morning?'

'No, you must come now!' Hiro shouted.

'Why, Hiro? What's wrong?' The tent had now fallen silent, expecting the worst.

'You must take a look now, while he is still drunk,' the guide began. And then all of a sudden, for everyone to see, Hiro made a circle with one hand and with the index finger of his other hand explained, 'He has problem with asshole!'

The tent walls shook as fits of hysteria erupted in the tent. Regardless of where we were from, everyone there that night clearly understood the international hand signal for asshole. To Monica's credit, she fought back the smile and managed to maintain her professional demeanour, agreeing to see the poor patient after dinner. As luck would have it, dessert arrived and it happened to be instant chocolate pudding. I couldn't miss the opportunity and I dug my finger into my bowl and raised my hand to ask Monica if I could make an appointment when she was finished with her next patient. But she didn't find it as funny as I did, or those cackling around me.

On some evenings the Tiger Dome would be turned into a movie house. The chairs would be pushed into rows and people would pile in and find a piece of floor. It was funny to watch how many gravitated around the heaters and not the television. We watched whatever movies were available to us on one of the hard drives someone had brought, often with mixed reactions, especially *Team America*, the animated movie by the creators of *South Park*. One evening Valerio, the only Italian in the team, insisted the movie of the night had to be *The Godfather*. The tent emptied out quite quickly, as Marlon Brando had us nodding off within minutes of the opening credits. But one movie that topped all others without a doubt was *Top Gun*. The cult classic had us all glued to the flat screen, oblivious to the call of our nice warm beds.

We would spend the week following our arrival in BC doing very little apart from eating, sleeping, reading and not much else. I am guilty of making our lives in Base Camp sound like a cushy holiday resort, but despite the creature comforts, there were many aspects that made mountain life difficult. First and foremost was the old climbing maxim, "everything is difficult at altitude".

What people often forget is that the starting point for the climb up Everest is already at an altitude which is just short of the summit of Kilimanjaro, Africa's highest mountain. The simplest task such as fetching a jacket from your tent would leave you breathless as you waited for your breathing and heart rate to return to normal.

While my body was taking time to adjust, my state of mind was working just as hard to come to terms with where I now found myself. Each day there was an internal squabble in my head between the voice that was my biggest fan and avid supporter, boosting my confidence, reminding me how far I had made it on the highest arena on Earth, trying desperately to plug the holes in the leaking bucket that was my self-confidence. The other voice, an unforgiving bully, would take cheap shots, undermining the list of accomplishments that had got me this far. As always, the two opposing forces within me would battle it out every waking moment, and often make their way into my dreams as well.

Having John nearby was a massive help. He had a failproof sense of logic and ability to restore calm to whatever insecurity was raging inside of my head. He was also a brilliant accomplice and our inane banter was often a source of entertainment for others.

During the time in Base Camp I also confided in Monica and told her that I usually took antidepressants, but had chosen not to take them here, based on a very uneducated observation I had made that the tablets had an adverse effect on my wellbeing. Over time, not having the medication turned out fine. On a day-to-day basis, my stress levels were manageable, but on days before the various moves in our acclimatisation process, I felt the familiar knot in my stomach, as though it was another Sunday night from my childhood.

CHAPTER 17

IN RUSS WE TRUST

On 12th April, two days after arriving at our new home, the Sherpa built a cubic stone pillar at the top of our camp ground. It was the chorten where we would have our puja ceremony. Before anyone in the team can set foot on the Mother Goddess of the Earth, it is customary to ask permission and to obtain Her blessing through offerings of rice, whiskey, various foods and sweet treats. Juniper is burnt and each climber is given the chance to place their climbing axe at the base of the chorten for blessing. The three-hour ceremony is then completed and a pole is erected on top of the chorten from which strings of prayer flags stretched in every direction to each perimeter of our camp. The flags are said to protect all those underneath them.

The remainder of the day is spent listening to music, dancing and consuming the leftover whiskey. The Sherpa men form a long line, locking arms like a massive scrum team, and sing traditional songs while they drum out the baseline with their feet stamping in unison. I was excited to be a part of one of the ceremonies that had always been a milestone in the Himalayan expeditions I had read about.

For the next five days we were tasked with doing not much more than growing red blood cells. Russell announced at our first expedition meeting that we would be heading back down the valley to the interim camp we had stayed in near the village of Lobuche.

About 12 kilometres from the comforts of Base Camp, in true military-style neatness which Himex is famous for, were two stores tents and two neat rows of yellow dome tents. The climbers and guides would be divided into two teams, one leaving the next day and the other leaving the day after that to go and climb Lobuche East, a 6,145 metre "trekking" peak. I felt surprised, anxious and excited having found out that in two days' time I was going to be climbing the second highest mountain I had ever climbed, second only to Aconcagua in the Argentinian Andes.

The reason for our unexpected jaunt was yet another practical ace that Russell had pulled from his sleeve. Being a trekking peak, there were no permit requirements for Lobuche East and getting to the summit would allow us to acclimatise to the same altitude as the first camp on Everest – which was pitched just out of sight on the other side of the notorious icefall at the beginning of the Western Cwm – but with considerably less danger of avalanche or crevasse falls.

My trepidation was founded in the fact that I was here to climb one very specific mountain, and I was worried that this trip would rob me of energy or weaken me, somehow affecting my performance when it was needed. It was as if I only had a certain number of steps. in me and I wanted to use them as wisely as possible.

But climb we did, and it was incredible.

After the walk back down the path to a cluster of tents on the last few slabs of granite before Lobuche's snow line, we spent a cold night in the camp before an early start. We awoke to one of the most incredible landscapes, as clouds rolled over Himalayan peaks that were framed by a spectacular spectrum of purple, pink and orange. We strapped our crampons – steel spikes that grip into the snow ice – to our boots before stepping onto the bright white ice. It was a tough day. It was my first day using an ascender on the ropes fixed to the mountain. The ascender device, or jumar, clips onto the rope and slides in one direction, locking when pulled on, allowing you to move up the ropes safely. This was nothing like those heroic steps I took in high school, on my way up the stairs to the last period biology.

The first climbers' footsteps on that route had now melted, forging indented steps in the mountain face which made it slightly easier for all the climbers who didn't have short, inflexible hobbit legs like mine. I reached the summit very near to the back of the group feeling more tired than elated, despite having summited my first Himalayan peak. We sat for about half an hour, drinking water and snapping some photos before the long, bone-jarring descent back to the interim camp for a good night's rest. The next day we would trek back to the "luxury" of Base Camp, and admittedly it was easier than the first time but still anything but a doddle. We spent the rest of that day tidying our tents, concocting gourmet savoury biscuits and having the usual "dinner and a show."

Six days after our return, Russell called another team gathering and told us we were going back to Lobuche again, this time moving from the tented camp to just below the summit in a single day. I honestly thought he was taking the piss. I nudged John and quietly asked if he was joking.

What I thought was a sick joke turned out to be an important exercise which would not only improve our acclimatisation, but give the guides a chance to evaluate the climbers and allocate us into the two summit teams, grouping the faster climbers in one group and the slower ones in another. This would be the last time John and I would climb side by side on this trip as he was possibly one of the strongest and fastest in the team, while I was the exact opposite. The rotation for climbing Lobuche for the second time meant that the faster team climbed one day before us.

It was on this second trip that Dave "Narli" McKinley, a New Zealand-based guide and I met. He had the role of sweeper, staying at the back of the group and herding in the last stragglers. As we neared the tents after a long day, I began to feel self-conscious of my slow pace. I told Narli to carry on and that I would be there shortly. He told me not to worry and then said 'As long as I'm around, you'll never be the last one into camp.' It wouldn't be the last time I'd hear it on the trip, but I would never forget it.

The first phase of our acclimatisation process was done. I felt like Russell was playing games with us sending us to go climb

Lobuche twice. I pictured the image of that clichéd high school football coach, punishing the team by forcing them to run laps of the field while he stands smugly on the sideline in a grey tracksuit and a steel whistle around his neck. But there was always method in his madness and many world-class expeditions now copy this acclimatisation model to avoid unnecessary trips through the icefall.

The night of 26th April brought the Tiger Dome to life. The television was replaced with raucous music. People danced. People laughed. And that night, my feelings of inadequacy and homesickness evaporated into the night. This was now my home.

As loud and joyous as that party was, I still managed to miss most of it. After one beer (partly responsibility, partly frugalness) John and I called it a night and went off to the sanctuary of our neighbouring tents. That night I was content and even somewhat pleased with myself. As the heat from my Nalgene bottle warmed the inside of my sleeping bag, I drifted off to sleep to the soothing heartbeat of the Tiger Dome.

Both expedition teams, the Yaks and the Yetis, were now acclimatised to 6,100 metres and the real climbing was about to begin.

CHAPTER 18

CAMP 1: INTO THE ICEFALL

Just as it had done every morning before, the alarm gong went off. It woke the climbers up but this time it was not summoning us to breakfast. The temperature was well below zero and the sun not yet up. The itinerary for 1st May was to move from Base Camp to Camp 1, which was approximately 600 metres higher at an altitude of 5,900 metres. I had got dressed into climbing gear in the dark on past climbing trips; it was a necessary evil for summit attempts. But this time we were preparing for the start line and it was as awkward and exhausting as ever. You can never become accustomed to it no matter how many times you do it.

I emerged from the tent, my bulky rigid boots exaggerating my limp as I made my way to eat some breakfast. When I say breakfast, I am referring to a piece of bread with chips of frozen butter and clumps of tinned jam that tore the slice into pieces. I wash it down with mouthfuls of sweet tea. And when I say eat, I am referring to the act of trying to force in some nutrition in between gagging episodes. Imagine a pelican gulping down sardines in slow motion – that was breakfast. But I would need to get it down to sustain me on the seven-hour climb. I put on my harness and fiddled with the last few details, ironically smearing sunscreen on while being blinded by the Discovery camera lights documenting our departure in the dead of night.

After bidding farewell to everyone who would keep Base Camp alive in our absence, we began our way along the path of rock and ice by the light of our head torches. After about forty minutes we arrived at Crampon Point, the last piece of relatively level ice where we could strap on our crampons and begin what had occupied my every thought for the last two years. I craned my neck upward to shine my torch beam into the labyrinth of ice formations announcing our entry into the Khumbu icefall and the most dangerous section of the entire climb. More climbers die before Camp 1 than anywhere else on Everest.

At Crampon Point, I sat awkwardly on a bulge of ice, lurched over my boots as I tussled with the straps, securing the metal teeth to my boots. My breakfast was perched at the back my throat and deep breaths prevented my "cookies" from being "tossed". The strategy of moving through the icefall as fast as possible has been drilled into each climber's mind, and I could think of nothing else. I was excited to be taking the first steps onto the mountain, but my energy was divided between the eight hours of climbing ahead and keeping my thoughts positive and the ferocious wolf named anxiety at bay.

From far away the icefall resembles a spilt box of popcorn, white bulbous kernels flowing down the Western Cwm. Face to face, the icefall is a glacier in motion. Gravity drags millions of tons of ice down into the valley and as it does, the seracs (or blocks) and slabs break up and slam together, some as large as school buildings and double-decker buses. Crevasses yawn and snap shut without notice, swallowing whatever prey is nearby.

The Kraken was lurking beneath me and could be released at any moment.

One of the expenses of an Everest expedition is the $10,000 permit fee payable by any climber moving above Base Camp. This exorbitant ticket covers the costs of the Sherpa team employed to maintain the icefall's ladders and the various administrative aspects of climbing.

I adjusted the strap on my helmet and rectified my torch so that the beam illuminated the ground in front of me. Straightening my backpack straps, I took a deep breath and took a $10,000 step forward into the notorious Khumbu icefall.

Within minutes our route became a deadly playground of blocks and bulges, ledges and ladders as we wound our way up in the dead of night. Each person kept to themselves, concentrating on each precarious step. We followed the fixed lines as the dark hours passed. The ice began to turn a pale blue as the sun began to rise behind us. As I stood catching my breath in a queue to mount one of the hundreds of seracs, I turned to see the east face of Pumori glowing pink, a startling contrast to the grey shadow of morning in the valleys.

Spirits were high and the conversation between us and several climbers from other teams improved with the addition of daylight. But with daylight comes the increased danger of movement and avalanches in the icefall, and so we were constantly pushed to keep going and keep rest breaks to an absolute minimum. Occasionally I would look up to see several strands of prayer flags strung overhead between blocks of ice for us to pass under. I only worked out later that the flags were placed over the more dubious of obstacles and precarious spots.

Just after sunrise I met with Big Jim Holliday (Vladimir the Bonecrusher from the first briefing) at a cluster of ropes where several lines converged. As I stepped over one of the lines, I caught the teeth of my crampon on one of the ropes and took a minor tumble, bruising my ego more than my elbow. But the fall had twisted my left ankle and it was now seriously painful and tender to put weight on. But considering we were not out of danger yet, I sucked it up and kept on going.

Jim had turned out to be one of the most caring, thoughtful and kind-hearted people I have ever met. I appreciated his quiet presence, and we enjoyed many conversations throughout the trip. I think it is safe to say that he is an incredibly intelligent man. I never learnt what his profession or background was, but without fail he always managed to get the seat closest to the heater in the dining tent.

The last section of the day's workout became quite tough, a culmination of several factors including fatigue, altitude and dehydration. The temperature rose dramatically in the last twenty minutes it took to move from the exit of the icefall to the tent pitched on a field of undisturbed white snow, our secret kingdom within the walls of Everest, Lhotse and Nuptse. Our trips up Lobuche had definitely paid off. We moved relatively quickly and confidently through the icefall, thus reducing the objective risks considerably.

I had reached Camp 1 on Everest. On *Everest*!

CHAPTER 19

FROM CAMP 2 TO 3:
VERTICAL ICE SKATING

I was told that Camp 2 lay beyond the rolling hills of snow, just out of sight at the foot of the south face of Everest. It was a gradual slope along the floor of the Cwm, punctuated by a few ladder crossings and a bit of a steep slope leading into the camp right at the end of the day's walk. From where I stood, I thought I was in for a relatively easy day and that I'd be enjoying some tea by lunch time. Let's just say that I woke up an optimist.

Thinking back, there was no reason why it should have been as tough as it was and I have to surmise that I just "hit the wall" that day. Perhaps I hadn't eaten enough or I was becoming despondent as the camp never seemed to get any closer as I walked. I was sore and stiff in my right foot especially and took painkillers with breakfast. Like the obstacle course we had played on the day before, I really enjoyed the crevasses and the other technical features we navigated along the otherwise featureless path. With a safety line on either side of me each attached to my harness, I can confidently say that I felt safe on the ladders. The gaping deep-blue maws below the aluminium makeshift bridges did not faze me, but I was still aware of the danger and took each one in my stride with prudence.

I had taken time to perfect my technique of walking the aluminium rungs of the ladders bridging each crevasse while in Base Camp.

About a week after we arrived at Base Camp, Russell arranged for a practice course to be set up for the team to perfect the various skills we would need higher up on the mountain in order to ensure safe passage on the route. Repetition would ensure that these crucial actions became second nature and reducing the chance of errors higher up – where it counted. While practising, I learnt that my size seven feet did not sit securely on the rungs like the other larger-footed climbers' did. Where they were able to place the crampon spikes under their heels on one rung and the front points on another, my crampons did not reach comfortably, so I quickly learnt to walk while balancing with one rung in the centre of my foot. It was a little trickier, but once mastered, the technique served me well.

There was ladder crossing after ladder crossing and the snow field seemed to never end, but eventually I would reach Camp 2. The six-hour journey felt like a marathon, and I immediately found a chair in the dining tent to take my boots off and soothe my throbbing feet. Nick Bonner the camera man was there to capture my sense of humour failure in a conversation that made the final cut of the episode. I came across as angry and despondent – there were more words beeped out than those that could be heard – but what I was feeling ran deeper than that.

While I appeared to be having a tantrum as I removed the compression bandages around my feet, in fact I was feeling a deep hole of self-doubt and embarrassment. I had burst into tears when I arrived and had hugged a fellow teammate. I was scared that someone would hand me a walkie-talkie at any moment and Russell would call me back down to Base Camp to pack my bags. One of the most dreadful feelings I often go through, even in recent years, is a distrust of my own body. This would not be the last time I would bear the consequences of the injuries I sustained in 2006. There would, in my future, be more than one expedition thwarted by the pain and inflammation in my ankles as well as the resulting lack of self-confidence and feelings of inferiority and failure.

How far can I push myself? I thought. *Will I be able to get out of bed tomorrow? Am I lying to myself, disguising this elaborate suicide mission as a dream?*

What if I can't handle this when all hell breaks loose?
I am the chink in the armour. I am the Achilles heel.

Before sunrise on 3rd May, the team and I got dressed into our down suits. For most of us, it was the first time they were being used for their real purpose. I had spent two days in mine in the back of a refrigerated truck as part of a PR event to raise awareness for the Climb of Hope campaign. Other than that, I hadn't worn it for more than thirty seconds at a time, as it sky-rocketed your body temperature if the weather was anything but freezing.

I was still stiff from the previous day's walk over the rolling snow hills and the final stretch of mixed rock and ice that is the garden path to the camp set up at 6,400 metres. After breakfast we shouldered our bags and began the slow walk to the base of the Lhotse Face. It was harder than any obstacle I had ever climbed to date. Even the notorious Canaleta – which is a soul-destroying grind over loose rocks and boulders that leads to the summit plateau of South America's highest mountain – did not compare to this.

After approximately ninety minutes of walking, the gentle slope forming the floor of the Western Cwm turned skyward and a bergschrund separated valley from face like a toothy grin. A bergschrund is a horizontal crack (crevasse) in an ice face caused by the weight of the ice lower down the slope, creating a tear in the face. This one was reasonably easy to cross, but a bergschrund can often gape open, creating severe difficulty and sometimes restricting passage on a particular route. This one was about one to two metres wide at worst, just enough to force you to use your knees to scramble awkwardly over it, leaving you out of breath with your heart thundering in your ears.

And then it was all uphill.

The best metaphor I can use to describe the surface of this face to most South Africans who, like myself, would never encounter anything like this, is to imagine an ice rink: hard as concrete, as slippery as wet glass and bone-chillingly cold. Hoist that ice rink on a giant crane to an angle of 60 degrees and there you have the Lhotse

Face. I failed to mention that the height from its base to the ledges where our camp was positioned, approximately three-quarters of the way up the face, is about 900 metres, the same height as Table Mountain in Cape Town. I almost shit myself out of fear and intimidation.

Immediately our ascender devices were clipped onto the safety rope and did not come off until we got into camp. A fall here would be fatal. Simple. Anything you dropped was as good as gone and had the potential to injure – or worse, kill – another climber. A dropped water bottle would become a projectile capable of breaking bones and, needless to say, wearing helmets on this section of the climb was compulsory. I was more afraid of dropping something on the wall than I was of being hit by something another climber sent down. It was more a fear of failure or fucking up than a fear for my own wellbeing.

Apart from one flying water bottle screaming past us about four metres away, the ascent of the day's climb was a monotonous uphill struggle as we kicked into the ice three steps at a time for nine hours straight. Rests were kept to a minimum, seeing that there was nowhere level to sit. The last three pitches of the day were a great opportunity to get acquainted with Dean Staples, our head guide, who had to coax me in the typical New Zealander no-bullshit guiding style around the last bulge, which was hiding the tented camp from sight. As usual I was exhausted.

The steep and unforgiving ice put immense strain on my ankles, especially my Achilles tendons which have almost no flexure, causing me to walk like a duck. Because of the way I had learnt to walk again my hamstrings were very short and weak, causing the load of each step to put all of the strain onto my quads instead of sharing it with all the muscle groups in my legs. Once again I was the last member to collapse into the camp. Not only did I feel the fatigue in my throbbing legs and the burning in my chest, but I could also feel the familiarity of self-doubt welling up inside of me. I was weak, slow and far from home and anyone who saw me could see that.

I couldn't ever discuss it or open up to someone about it. By the time you reach Camp 3 on Everest, it is a given that you are fully capable of keeping your shit together. The cluster of tents poised on the wall of ice – up at seven and a half kilometres above sea level – is not a safe place for sharing by any stretch of the imagination. Everyone up there is preoccupied with their own agenda, which consists of one thing: not dying.

But despite how I felt lying there flat on my back, my chest still heaving to gain purchase on the thinning air, I had reached 7,500 metres and set a new altitude record for myself. I felt a lopsided smile spread across my face. Reaching Camp 3 was purely an acclimatisation exercise and, after spending a night there, we would retreat back down to Camp 2. Camp 2 lay almost a kilometre vertically below us in the shadow of Everest and Nupste. We would spend another night at altitude there before retreating to the comfort of Base Camp.

And then all that was left to do was wait for a weather window, the green flag for a summit attempt. That came on 6th May.

CHAPTER 20

AVALANCHE!

Back in the confines of our village in the valley, life returned to its routine of eating, sleeping, tidying and organising our tents, playing Scrabble and whatever else used up time.

On the morning after my team had successfully arrived back from our acclimatisation rotation, I started the process of making a call home. I distinctly remember it was 7th May, my brother Mark's birthday. In 2009, the only way to get a call out was to make sure the Began satellite modem was fully charged and then find a place that was out of the wind, away from the noise of camp life and somewhere where you could get a good signal. The modem was the size of an encyclopaedia and needed to be propped up very precisely with rocks in order to maintain a good signal. You could then plug in the handset and dial out.

I was about two or three sentences into the conversation with Mark when the peace of the camp was interrupted by a sound so all-consuming it seemed to come from every direction, even the ground. It was frightening and disorienting and my reflex reaction told me it was a bomb blast. But then within a fraction of a second I came to the realisation that it was in fact an avalanche.

Out of fear of being buried, I immediately disconnected the call and exited the tent I had made into my phone booth.

Outside, everyone was staring in the same direction. The left-hand wall of the icefall was in motion. A massive hanging serac had dislodged from its precarious place on the sheer cliff face that is the Western Shoulder of Everest. By the time I had got out of the tent the ice had hit the bottom of the face, dumping thousands of tons of ice and snow into the icefall and causing a white cloud that was now moving towards us. My only reference to something this big were the cumulonimbus clouds of the Highveld's thunderstorms. This was ten times bigger and growing, as the giant white nexus engulfed the Khumbu Valley. Some people had managed to catch the avalanche on film, but within a minute or two their footage would turn to grey as the ice storm showered the entire Base Camp settlement.

The Sherpa staff started shouting and awe turned into panic. There were people up there.

The rest day in camp was now a rescue operation. The radios burst into action and all hell seemed to break loose: there was running and shouting, stretchers and oxygen bottles, picks and spades. Amidst the chaos, Russell stood with the radio glued to his hand and said something that reinforced the reason why they call him Big Boss. He personified leadership and what it means to be cool under pressure. Calmly he instructed the Sirdar Phurba Tashi to "send six boys". My immediate reaction was one of shock. Six? We had at least twenty capable Sherpa to go and help those stranded in the icefall. Why would we only send six?

Before I could ask, Russell turned to one of the other climbers and, as if reading our minds, he explained that he was only sending six in case any further avalanches happened shortly after the initial fall, which was not uncommon. A small team of six could be easily deployed and managed while the other Sherpa staff would be rested and alert and able to help once the injured were brought into camp. Once again Russell Brice proved that this was not his first rodeo.

That day there were several minor injuries and one death. A Sherpa climber was blasted into a crevasse while returning from a trip to stock supplies at Camp 2. The only thing that was found was one of his boots and a water bottle. Our team members who were up in the icefall at the time managed to find cover but were terrified and shaken as "pieces of ice the size of televisions" flew past them in a cyclone of ice and snow. Our South African teammate Gilad Stern was one of the climbers who was stuck in the middle of it all and he was badly rattled. In the hours that followed, Gilad chose to bow out of the expedition, having experienced what every climber dreads ever happening.

The next day, Gilad broke the news of his departure. Carrying on with the climb meant having to venture into the icefall and back once more, something he vowed never to do again. Feeling sad, John and I bid him farewell and watched our friend and countryman as he walked out of camp and homeward. I have always admired Gilad for his ability to weigh up risk versus reward, and this time his decision was in favour of everything that awaited him back home, outweighing whatever was possibly waiting for him on the summit.

The mood in camp reflected what had transpired that day. The deceased Sherpa was not from the Himex team, but was a relative of one of the Himex Sherpas. While I was grateful to have escaped the temper of Madam Everest, I was severely shaken, having realised that I had been directly under that serac almost twenty-four hours to the minute the previous day. I even remember Dean "Dino" Staples pointing it out to the group while we discussed the temperature rising with the approach of midday.

It was now more apparent than ever that my slow, unsteady pace could put an end to more than just my expedition. This was not the place to just do "my best". This was Mount Fucking Everest.

From then on, one day blended into another as we went about our lives. The excitement of having acclimatised without any major complications was mixed with the impatience of not knowing when our chance to attempt the summit would come. Any illness or injury in this waiting period would put all expense and physical hardship to waste. We were at the mercy of the mountain – her temper, her tantrums and also the weather.

Weather on Everest is the one factor that no amount of money, training, preparation or research can alter. Over time, modern forecasting technology – combined with a greater accessibility of such information – has made weather prediction one of the biggest differentiators among Himalayan operators, and also the rate of success of the expeditions they offer. As one of the pioneers of modern-day Everest climbing, Russell's weather forecasts and his interpretations of them have played a pivotal role in getting his clients and Sherpa team to the top and back alive.

But this information comes at a price. In another expedition meeting we were all instructed that in no uncertain terms were we to divulge any information with regards to our summit attempts to any sources outside the confines of the Himex camp. It had become obvious that other expeditions on the mountain were reading Himex team members' blogs and websites. Going to the expense and effort of obtaining highly accurate weather information and then only sharing it with the rest of the teams in Base Camp was not an act of selfishness, but rather a way of managing the many objective risks. The repercussions of other teams learning of our plans to take advantage of upcoming breaks in the weather would result in high traffic on the safety lines and crowding at the various bottlenecks along the route, exponentially increasing the likelihood of accidents, injury and death due to exposure.

So until further notice we were to stay healthy, stay focused and be ready to head off back up the mountain on just twelve hours' notice. We were not allowed to communicate anything specific to our families back home or those who read our blog posts, as it could jeopardise everything we had endured until now.

Sixteen days is a long time to sit on a rock and stare up at the sky, wondering if tomorrow is going to be the day you are going to take on the biggest mountain on the planet.

CHAPTER 21

LIKE SOLDIERS OFF TO WAR

After breakfast on the morning of 15th May, we were instructed to gather outside the Tiger Dome for an expedition meeting. This was a welcome break from the routine we'd found ourselves in. The final summit teams had been selected and this time the entire Sherpa complement joined us in a massive circle. Each climber is paired with a high-altitude Sherpa for the climb from Camp 4 to the summit and back and so one by one we were introduced to our "summit buddies" with a solid handshake and more often than not a big hug. The Sherpa's responsibility is to ensure the safety of themselves and their client on a one to one basis. A Sherpa is a guardian angel who accompanies you into the depths of hell and back.

Finally, I was called up to meet Lhakpa Nuru, a man possibly five or six years younger than me but very similar to me in height and build. This was the guy with whom I would hopefully stand on top of the world within a few days' time ... if that damn day ever arrived.

By now eleven days had crept past since the completion of the rotations and we were all trying hard to manage our impatience and tension. Chores such as laundry and landscaping were treated like meeting requests, something we could plan our days around. There had already been one false alarm a few days before when a short window appeared and with it a plan to send the faster Yeti team up. Should they have failed, being stronger and faster climbers, they would be fitter and more capable of trying again later on. But quickly they decided not to make the attempt. It was a good decision, but the false alarm left the climbers concerned a little unsettled and anxious.

And then one day it happened. After several hours of huddling around the laptop, Russell – together with the team of guides – identified a possible window. News spread through camp like diarrhoea at a music festival. The Yetis would be leaving in the next day or so and the Yaks would trail them, 48 hours behind. The announcement was made. This was it! John would be leaving the next day.

We both went about preparing and packing. We had probably been through the motions a hundred times each, but this time it was for real. As midnight on 19th May arrived, neither John nor I slept much. And yet despite the fact that I was wide awake, prying myself from my bed to wish John and the rest of the Yeti team farewell was no easy task. We watched as the string of head torches disappeared across the frozen wasteland.

I wrestled with the thought that it was soon going to be my turn to trundle off into the darkness in the direction of triumph. This was the real thing. This was the reason we had come.

Starting now, there were 48 hours on the clock.

My turn did, eventually, arrive. It is safe to say that I am even less of a midnight person than I am a morning person. The clanging of the alarm pot set both me and my bowels into motion. My nerves were in perfect working order and a visit to the bog was not how I imagined my conquest of Everest beginning. Breakfast at -10°C never gets better, and once again I re-enacted the slow-motion pelican move, gagging down chunks of butter and toast with mouthfuls of sweet milky tea. Out came the camera again, panning across our glum faces as we winced in the beam of its "sun gun". I don't recall what the camera guys asked me that night. I was a ball of nerves as I fumbled with my gloves and dug around in my bag for God knows what. It's not like I could forget anything massively important. I had had over two weeks to make a list.

We could not avoid the inevitable much longer and soon it was time to say goodbye. Lachu and Tashi Tashi, the proud kitchen staff, stood smiling widely as if it was their own sons and daughters heading off to school for the first time. Russell shook our hands and I got the compulsory hug from Monica. I had grown very fond of the team doctor, having first watched her on Discovery's first two seasons of *Everest*. Over the course of the trip we'd enjoyed several discussions about everything from my decrepit ankles to her pet donkey back home in Spain.

In my mind I had created an ally, a sympathiser for when my disability would get the better of me. A doctor would understand and vouch for me when my pain levels became too great to continue. I had already thought this through before I had even climbed onto the plane. Throughout the trip, the possibility of failure was there. It was bound to happen. I mean, what do you expect? After all, I am the Achilles heel.

We put on our head torches and backpacks, and then off we marched. I distinctly remember the smell of the juniper branches burning on the camp's stone chorten, an offering to the Mother Goddess of the Earth to allow safe passage and, more importantly, a safe return.

Just as we had done on our previous trip, we arrived at Crampon Point and strapped our boots to their gleaming teeth. We were suited up like warriors heading into battle, putting on layer upon layer of Gore-Tex armour, our helmets and spiked axes.

As if we'd even stand a chance if the enemy were to attack.

The icefall by nature is ever-changing as blocks shift and crevasses open. Our path would not be the same as the previous time we had tempted fate and since the avalanche on 7th May. We had no idea what to expect. But one thing had not changed: we still needed to move fast, avoid unnecessary risk and get through this white-walled maze as soon as possible.

The day unfolded thankfully without any incidents worthy of note. I moved through the icefall nearly 90 minutes faster than my previous rotation, which was partly due to being acclimatised and partly the memory of the avalanche. Up there it is not a case of *if* anything happens, it is more likely *when* something happens. Once again we crested the ridge leading into the Western Cwm, except this time our stop-over was no longer than a few minutes as the destination for the day was Camp 2, just on the other side of those gentle rolling hills and up a scree slope.

That afternoon saw me enter the camp in slightly better shape than the last time. No tears this time, but the same amount of pain coursing through my lower legs.

If anyone asked, I was fine. This was my only shot at the summit and I would be damned if I was going to let on that beneath my world-class shell of down and nylon was a boy somewhere on a very big rock, scared out of his mind and wondering if he was even big enough for this mountain.

As the sun set, turning Lhotse ochre yellow in the fading light, I stared up at the wall. A gentle breeze blew across the camp, causing the flaps of my hood to sway gently. The day was drawing to an end. The hum of human activity in the alien landscape began to fade while the Himalaya's eyes began to droop. I turned to steal one more gaze of Everest, towering into the heavens like the Tower of Babel. I drew too deep a breath into the depths of my lungs

... and promptly vomited my lunch onto the rocks at my feet.

I had twelve hours to convince myself that I was indeed the man for the job, because tomorrow was going to be a mother fucker of a day. I either had it in me, or I didn't. Regardless of whatever my excuse was, the mountain wasn't interested in hearing it.

CHAPTER 22

MAN DOWN

The 21st May was one of the toughest days of my life and one I will remember forever. We crept at snail's pace up a 60-degree slope of blue ice, moving from one awkwardly spaced foot hole to the next in the blistering heat of midday.

That bad day was a result of a series of mishaps that, in retrospect, could have cost us the expedition. After a slow start out of camp, approximately ninety minutes from the tents, Big Jim collapsed at the foot of the ice wall and was lying motionless on the ground about a hundred metres in front of me. Instinctively I began running as fast as the thin air would let me, which was probably as futile as it was ridiculous. The climbers in front of him had also noticed him fall and they too came to his rescue.

The six-foot-plenty American – a goliath of a man with a heart of 48-carat gold – sprawled across the ice and his eyes were rolled back in his head. He was unconscious and shivering uncontrollably. We grappled Big Jim onto his back and I kneeled next to his head. I began to talk to him, encouraging him to stay with us, telling him that everything was absolutely fine and help was on the way. Within a minute or so a crowd had gathered around him, including Shinji Tamura, the second Japanese guide, Mark Woodward (Woody) and Narli. Two of the New Zealander guides were already on their radios, calling the incident in and requesting Sherpa support to bring oxygen up from Camp 2 to where we were.

The twenty-odd seconds it took for everyone to congregate around our fallen friend felt like an eternity. Big Jim's eyelids fluttered. He was barely conscious, incapable of speaking or standing. In a stroke of luck, among the impromptu mob was an Austrian climber who was a qualified emergency nurse. Within a few seconds she was injecting Jim with dexamethasone, a steroid used to treat cerebral oedema. Years later I would discover that the woman who came to our aid that morning was Gerlinde Kaltenbrunner. She is indeed a trained nurse but also happens to be one of only two women ever to summit all fourteen of the mountains on Earth higher than 8,000 metres, and in addition to this incredible feat, she did so without the use of supplemental oxygen and high-altitude porter support.

Then the unassuming Florence Nightingale disappeared as quickly as she had appeared. That year Kaltenbrunner scaled Lhotse, the fourth highest peak in the world, and would return the next year to summit Everest and the infamous K2 the year after that.

Back on the ice, Big Jim was still "man down". As an effect of altitude, fluid had begun to accumulate around his brain. This commonly causes dizziness, confusion and in this case, a loss of consciousness. The syringe did not find its way into Big Jim's thigh easily and before long there were blood smears on his skin and clothing. Considering the circumstances, where we were and the urgency of the situation, the outcome was nothing short of miraculous as, a mere twenty minutes after the call to Camp 2 was made, two Sherpa staff arrived with an oxygen bottle, face mask and a flask of piping hot tea. What had taken me just over an hour was a morning stroll for the Sherpa staff stationed at Camp 2. The strength and agility of the Sherpa climbers never ceased to amaze or humble me. They immediately covered Big Jim's mouth and nose with the rubber oxygen mask and he reacted to it instantaneously. His pupils contracted again and he was able to comprehend the commands being issued to him through the madness. Minutes passed and Jim was finally assisted to his feet and he began a slow and heartbreaking walk back down the Cwm to Camp 2, effectively striking his name from the summit team.

He was lucky to escape with his life. His collapse could very easily have been a stroke, a heart attack or worse. He would live to tell the tale, but also live to endure the bitter taste of giving up. Unsurprisingly, Big Jim would return the following year and have his moment of glory on the summit of Everest, closing that chapter in his life.

The tragedy was avoided but had cost the team an hour and a half. That was ninety minutes of precious time before the Western Cwm began to heat up like a reflector oven. The midday sunshine bounces off the white walls, pushing the temperature into the high 30s. We had left Camp 2 as the sun was rising in order to be in the tents of Camp 3 by noon, but after the delay caused by Jim's collapse, the team crossed the bergschrund that announces the start of the Lhotse Face and began the ascent of the icy mirror much later than planned. Before long I was at the back of the queue and would only arrive in Camp 3 after 1 pm, sunburnt, despondent with exhaustion and in a lot of pain.

From spending nearly eleven months in a wheelchair, my Achilles' tendons have become shortened and incredibly stiff, and despite surgery to lengthen them I still have very limited flexure in my ankle joints and feet. I would also only discover after a visit to a podiatrist in 2012 that there was a lot of scarification from tearing the plantar fascia of both my feet, further limiting the range of movement and causing excruciating pain in the arches of my feet. The result forces me to walk up steep inclines with both feet turned outward like Charlie Chaplin, minus the laughs. My awkward and clumsy gait eventually did get me to my destination but dehydration, bruised knees and depleted self-confidence were the price I would pay. I had climbed to Camp 3 once before on our acclimatisation cycle so I knew I was capable of it, but whether I had a second trip within me was always in the back of my mind.

By now John and the rest of "the fast team" – the Yetis – had summited, and some of them were making their way down from the top. I was in the team that made Russell work for his money. And so as luck would have it, both John and I arrived in Camp 3 at the same time, he from above and I from below. We were both shattered and borderline delirious with exhaustion and taking considerable strain in the heat of the day. We sat for a while and I congratulated him to the best of my ability. He spoke briefly about the route and how his summit day had gone.

We then shared the best tasting water I have ever experienced in my life. The climbers that had arrived before us were melting snow and graciously fed us cereal bowl after cereal bowl of the sweet nectar. We both began to feel a lot better as the water started to revive us. As we slouched on a snow ledge at 7,500 metres high, I sheepishly asked John if I could take his camera to the summit as I had left mine nestled snugly in my tent just two kilometres below. I remembered fumbling through the top pouch of my backpack for nothing in particular back in Base Camp, only to realise while approaching Camp 2 that it was my camera I had left in the tent. Of all the things a climber could forget to take on an Everest summit bid!

John was obliging and handed over his camera, but everything in life comes at a price. To this day I am still paying for it every time the topic of cameras or summit photos come up in conversation. It's one of those mistakes that a climber can make which won't cost you your life, just your pride.

John asked me how I was feeling and we got talking about my exhaustion and pain levels. We also discussed the fact that I was worried about the days ahead and whether I had the ability, tenacity or attitude to summit in two days' time. I didn't mince my words as I expressed the self-doubt and fear I was wrestling. As my closest friend, John knows one of my biggest shortcomings (apart from my height) is my self-doubt and my easily rattled self-confidence. And so in true John Black fashion, he managed to renew my confidence and give me a pep talk, and he did it with just two words. 'Back yourself.'

And just like that he'd managed to get my head straight. I was back in the game.

As the years pass I still have to remind myself of those two simple words. *Back yourself*. Even sitting at this keyboard is a direct result of John's sage words. So often I find myself questioning my actions, the projects I undertake and the content I speak on. But I have to remind myself that I have made it this far and perhaps I need to afford a little credit where it is due. I didn't come this far only to come this far.

After about 40 minutes John and I parted ways. He continued his journey down, one that he would later describe as torturous. He was on the brink of delirium as he arm-wrapped each pitch down the Lhotse Face, finally coming to rest in Camp 2 merely hours after standing on the summit.

I looked around the abstract surroundings of the camp dug into the mountainside at an altitude higher than any other mountain outside of the Himalaya. The world disappeared beneath me as I sat trying to absorb the panorama before me, the massively exposed Western Cwm. Behind me stood the summit of Lhotse, the fourth highest mountain on Earth. I looked from left to right; Nuptse formed the left-hand flank of the Western Cwm with the Khumbu Icefall, Everest Base Camp and Pumori.

I started making a list of the things I had achieved and the milestones I had reached to get to where I was now, sitting in the snow-dubbed Camp 3, the launch pad for my attempt on the biggest mountain in the world. It was massively rewarding to remind myself of exactly where I was, perched in the snow on that sweltering afternoon at 7,500 metres above sea level, over 600 vertical metres higher than my previous altitude record on Aconcagua in Argentina six years before. The day's work was done and I could retreat to the tent and rest.

CHAPTER 23

THE GATES OF HELL

After approximately three spoonfuls of vienna sausages and baked beans from the vacuum-packed boil-in-the-bag meal I had lugged up there, Chris and I spent a reasonably comfortable night in our tent perched at the top of Lhotse Face. Chris and I had partnered up when we were both assigned to the slower of the two Himex teams for the final summit bid. He is a lawyer from England and a great friend with a devious sense of humour and the sophisticated accent of an Eton schoolboy. It was the first night either of us had slept on oxygen and it went very well, considering I only woke up a few times to readjust my rubber face mask or to inspect the regulator dial in fits of unnecessary paranoia. The morning was cold and before I had even emerged from my down cocoon, the trauma of the previous day's "vertical ballet" was already evident. I stretched and yawned just like I did most mornings, and in doing so I felt that my ankles were rigid and tender. It wasn't exactly the start I wanted for the day, but at least it came as no surprise.

I stepped out of the relative comfort of my tent into the icy wind of Camp 3, the threshold of Hades. This would be my second journey into hell, but this time it was all my doing. My last journey into the underworld had not been my choice; I had been a broken person then, with broken bones and broken dreams. Now every grimace, every tear, every step further away from my humanity, every moment of anguish was a product of my own choices.

As a result of the effects of altitude combined with exhaustion, dehydration and oxygen deprivation, I have large gaps in my memory regarding the ascent from Camp 3 to the summit of Everest. My recollection of that day is a series of still images and not a fluid sequence, as if my brain switched from recording video to snapping photos.

The day had started just after sunrise on 22nd May, after we had packed our bags and washed down as much cereal as my gag reflex would allow. We departed Camp 3 for higher ground, heading towards Camp 4. A distance of just over a kilometre on foot would take me an agonising 10 hours to complete. I was hobbling badly and was far from alert, having taken at least eight Synap Forte tablets – those same painkillers I'd almost taken when considering suicide – since breakfast. I was a semi-functional junkie at best.

The queue of climbers ahead of me started at a slow pace, stopping often for various team members to adjust gear and shift oxygen bottles. But despite the gentle start along the faint path, any effort to gain some movement in my right ankle joint proved futile. It felt as if a nerve was trapped underneath my outer ankle bone and bearing weight on it was painful. But it was a pain I was going to have to make friends with. The swelling and inflammation from the exertion of yesterday's climb had left me with about 10% movement in that foot. I wasn't worried, but it was just another factor to consider. My pace was slow, which meant I would take longer to reach the next camp. I had to pace myself and time my food and water intake. I had come to terms with my spot at the bottom of the leader board.

The path leading out of Camp 3 heads up to the remainder of the Lhotse Wall and veers off to the left to the Yellow Band, a slip-and-slide of glass-like rock and ice. Crossing this famous section of rock was tricky. My rigid limbs made balancing incredibly hard and at times I found myself on my hands and knees. A fall here could put an abrupt end to my expedition as well as anyone I might have bowled over on the way down.

I was the only climber not getting impatient with the slow pace. With my right foot being upslope and the Lhotse Wall disappearing nearly 2,000 metres down to my left, it wasn't long before I was almost stone last in the queue. Climbers would move past me on the lines as I had to stop often to try to "jiggle" some movement into my wooden club foot, a technique that had proved successful in the past but now grew more fruitless with each attempt.

Where the ice met the ochre striations of the granite belt, I looked up to see a group of three or four Sherpa from our team – along with Adrian Ballinger – crowded around a large battery-powered drill. They were placing an expansion bolt, which would act as a sturdy anchor for the fixed lines. The smoothness of the rock lacks the cracks and crevasses that usually provide adequate placements, making this section of the traverse dangerously unprotected. I passed the gathering of labourers and an argument flared up in my head. Firstly, I was irritated that I was barely vertical while they were operating power tools. Someone had had the strength to carry them up 4,000 vertical metres above Base Camp (my maths was about as sturdy as my legs at that stage). I was so jealous of their strength.

The second voice started questioning the ethical impact of drilling into hallowed ground and what the purists would have to say about the abomination that is modern-day climbing. A third voice weighed in immediately, promoting the safety of the climbers and the value of human life. But the argument fizzled as fast as it had begun. My levels of physical and mental exhaustion put all arguments to bed as I sighed an unceremonious 'Ah, fuck it.'

After the Yellow Band, the mountain reveals the rest of the curved slope heading leftward up to the Geneva Spur, a small ridge hiding Camp 4 from view. I managed to stumble another 200 metres past the Yellow Band until I eventually collapsed to my knees. Tears came easily, a sour mixture of pain, frustration and embarrassment. I looked up the slender couloir leading to Lhotse's summit, a thin strip of ice at 45 degrees. 'What a shitty place to die,' I said out loud.

I turned over to sit on the hard mountainside and dug my crampons in to avoid a slide back down the Cwm.

And then the internal monologue began. *Is this it, Rob? Is this the obstacle that is going to turn you around? You made it this far, but now you're fucked.*

'You can't climb Everest on your hands and knees,' I uttered in a New Zealander accent, mimicking Russell's conversation with Tim Medvetz from the first season of the Discovery Channel documentary *Everest: Beyond the Limit*. 'Is this the obstacle you choose to end your one shot at Everest?' I asked again, my voice quaking like a nervous child. My oxygen set was still in place on my face, despite it only delivering two litres of oxygen per minute. In my bag was a packet of Synap Forte, the tablets which only three years before were intended to spell the end of me.

Unscrewing the lid of my pink Nalgene bottle, I swigged a mouthful of the icy water, sending the first four tablets to work and leaving an aftertaste of bitterness and whatever was left in the pot when we had melted water the night before. I closed my eyes for a moment, but the feeling of slipping out my seat and out of control overwhelmed me.

The entire time I sat there, I kept pumping my right foot up and down as if on an imaginary accelerator pedal in the hopes of regaining some movement in what I was now calling "this fucking foot." After 10 minutes or so I scrambled to my feet and attempted to carry on, but within a few steps I found myself on my knees, my rigid boots digging into my shins. I looked at the rope, a bright red thread leading the way to Camp 4 and my new goal. With my right hand I slid the ascender device a foot or so forward and crawled two steps forward on my knees. Again I slid the ascender and crawled another two steps forward. Despite the thick padding of my down suit, the hard ice was digging into my knees and it felt as if it would split the skin each time I moved forward.

Then I found myself in what, to this day, is one of the most awe-inspiring and magnificent places I have ever been, with a panoramic view that stretches for literally hundreds of kilometres in every direction. But I was too sore to give a fuck.

Going nowhere; once more I dug out the plastic bag stashed in the lid of my backpack and down the hatch went the next four tablets. After later researching the drug on the internet, it became apparent that I put myself in grave danger of kidney malfunction, especially in that state of severe dehydration. But in all honesty, had I known the risk I faced, I would still have done it. This was not the obstacle that was going to send me home.

There is video footage of me on this section of the route, skidding awkwardly down the Lhotse Face several times, tripping over my own immobile feet and coming to a jarring holt on the fixed line. It looks like I'm wearing roller skates, not crampons. The camera may add 10 pounds, but it cannot hide the fact that I was living up to the title I was given in the final edit of the documentary: "Russell's weakest climber". I think a label like that would have hurt a lot more, had I not resigned myself to how fitting and accurate it was.

As Satan's little helpers dissolved in my stomach, each step closer to the safety of the camp became slower and more reckless. A few hundred metres before the path snakes its way up the Geneva Spur, the traverse was as blurred as it was flat. With the safety line on my right side, it felt as if I was taking leave from my body, watching a drunkard stumble his way home after a heavy night out. Suddenly I felt a jolt as my right crampon caught the strap on my left crampon and I realised I'd become a monopod. I was falling, and with no effort to stop myself I toppled over to my left on a trajectory that could have potentially found me in Camp 2 – and dead. A fall of that magnitude was nicknamed "the Grand Tour" and it was often used in jest, but everybody knew that unless you had a safety line to catch you like I did, it spelled death in no uncertain terms.

In retrospect, there were no moments of my life flashing before my eyes, no dark tunnels with bright beckoning lights and no visits from a dead relative offering cryptic advice. I cartwheeled in a mess of arms and legs, top heavy from my backpack and oxygen bottle, until the fixed line I was tethered to took the tension of my weight and I came to a dead stop, flat on my back, head facing the bottom of the valley and feeling completely unperturbed.

It felt so good to just lie there. For what must have been thirty to forty seconds, I stayed there staring into nothing, enjoying not having any weight on my feet. But then instinct took over and I began systematically feeling my elbows and forearms, expecting to find a glove full of blood and feathers. I ran my hands down over my hips and thighs. No blood. I sat up and ran my hands over my knees and shins. Nothing broken, no blood. *Well, fancy that!* Back to the task at hand.

Standing up again reminded me how angry I had grown with my situation, how angry I was with "this fucking foot." I cursed like a sailor as I scrambled my way back to the path over a minefield of rocks and ice, muttering to myself about how surprised I was that I didn't tear myself a new asshole on the sharp rocks. Back on the path I was met by cameraman Mark Fetu. He had caught up to me during my brief time-out and greeted me with a hand on my shoulder.

'Jesus mate, I thought you were a goner!' he said.

I smiled under my oxygen mask. 'I'm fine, just shaken up.'

He looked at me again, a smile creeping up his face. 'The camera wasn't rolling, mate,' he said. 'Do you mind trying that again?'

I was grateful to have Mark with me, just a few steps behind, for the remaining hour it took me to cover the last 450 metres of shattered granite, its jagged edges sharpening as fast as my mind was blurring. Mark Fetu is an Everest veteran. Built like a Russian tank with a shaven head, he appears to be a rough and tough looking guy, not the kind of guy you would want to meet in a dark alley. Or any alley, in fact.

As the expedition progressed, I would learn that behind his intimidating appearance lies a warm and hilarious character. Mark is best known for his heroic 8,000-metre high bivouac on Everest, where he refused to leave an exhausted client he was guiding. Record has it that when morning came after a night in the Death Zone with no tent, Mark awoke to find the client dead, so he abandoned the corpse and walked down and subsequently into a hospital theatre, where he would have all ten of his toes amputated.

I cannot get the image of his square-ended feet out of my head – it was a stark reminder of everything this mountain was capable of taking from anyone, regardless of the résumé you had brought with you.

Reviewing the footage of me arriving in Camp 4, I can't help but fixate on the distinct angle at which my ankles are frozen, even with the three rigid layers of insulating nylon, neoprene and Gore-Tex of my boots. I was in agony, but still I announced 'I got into Camp 4!' to the camera as I arrived, pumping my fist in the air before surrendering to a coughing fit.

I was also captured on camera saying that Camp 4 is the shittiest place I have ever been to in my whole life. 'I don't see a big postcard industry for this place, I must be honest,' I said in my best Jo'burg East Rand accent. That has become one of the most memorable quotes from the episode and friends of mine remark on it often. That being said, the South Col – where Camp 4 is strategically placed, despite being a level field of gravel and boulders in the saddle between Everest and Lohtse and situated at approximately 8000 m above sea level – is no paradise either. Winds funnel through this passageway between the upper reaches of Lhotse and the summit pyramid of Everest at such speeds that little snow collects on the ground.

It was around 4 pm once I had settled into the tent. When I say "settled", I mean collapsed. Despite being exhausted and in a state of dementia, I can still remember marvelling at the neat pile of oxygen bottles, stacked like a barricade among the yellow dome tents that turned this Arctic wasteland into a village. This is the killing field where climbers literally froze to death just metres from their tents on 11th May 1996. Some of their bodies still lie where they fell all those years ago. But for the restless hours until midnight, this cemetery had to be home.

CHAPTER 24

CHECK. DOUBLE CHECK. TRIPLE CHECK.

My gloved hands find my goggles perched on the top of my head. Check. Sunglasses. Check. Gloves, spare gloves. Check, check. Water, GU sachets, sunscreen. Check, check, check. Summit banner. Scout scarf. Bank bag. Spudd. Check.

Goggles. Sunglasses. Gloves, spare gloves. Camera. Water, GU sachets. Sunscreen. Summit banner. Scout scarf. Bank bag. Spudd. Check. Double check. Triple quadruple quintuple check.

The wind is flattening the tent from side to side, making me anxious and claustrophobic. Chris is sick, *I think*. He has the squirts and that fucker better not give it to me. Keep your oxygen mask on. Breathe clean air. Don't get what Chris has. Fuck. My stomach is churning. No, it's not. Drink Imodium.

Goggles. Sunglasses. Gloves, spare gloves. Camera. Water, GU sachets. Sunscreen. Summit banner. Scout scarf. Bank bag. Spudd.

I close my eyes. Wait. What's the time? *I think*. 21:30. Two hours, thirty minutes until "go time".

CHAPTER 25

GO TIME

I was warm and it was quiet. Until Chris grabbed my shoulder and scared me awake. I jolted upright and looked at my watch. *23:50. Fuck! It's time!*

The wind was screaming like demons on the other side of the nylon wall. I kicked off my sleeping bag that was wrapped around my legs and began the ritual. Getting dressed by torchlight in a tent while sharing with someone who has just as much gear as you do is not easy. It's downright exhausting. The only thing is was smearing cold greasy sunscreen over every inch of exposed skin in the dead of night at -20° Celsius. Chris cranked up the stove to boil our last cup of tea and I swigged another four painkillers with a sachet of Hammer, a high-energy, carbohydrate paste, the last "solid" food I would eat for the next thirty-six hours.

As I finished lacing my boots over two pairs of socks and compression bandages, Ed Wardle burst through the tent door, blinding me with his camera light. 'Are your feet all right?' he asked me, prodding for a soundbite to juice up the documentary footage. I explained the process of wrapping my feet and inserting my battery-heated inner soles. 'Better do, I guess.' The words slid out of my mouth as if I had had a choice in the matter. Ed probed about the wind and both Chris and I revealed our fear for the time we would be exposed out there.

'That wind is going to cut through us all day!' I gestured, chopping my one hand into the other to emphasise its severity.

'You don't have to go,' Ed replied.

Thankfully my response to Ed's statement appeared less aggressive on film. Leaning forward to confront the faceless light, I said, 'Sorry? I don't have to go up?' I was furious at how easy Ed made quitting sound. 'Yes, it's a choice,' I continued, looking away. 'But it's not one I am willing to make at this stage. I am still getting one foot in front of the other ... so, still going.'

That's what it had come down to. No glory, no romance, just the fact I was able to get one foot in front of the other. A fool's errand if ever there was one.

During the course of the evening, Russell postponed our departure time from 11 pm to 1.30 am. He was monitoring the encroaching weather systems and its associated wind speeds from his temporary camp, pitched 500 metres above Base Camp on Pumori. And that's where he conducted our well-planned orchestra from, nearly three kilometres away as the crow flies.

Truth be told, in the event of an emergency, any attempt to reach us would have taken between thirty-six hours and three days depending on the position of the climbing Sherpa teams and prevailing weather conditions. We may as well have been on the moon. The weather report was forecasting that the wind would die down around 1.30 am, giving us another 150 minutes of sheltered comfort, but 150 fewer minutes to get up there and back alive. The weather window would be closing soon. There was a cold front carrying heavy snow which would drop temperatures to well below −40°C with high winds coming from the Bay of Bengal. And it was gaining on us.

We were taught very early in the expedition to negotiate our time to the minute. Departure times were as rigid as the tent floor I had just spent the last few hours on. If the plan was to leave at 1.30 am it meant just that. Not a minute later, nor a minute earlier. If a climber left their tent ten minutes early it means they would be exposed to the elements, losing valuable heat and energy just standing still.

Similarly, a climber emerging from their tent ten minutes late puts the rest of the team in the same danger, so 1.30 am meant 1.30 am.

I exited the tent on my hands and knees and bungled to my feet. The uneven stones and gravel surrounding the cluster of tents made it hard to balance and I stumbled forward and back like an alcoholic searching for their car keys. I could hear the familiar voices muffled under the rubber masks as the team congregated among the glowing orange domes. It was difficult to see any faces because our head torches blinded whoever you were looking at, so out of consideration I kept my eyes at my feet as I clipped the sternum strap of my backpack. I checked the tethers keeping my mittens attached to the sleeves of my down suit. There was a tangle; my glove had landed up on one side of the shoulder strap and my hand on the other. It was a simple dilemma to solve, but this feat took me nearly two minutes to fix. I knelt down to adjust the battery-powered heaters in my boots. The elements had heated fully and were starting to burn the balls of my feet. Before I could get my second glove off, Lhakpa Nuru's face appeared and he asked what the matter was. I could tell by his squinting eyes that he was smiling under his face mask as he fiddled the heating pads down to their lowest setting.

Just as quickly as he had appeared, he jumped to his feet and was digging in my bag to check the dial on my oxygen regulator. The dial clicked and I immediately felt the cold air blowing harder on my top lip. Four litres per minute when walking, two while resting in the tent and sleeping. We were gassed up and ready to go.

Woody raised his arm in the air and gestured a big circle. I didn't hear what he said but I understood full well it was "go time". Lhakpa patted my shoulder twice to signal our departure, but I held out an arm and told him we would join the back of the queue. I knew it would not be long before the climbers behind me would want to pass and I thought we could avoid the awkward dance move as they passed me on the fixed lines. That and the fact that we would encounter less of the team when the time came for me to turn around and descend back down to reality.

You can barely walk, Robert, I thought to myself. *This is Mount Fucking Everest! What the fuck were you thinking?*

I am the chink in the armour. I am the Achilles heel.

CHAPTER 26

CHASING SCORPIO

My memory of the climb between the South Col and the Balcony (a landmark on the way to the summit where the path reaches the top of the south-west face and continues along a ridge line in a westerly direction, which leads up to the South Summit) is scattered and thin. Leaving the tents, we joined an already long line of headlamps spread out all the way up to what I suspect was the Balcony. The gentle gradient gradually worsened and the path became a monotonous back and forth of switchbacks as we edged closer to the illusive summit, the ultimate goal, which was as far away as it was all-consuming.

In the pitch black I would pause every four steps to ease the burning in my thighs and the feeling of suffocation. In the darkness, only the pinpricks of light from the climbers' headlamps were visible against the 60-degree slope in front of me. They would disappear over the edge as the path turned left at the Balcony and continued towards the South Summit. I imagined myself floating in space. It was black in every direction I looked – except down. The yellow stars on the path ahead of me made the perfect constellation of the scorpion's tail.

That is the extent of my memories of those next few hours as left followed right, followed left, followed right.

At one point the path had devolved into a series of small stone ledges, which had slowed the pace considerably. For a short while

I had company, even if it was in the form of a queue. Being alone in the Death Zone multiplies your chances of dying up there, so the thought of having people around me, regardless of who they were, was very comforting.

The novelty of my very own summit day on Mount Everest lifted my spirits. I had moments of welling excitement and I smiled widely under my breathing apparatus.

Summit day on Everest. Don't pinch me, I'm enjoying this.

The next image I have from that night – in the stack of Polaroid shots in my head – is a climber sitting in the middle of the path. There he sat, calm and coherent. Nobody was panicking or trying to communicate with him. *This is going to be a cluster-fuck* was my first reaction as visions from the volumes I had read about the 1996 disaster flashed through my head.

Who is this? Is he one of ours? Is this guy going to die here? Confusion set in immediately. I wanted to stop and assist this guy. Nobody else was stopping to help.

'You okay?' I managed to ask the collapsed figure, and he nodded in response. We were like neighbours greeting each other casually as if we were out walking our dogs. I would learn later that he was an independent climber who had run out of oxygen only three to four hours from Camp 4. Russell Brice assisted by sending some of his "boys" up to him with additional bottles and they escorted the man back down to the safety of High Camp. That's how people die up there – recklessly embarking on a summit bid without ticking every single box.

Hours passed and it began snowing lightly. To the east I could see the faint line of morning starting to glow purple and orange and the silhouette of Makalu, the world's fifth highest mountain, becoming clearer in the distance. Its summit lay right in line with where I stood. I fumbled for the camera in the chest pocket of my down suit and pointed it in the general direction of the neighbouring giant. The photos later revealed that the flash reflected off the falling snow immediately in front of me, and the image was useless.

Tick followed tock followed tick followed tock. Left foot followed right followed left, and by 5 am I crested the Balcony just as the sun peaked that morning, painting the slopes pink and orange for a few brief minutes. The serene beauty of this jaw-dropping vista was shattered as I stepped onto the crest of the Balcony and directly into the coldest, most brutal wind I have ever experienced. The scouring snow and frigid blast of air felt like rock salt fired from a shotgun, stinging every exposed piece of skin. I quickly cowered for shelter behind an oddly placed boulder to regain my composure and swap the regulator from one bottle of air to the next. As if from nowhere, Lhakpa's hands were on the regulator first and once more, with smiling eyes he came to my rescue. Between the stranded climber and the Balcony, I have no recollection of Lhakpa Nuru being anywhere near me, yet the moment I needed a helping hand he appeared from thin air, as if he was made of it.

Several precious minutes passed and I could no longer postpone what needed to happen. Without drinking or eating anything as planned, I slung the hood of my suit up onto my head and pulled it skew in an effort to shield my face from the airborne spray of invisible daggers. I looked up at the next leg of the route and saw steeper, rockier, knee-deep snow steps towards the South Summit, a false peak which can be seen in photos of the south face of Everest as a kink in the slope to the right of the summit. And a fucking queue.

When you are born with your arse as close to the ground as I was, the snow steps feel like a history essay assigned on the last day of the school term. Each step was difficult, being significantly bigger than a step I would normally take. With the added weight of my double layer boots and crampons caked with snow, it became a monstrous effort to lift each foot. The sun had risen above the horizon now but its warmth was deficient and the wind that was forecast to die down was still alive and well, causing me to hide behind the baffle of nylon and down.

The next hour or so passed with me taking three steps at a time up towards the South Summit. I wrestled with my windswept hood and chose the least-weathered fixed line at each anchor, making the way up to our next oxygen cache slow. But we gained altitude steadily and efficiently, three frustrating steps at a time.

The price for our slow pace was to be paid then and there as the weather closed in around the back half of the queue heading for the summit. Each year around the third week of May (during the summit season) there are two or three short breaks in the weather on top of Everest known as the window period. Each window is approximately three to four days long and we were heading to the top as the last window of the season was engulfing us with each passing minute.

By the time I reached the South Summit, visibility was down to just a few metres and now mist was added to the list of elements that were out to kill us. It was not necessary for a bottle change at that stage so we descended the scree slope and continued past the stack of aluminium bottles, shredded prayer flags and the remains of what looked like a tent. Once we were on the corniced traverse the wind halved in power but still cut deeply into the tiny pieces of my face between my goggles and face mask.

The corniced traverse is a precariously exposed section of the route which has steep drop-offs on either side, like walking up a dragon's spine. A fall to the left takes you two kilometres down the south-west face of Everest, directly into the Western Cwm. A fall to the right takes you down the Kangshung Face into Tibet, equally steep, equally high, and equally fatal. I was lucky enough to be given a portion of the footage that was shot with Lhakpa's helmet camera from the editing room floor of Tigris Productions. On screen, Lhakpa and I can be seen talking and exchanging high fives at the first sighting of the Hillary Step.

But my joy was short-lived. Within a few steps a queue of climbers were stacked all the way up the wall and onto the summit ridge. They were standing, waiting and burning daylight, but more importantly sucking precious O^2.

By now it was around 7 am and the temperature was lurking well below –30˚C. It was impossible to make out who the other climbers were, as we were all reduced to an assembly of equipment, Gore-Tex and down, differentiated only by the colour of our suits and the boots we wore. Up there I was "red and grey down suit with red and black boots". My oversized Oakley Wisdom goggles with a snow-camo frame, orange fleece beanie and the fighter pilot rubber face mask from my oxygen set all contributed to me looking less than human. But considering where I was, maybe that was fitting.

As a teenager I saw a magazine advert featuring The North Face in one of the many climbing magazines I repeatedly thumbed through. The magazines were outdated and dog-eared, but I committed each one to memory. I scoured each photo and each piece of gear that I dreamt would one day hang in a cupboard of mine. The advert headline read "My Body Wasn't Made For This, But My Soul Was." As a copywriter who has paid my dues in the trenches of the advertising frontline, I admired and cursed the talented bastard who wrote it. As a mountaineer it is one of those adages you keep in the back of your mind that reminds you why you are five miles high on a chunk of ice in a screaming gale, beyond any hint of happiness, reason or sensibility. Today was one of those beautiful days.

Back on the corniced traverse, the hoard of down suits wasn't moving fast. About a hundred metres or so along the path was the Hillary Step. Every time a gap appeared a descending climber would swing over the edge of the jagged rocks and abseil down the Step, creating more anxious tension with every missed chance of ascending.

Summits are forfeited and lives are lost when people in cold places stand still for too long. Each lost minute is a minute of daylight, a minute of supplemental air, a minute closer to the approaching weather system and a minute closer to the unfolding of a potentially fatal disaster.

The Hillary Step is the only part of the south-east route to the summit of Everest that requires any kind of rock-climbing skill. At 8,800 metres above sea level, this moderate scramble becomes a technical nightmare of rock and ice, creating the last obstacle between any climber and their goal. Named after Sir Edmund Hillary for his first ascent of this boulder, the Step is 12 metres of cracked slabs consisting of rock and ice which climbers try to scramble across. The sheer exposure adds to the psychological difficulty of the Step as you stare down to the little coloured dots that make up Camp 2, pitched 2,400 metres directly below you. Several weathered ropes are strung along the route, sun-bleached and brittle, attached to the mountainside with steel pitons hammered into cracks and crannies, probably decades ago.

Up ahead, Woody was waving his arms at the climbers perched at the top of the last rocks, abseil devices in hand. I wasn't close enough to hear Woody over the surging wind, but having become well acquainted with the New Zealander over the previous few weeks, I can guarantee that he wasn't challenging the oncoming climbers to start a Mexican wave. A few robotic climbers scrambled their way up the face and out of sight.

Within about twenty minutes I was standing at the bottom of the most famous piece of rock in the world. I clipped into the fixed line and kicked hard into the ice on either side of the stack of boulders. I edged my way up awkwardly as my crampons screeched like nails on a chalkboard. Each step was off balance as the ropes were anchored above and to the left of me, constantly pulling me off balance. Any slip now would send me swinging uncontrollably, dangling literally kilometres above Camp 2. I hung on the fixed line, yanking at my ascender with absolutely no evidence of my sixteen years of experience as a rock climber.

I clambered to the top of the final bulge that brings the scramble to an end. I must have bashed my knees in the process and I ran my hand over my throbbing patella, once again checking for blood. I took a few fast breaths in an effort to ease the sound of my pulse thundering in my ears while using this opportunity to switch my safety leash and clip both karabiners to the business end of the fixed line that led to the top.

As I stood up I almost scraped O^2 masks with a figure leaning absently in front of me. "Blue down suit and red Millet boots" lent against the rock face, standing in an upright version of the recovery position from page sixteen of my First Aid Manual. We almost collided face to face and she didn't even blink. No more than two steps behind the catatonic woman was the Sherpa guide who was short-roping her. (A short rope is used to keep a climber within a metre or two of the person guiding them. It is also a clear sign that the person being short-roped is in a world of shit.) Unsympathetically he put his gloved hand on her shoulder and shook her in an effort to bully her to the top of the abseil.

In a blog post I later wrote upon returning to Base Camp, I wrote:

"I looked up to be met with the blank gaze of a woman who looked like she had seen Hillary's ghost. Her eyes were wide and she was speechless, her face a cold and pale suede. Her Sherpa was short-roping her down from the summit, her victory packed somewhere safely. She was apparently a sixty-year-old USA climber ... I hope she still is."

From the top of Hillary Step, the summit lies silent but within sight. We were now out of the relative shelter of the corniced traverse again and everything that was said had to be shouted, even though Lhakpa and I were an arm's length apart.

Lhakpa received a radio call but I didn't hear it, so he repeated Russell's message into my ear. 'Big Boss say no so far now.' I give him the thumbs up and we begin moving again. After clipping my cow's tail from one pitch of rope to the next, I took a few steps before coming to an awkward halt. "Royal blue suit, red boots" – the crazy Frenchman from our team – was on his way down and we kind of shook hands. It was more a bumping of gloves than a handshake. With a new sense of urgency, Lhakpa slapped my shoulder and in a single word summed up everything. 'Summiiit!'

That was what we were looking at. It was why we were there and a reassurance that everything was going to be okay. I pivoted around, keeping my aching feet firmly anchored in the snow, to shake Lhakpa's mitten with both of my hands.

And then I began the last few steps to meet Madam Everest.

CHAPTER 27

09:21 AM, 23RD MAY 2009

That was the precise moment I stumbled to the highest point on the planet – 09:21 am NPT, 23rd May, 2009.

There were still about twelve people strewn on the summit mound, with the last few climbers arriving intermittently. The bright colours of everyone's down suits and the strings of prayer flags up there made it look like a small plane had crashed into a paint factory. People collapsed on their sides; others kneeled and onlookers huddled around the scene.

I spent twenty-two minutes there. I wasn't victoriously posturing to the soundtrack of Dvorak's 1812 Overture with my chest expanded and my hands on my hips. Nope. I sat.

I'm not sure what I expected to see at the pinnacle of the Earth, but I was surprised nonetheless to find a litter of heroes and strings of prayer flags frayed by icy winds. There was a small wooden-framed box with glass sides on a short post planted firmly in the snow. The yellow painted shrine contained a statue of Buddha, seated quietly and serene, oblivious to the screaming demons of the Death Zone. The box's sides were old, scratched glass panes holding a few photos of people from all corners of the world. Some climbers had stuck a few stickers on the glass and wedged into one of the corners of the box was a photograph of the Dalai Lama.

Visualisation of any goal is said to be a brilliant tool to prepare people, especially athletes, for big events or races. Creating a picture of success in your head during the preparation stages makes the goal more tangible and in turn increases motivation levels. In the months leading up to the expedition I had created a mental movie clip of my summit moment, including the wind cutting deeply into my numb lips and cheeks. But in reality the scene was far from the picture I had painted in my head. There is no way to imagine the scathing cold or how isolated and exposed I felt.

For those twenty-two precious minutes the world stood still.

Behind me, Lhakpa dug into my bag and grabbed a handful of the summit banner I had carried up. The miracle of dreams. Since its early inception at my desk in the corner of the studio, the banner had evolved into a mammoth sail measuring over three metres wide and as high as I am tall. It was a mosaic of photos, logos, inspiring quotes and even a marriage proposal. Each block represented the support that had driven me to where I was now sitting. I imagined holding the banner between two people, stretching it across the summit for the world to see, but the high winds forced me to sling it across my shoulders like a giant winter scarf. Cameras clicked all around me and my camera was passed from Lhakpa to a faceless cameraman and back. Then I turned and asked my guardian angel if he could fetch the plastic bag I had also carted up there. His whole body disappeared into my bag and reappeared, holding my most sacred of possessions. Tightly stuffed in the Ziploc bag was a handmade bear called Spudd, two tattered Scout badges and a leather thong with two wooden beads dangling from each end.

Spudd was a gift from my mother which she had hand stitched herself. Before my first trip to the high mountains she gave me the awkward little bear, which had coarse textured fur and black beady eyes. His black cotton nose and mouth give Spudd a curious expression that seems to ask, 'What the hell are we doing now, Rob?' That brave bear is now 19 years old and has climbed on six of the seven continents, boasting more time in the Himalayas than almost every human I know.

One of the Scout badges in the packet was a bottle-green Springbok Scout Award badge. It belonged to Hans. It was my way of saying thank you to him for the life he had led, the example he had set and the motivation he had poured into me during my formative years.

If I could climb to the top of the world with a small symbol of everything Hans had been to me and could spread some of his indomitable spirit with a message of hope for those facing cancer, then maybe his death had not been in vain.

The leather thong was my Wood Badge, a globally recognised scouting award signifying my qualification as an adult leader in the Scout movement. Throughout the training process I had been assigned a mentor called Mike Dickinson. He too would succumb to cancer. It took his body cell by cell, but it could never have conquered the man.

I brought the Wood Badge back and gave it to Mike's son, Allan. As time has passed, Allan and I have become incredible friends and I often smile to myself on the occasions I see Allan's father's mannerisms in the things he does and says.

I turned and clawed a small divot in the snow. I then placed Hans' badges into the hole and covered them with a handful of snow. Pressing the lump down firmly with my knuckles, I whispered a reverent 'thank you'. I was thanking the Mother Goddess of the Earth for letting me be there, thanking every person who had believed this was possible. A heartfelt expression of gratitude to be in that exact place at that exact point in time.

Zero visibility. Atrocious weather. Utter exhaustion. But perfect.

The radio hissed to life again. It was Russell and this time he was talking directly to me. 'Nice one, Robby. It's time to get down.' He was as calm as ever. That was a good sign. There was no applause, no cheers from the crowds, nothing. Just sage advice from the man who has never had a client die in his care on Everest. Over twenty-one years of shepherding people into the Death Zone and back, and every single one of them have returned alive.

'Robby here. We are starting the descent now,' I said into the walkie-talkie that was attached to Lhakpa's down suit like an umbilical cord connecting us to the real world. I had to over-emphasise each word as I battled the numbness in my face. Somewhere during the ascent, near the foot of the Hillary Step, I was forced to turn my radio off. It was not working well and beeped repeatedly which became irritating and any communication coming through it was inaudible. Having confirmed that we were on our way back safely, I slipped my mitten back over my hand and turned to face down the summit ridge.

It was at that precise moment that I felt the adrenaline ebbing from me, giving way to a muted sense of panic and exhaustion.

The walk ahead promised to be a long way down, demanding every bit of my concentration and endurance. Getting back down would be as demanding, if not more, than what I had just gone through to reach the summit.

New challenge. Same dodgy legs. Ten hours in.

CHAPTER 28

BLUE SUIT, BLACK BOOTS

It took almost as long to get back to the relative shelter of Camp 4, which was lying bare and exposed in the hurricane funnel of the South Col. Within minutes I found myself back at the Hillary Step, this time looking down at the last stragglers who were fumbling at the fixed ropes like zombies clawing at a locked door. I sat down, leaning against the rocks that marked the end of this section of the ascent.

I threaded my belay device with utmost care. Dropping it would not only make the abseil even more risky and awkward than it already was, but we were directly above Camp 2 and that piece of steel would become a lethal projectile for anyone in the vicinity 2000 metres below if I were to fumble. I also couldn't stop thinking about the fact that Bruce Herrod's body was found at the bottom of the Hillary Step in 2009, still attached to the ropes. It is speculated that Bruce slipped or inverted on the abseil and lost consciousness. His body was moved a year later and laid to rest nearby by American climbing legend and leader of the IMAX Team, Pete Athans.

The descent of the rocky obstacle was anything but graceful. My crampons were more cumbersome and unhelpful than on the way up and I skidded and screeched my way across the icy rock face, bashing my knees and clutching at the rope as if it was my first time in a harness. Only once we were out of the bottleneck and firmly standing on the relative safety of the corniced traverse did I feel some sort of relief.

I was instantly made aware of how exposed this section of the path is. Climbers shuffling their way along the path leaned clumsily into the incessant gale that whipped over the knife edge of ice and snow. The pace was frustratingly slow near the back of the queue as we plodded forward five steps at a time to halt and wait in a human traffic jam. At least the wind was now on the opposite side of my face, which made for a nice change. We continued through the whiteout along the trampled path, following the blob of colour ahead of us and the occasional spot of scree and granite. The pile of cached oxygen bottles at the base of the South Summit reminded me to check on my own bottle. I had no idea how long it had been since last it was checked or changed.

As if he had read my mind, Lhakpa had his hands in the top of my backpack and was wiping the ice off the regulator dial. 'Is okay. Change little bit,' he said, gesturing with his giant red glove.

Chris was about twenty climbers ahead of me in the queue as we edged our way down. Every time the conga line came to a stop, my English tent-mate would collapse onto his side out of utter exhaustion. But he was moving, albeit slowly, closer to camp and closer to a safer altitude.

I learnt quickly that when Lhakpa says "little bit", it is approximately an hour. Within 100 metres of the Balcony, the skyline started to distort and fade as though I was looking through a fish-eye lens, and I became suddenly dizzy. Within seconds I found myself looking for somewhere to sit. And then everything went black.

I realised immediately that I was sitting and Lhakpa was stuffing the full replacement bottle back into my bag. The gap in time was startling, and whether or not I lost consciousness is still debatable. A shiver of fright ran down my spine at the realisation of how quickly the situation had become unmanageable once my oxygen supply was depleted.

With the new bottle attached and packed away, I got up onto my feet. We made our way down past the Balcony in clear sight of Camp

4, the ant farm of tents below, blurred intermittently by the cloud rushing between Everest and Lhotse.

By now the pounding in my feet had spread up to my knees, making one inseparable ache that surged with every step. Every foot placement was a stark indication of my vulnerability, each movement a reminder of that April night when my life changed in the time it took to fall two and a half metres. Each step took me closer to the little yellow and orange dome tents. Fortunately, the terrain had "simplified" and the awkward bone-jarring rock steps were replaced by a relatively smooth snow slope, allowing me to gain some distance away from the Balcony in a short span of time.

A few hundred metres below the Balcony lies the lifeless body of a climber. In silence, he lies with his head hidden under a thick sheet of blue ice. The fabric of his down suit is bleached by the harshness of the high-altitude sun. What was probably a rich aqua colour is now a pale sky blue, almost grey. About five years previously, this guy was a climber just like me. I imagine him as he was then – "blue suit, black boots". He probably sat down to rest and didn't stand up again. Unscathed, the webbing of his harness is still intact now around his withered thighs and waist. His feet are partially buried by a porcelain layer of ice, as if his body is sinking into a pit of ghostly quicksand. His arms lie peacefully at his sides. His bare fragile hands, closed in loose fists, are blackish-brown as if the desiccated layer of skin covering them had been applied with a paintbrush. The body is in full view to every passerby, maybe two or so metres away from the fixed lines on a gentle ice slope.

'What happened to you?' I asked him out loud, almost expecting an answer. From where I was standing the terrain was relatively gentle, a gradual slope punctuated with the odd boulder strewn across this abstract landscape. Nothing about his position or the relaxed pose he rests in now showed any sign of trauma. There were no twisted limbs or fractured bones, so I ruled out the possibility of a fall. He was poised deliberately with his legs pointing downhill, the same way I had sat down on the slope leading to the Geneva Spur just twenty-four hours earlier. He was there on purpose.

'Why you and not me?' I asked, like Lady Macbeth addressing Thane of Fife. What could possibly have happened that I, the chink in the armour, stood breathing while another climber lay dead at my swollen, fatigued feet? Nobody chooses to die.

But even in my state of exhaustion, I could see that this was no accident. I had assumed this exact pose just yesterday. I had stopped to rest, also facing downhill, and instinctively given in to the weight of the pack on my shoulders. For a while you can close your eyes and escape this blanched hell while you concentrate on slowing your breathing and stopping your heart from hammering its way out of your chest.

In time I would realise that the difference between the departed and me was simple; it lay in the decision to carry on. There was no way to tell the details of this man's demise, whether he had fallen victim to sickness or run out of oxygen. But what did happen to that climber was that he accepted that this was going to be the obstacle that would be the end. That decision was to stop him, less than a two-hour walk from the sanctuary of the South Col. Once you have made your decision to quit, Madam Everest takes care of the details.

Within minutes, lethargy and hypothermia take hold, like steel chains shackling you to your icy grave. Consciousness fades and you slip into a deep sleep, and death is not far behind. In the advanced stages of hypothermia the brain sends false signals, creating the sensation of warmth which engulfs your body, and in a twisted irony, several climber's bodies have been found with their gloves taken off and their down suits unzipped due to a delirium that secured the final nails in their granite coffins.

A deep sigh eventually set me free from the daydream and I turned to continue the jarring descent to camp. Never before had I been that close to a dead body, and walking away I was surprised at my lack of fear or reluctance to be in his presence. Instead I held a rational and cold conversation with what was once a man with dreams and ambitions just like mine but is now an icy monument in remembrance of himself and nothing more.

From what I could gather through research, the deceased was a Korean climber who passed away in 2004 or 2005. In recent years, social media and various tabloid websites have sensationalised the presence of dead bodies on Everest. Headlines have distorted the truth, conjuring images in the minds of the general public of climbers stepping over corpses like drunk students at a music festival. "Climbers' Bodies Used as Landmarks on Everest" was one of the headlines I found, right next to one of those "13 Celebrities You Never Knew Wore Braces!" "interest" pieces.

Everest's history is stained with tragedy and at one stage the statistics showed a one in ten ratio of fatalities on the mountain. There are an estimated 200 corpses on Everest, the majority of which are not visible to climbers en route to the summit. Wherever possible the deceased are moved away from sight and committed to a crevasse or buried with stones and snow. Unfortunately, there are some bodies that have been given nicknames, stripping them of both their identity and their humanity. Most famous of these is "Green boots", a climber of Indian descent called Tsewang Paljor. He took refuge in a small hollow under some overhanging rock during his ascent of the north face in 1996. He subsequently died from exposure and his body lies in plain sight to every climber going to the summit. The cave has been called Green Boots Cave by teams on that route, not in flippant disrespect or bravado, but as a waypoint to gauge the location of climbers on the route. In a context of safety, rescue and oxygen supply, geographical markers can mean the difference between life or further death.

Adding insult to injury, the late British climber called David Sharp also took refuge in the already infamous cave during a storm. His body was also visible, resting on his haunches with his arms hugging his legs tightly. The circumstance around Sharp's death caused a controversy which I will not go into. His body was moved a year later in 2007 at request of his family.

Death on Everest evokes a range of responses from climbers and non-climbers alike. There are as many opinions on the topic as there are people. One of the most accurate analogies I have come up with having discussed this conundrum at length is this: imagine you are a runner in an ultra-marathon. In the last kilometre of your 90-kilometre race, you encounter a runner who is unable to carry on. Consider trying to hoist him over your shoulder or even piggyback him to the finish line and the medical attention he needs. It would be irresponsible to even try to pick that runner up and carry him the remaining distance, considering your advanced state of exhaustion and fatigue. Before long the sweeper vehicle would be loading two people into the ambulance, the number of casualties now doubled. At altitude the stakes are even higher; it is not a race. Instead of a finisher's medal, mountaineers are rewarded with their own lives. Rescue attempts, as straightforward as they may seem, are anything but that. Up there the risks of injury and exposure to extreme weather conditions for prolonged periods of time are fatal in most cases. The Hollywood image of one bearded mountain man helping the other by putting his arm over his shoulder as they limp towards the thunder of an approaching helicopter is as ridiculous as it is far-fetched and idealistic.

When deciding to go to Everest I had to resign myself to the fact that a rescue above 8,000 metres is virtually impossible. It is also selfish to put others at risk, possibly increasing the death toll and burdening them with your fate for the rest of their lives.

I told myself this on several occasions leading up to and while on the expedition, as a reminder to myself to keep moving. *Nobody can walk for you and if you are unconscious, you are regarded as dead. That's how it is.* After all, it was my signature on the Himalayan Experience's indemnity form.

Looking at the body of this man on my way down made it all too apparent why the majority of the bodies are still where they died and cannot be brought down. A lot of them are now cast in compacted ice. Removal would require chipping away inches and inches of solid ice, requiring several hours of hard labour at extreme altitude and low temperatures. Carrying a 60–70 kilogram body down a steep snow slope would prove exhausting and slow, once again exposing the rescuers to prolonged periods of exposure. Moving an immobile climber on a mountain has been compared to carrying two bags of cement down the stairs of a wet fire escape on roller skates. On rare occasions, bodies are wrapped in foam sleeping pads or discarded tent fabric before being slid down the mountain, but still at a great risk to the team responsible for controlling the descent.

I snapped back to reality. My feet were now screaming from not shifting my weight for a while. Who knows how long I had stood there, as still and as vacant as the deceased "Blue Suit, Black Boots" and I eventually parted ways and I continued to make my way back to the tents, slowly and awkwardly, each step thick and heavy in my boots. My shins and ankles were now swollen and raw. I used every opportunity to rest and adjust the angle my foot had taken inside my boot, alternating each leg, lifting each foot up like an indecisive flamingo. I had no idea where Chris or Lhakpa were. I have no recollection of my guardian angel during the descent. I think he hung back by a few minutes, perhaps discussing the day's work with the other Sherpa climbers and guides.

The way back was pretty much straightforward and we were descending to a safer altitude, so it was not entirely necessary for him to be babysitting me at this point in the day. With the amount of pain I was in, I was aware of very little around me. Apart from stopping at that body, the walk down was more about trying to get down as soon as possible and getting my weight off these cement feet. All I was concerned with was finding my tent so I could collapse in the "safety" of Camp 4.

I was met at the tents by one of the Sherpas who was yielding a flask of lemon tea, a dose of piping hot magic in a desert storm of ice. I drank deeply, clouds of steam bellowing as I attacked the cup and seared my wooden lips. The sheer joy of hot tea coursing into my body outweighed the agony of the hot, acidic liquid cauterising the cracks in my blistered lips. By now it was late in the afternoon, around 4 pm. I had been walking since just after midnight. The wind was still howling around the ghost town that was our camp. Whoever wasn't already horizontal in their tent was probably still descending behind me.

After a further two cups of tea I fumbled out of my crampons and backpack and collapsed next to Chris. He had made it down alive and was semi-comatose in the tent. That makes it sound more planned and composed than it really was. In reality he had collapsed, mostly on his side of the tent. His down sleeping bag was pulled across his torso and his face was hidden behind the mask of his oxygen set. I was greeted by his eyebrow lifting enough to acknowledge my entrance. It was not the hearty backslapping welcome one expects on returning from a journey out of the troposphere and into the Death Zone. Too tired to eat, shit or cry, I joined the pile of down and nylon that was Chris and my body hit the tent floor like a stack of newspapers on a pavement.

And that is where I stayed.

Reviewing the video footage, the tent door was still open and flapping in the gale as we lay there. I lifted one arm, having found the camera inside my chest pocket, and snapped a handful of the worst photos ever recorded. I wasn't even aiming but one unplanned selfie shows me lying on top of a sleeping bag, my face sideways in the picture, blankly staring through the camera. My bloodshot eyes and wind-burnt face are exaggerated by the harsh yellow glow of the tent, but my expression is one of bewilderment and can only be described as absent at best.

I dropped the camera next to where I lay before closing my eyes. *What the fuck just happened?* I thought.

At some point in the early evening I awoke, shivering. My boots were still on, my gloves still tethered to my sleeves. I got up and zipped the tent door closed as the last rays of sunshine were leaving the Col. Chris was breathing.

'You okay?' I gestured at him, as if there was anything in my power to help the guy out.

'Bloody shite,' he mumbled, before closing his eyes. I heard the heavy rhythm of his laboured breath.

The night passed slowly. Chris was a mess, literally. Above 8,000 metres Imodium had little effect on his frequent surges of diarrhoea, which had worsened beyond control on the descent back to camp. Considering the temperature was 40°C below zero and gales were pumping relentlessly, Chris' life could easily have ended had he risked opening his down suit to relieve himself. The tent was thick with the smell of human shit. The yellow nylon walls wrestled in the wind and despite extreme exhaustion, I was semi-conscious as each minute ambled past. I spent the dark hours trying to bury my entire head into my oxygen mask as morning played hide and seek outside our little round gas chamber. "Cracking a window" was not an option.

One thing does remain clear in my memory. As I lay there, I repeated to myself, *you've just climbed the highest mountain in the world*. Over and over. At one point I'm sure I said it out loud. Chris didn't respond. He was going to die soon anyway and I was too depleted to do anything about it.

And then the question popped into my head, ricocheting inside my skull. *But what does it mean?*

For the next 10 hours, Chris and I lay almost motionless. I moved only to ease my aching feet or twist my neck, peering through the corner of a half-opened eye to catch a glimpse of the down-covered heap that was my neighbour. If the sleeping bag was moving it meant he was still alive.

I had reached a state of utter exhaustion in which my body was too heavy and tired to do anything at all. My mind was still racing back and forth in intervals of deep thought (within the limitations of where we were) and a blurred delirium, flitting in and out of sleep. In between bouts of restless slumber, I felt something hard jabbing into my ribs. Half-lifting myself up to try to see what it was, I was completely confused, feeling the mat around the obstruction only to realise several seconds later that the pain was coming from the digital camera under me. I must have dropped it after snapping off those few post-summit glory shots.

It was only when reviewing the contents of the memory card a week or so later, that I realised that I had taken those lopsided photos in the tent. There is also a video of the inside of the tent, dancing in the afternoon winds of the South Col, badly framed with no real point to it at all. The pictures on the card capture the nonsensical existence I experienced that afternoon, all taken from the flat of my back.

And there I lay. I had achieved the epitome of success. From the age of fifteen I had been drawn to the idea of Mount Everest – not just climbing it, but its entire heritage and history, the magic and mystery of it. I can still spend hours thumbing through the many picture books from my tightly packed bookshelf. The picture on the wall of our kitchen is an A0-sized block-mounted photograph of a climber on the corniced traverse, taken from the South Summit. This mountain has never been a hobby, but more of a deep-seated obsession.

And now it was mine in all its glory.

CHAPTER 29

SUCCESS AND HAPPINESS

Success is usually associated with wealthy individuals in tailored suits, drinking a fine whiskey while enjoying the sunset from the deck of a beachfront summer home, not some guy from Germiston with dodgy ankles, wearing a sleeping bag with legs while smelling like a wet dog. But success and mountaineering have always been closely twinned. We have all seen those oversized posters in thick black frames on office walls, dramatic photographs of a nameless climber forging his way through an oncoming blizzard with a title like "LEADERSHIP" or "INTEGRITY" in elegant block letters. Normally it is followed by a qualifying statement underneath it, quoting some or other maxim.

Upon closer inspection the chasm between the two could not be greater. Professor Shawn Achor, the author of *The Happiness Advantage*, professes that the link between success and happiness is both broken and backwards. He goes on to explain that during our entire lives we are taught that happiness is a result of success. Study hard so that you can be accepted into a decent university. Then before the champagne cork has landed, the new message we're told is to work our butts off and get a degree in order to get into the right law firm or advertising agency or financial institution. Because that's where success awaits, and with success comes happiness. You graduate at the top of your class and are immediately thrust straight into the corporate arena, cleverly disguised as a cubicle with a laptop and a coffee cup. And happiness has moved again, hiding behind your first promotion.

All that is happening is that happiness is being moved further and further away, making it something we are always chasing and never truly experiencing. It is human nature for us to constantly shift the goal posts further and further away in the name of growth. That growth is often in an upward direction and success is not far behind. You adjust the cufflink in your Egyptian cotton shirt sleeve on the way out of a very productive meeting before climbing into the leather seat of your luxury car. You are at the top of your game. You are successful.

Yet ironically, in the mountaineering game, successful CEOs of the guiding companies, sponsored athletes, and the elite certainly do spend a lot of their nights sleeping in a tent and eating out of an aluminium pot, despite being undoubtedly at the top of their game. So perhaps there is some truth in Achor's work. Success to a large degree lies in experiencing the things that make us happy, and not the other way around.

However, the definition of success differs greatly from person to person, making it difficult to gauge one idea against the other objectively. For fifteen years of my life, the milestone of my success was an area of snow the size of a double bed, waiting for me at -47°C on top of a hill. To many people that is nowhere close to their embodiment of success, and is often dismissed as crazy or downright stupid.

I had joined the exclusive ranks of the Everest Club, the cream of the alpine crop, the iconic epitome of success. The man on top of the world, I had sung from the mountain tops and returned triumphant. But there, lying on the floor, slurring and sunburnt like a homeless person, neither happiness nor success were anywhere to be found. They were abstract ideas, far too complex for my tired and oxygen-starved brain to deal with.

Climbing Mount Everest has been described as "the ultimate endeavour of the human spirit" beyond the realm of mere mortals, never mind me. What the hell was I doing there?

CHAPTER 30

THE WAY DOWN

The first light of morning came, giving rise to one of the clearest and calmest days we had experienced during the trip. The wind was still moving bad weather our way, but for now the deep-blue sky stretched over us in every direction as far as the eye could see, which, considering where we stood, was far. But the brilliant conditions of daybreak went unnoticed.

We had made it through a second night at 8,000 metres above sea level, but Chris was unresponsive. His words during those fleeting conscious moments were garbled and incoherent, so I alerted the guides to the situation that was unravelling fast. Narli arrived in the tent entrance and began to scope out the severity of the problem. He and I had become quite familiar – it was bound to happen. Narli was the sweeper guide, the shepherd, and I the last sheep. Today his light-hearted optimism was nowhere to be seen.

The radio crackled to life as we got the expedition doctor, Monica, on the line. On the other end Mon and Russell were scratching their heads, powerless to do anything more than dose Chris with as much Codeine and Imodium as we could muster.

Despite my intention to stay with Chris, I was sent packing and in no uncertain terms. Before I left, I grabbed Chris' hand in mine as he lay near the door of the tent and held it to my forehead. 'Chris, you gotta get up and move now, okay?' I said. I slapped his thigh, hoping to evoke some kind of response. He muttered something about seeing him later in Camp 2.

Woody and Narli knew I was slow on my feet and sent me off without any further delay, back down to reverse the path I had limped up less than two days before. The phrase "as useless as tits on a bull" was used when I suggested helping them get what looked like an upright corpse out of camp. So I walked off to find the start of the fixed lines.

I looked back to see Chris being harassed to his feet. The New Zealanders are known for many things, but diplomacy is not one of them. As subtle as blunt axes, Narli and Woody strong-armed Chris into some resemblance of a mountaineer and their journey home started ... three steps at a time.

On a long enough timeline, everybody's chances of survival in the Death Zone diminish to zero. Get up there, tag the top and get the hell out. No rehearsals, no long tracking dramatic shot, no theme music. This selfish mindset trumped any bruising to my ego that had been caused by being more of a hindrance than anything else. I had to get my head around the task at hand: getting down alive.

In the back of my mind I was surprised Chris had made it through the night, but he was not in the clear just yet, and the question of whether he would be able to make it down off the mountain was still unanswered. Saying farewell to him back at the tent, I had found myself swallowing the lump in my throat as part of me was resigned to the fact that this would be the last of Christopher Macklin.

I peered over my shoulder one last time and saw Chris lying on his side a few paces from where he had started. I muttered something resembling a prayer, which probably came across as more of a command than a request. *They gotta get him down off this hill. They just have to keep pushing him down.*

The way back home traversed around a bulge of shattered slate, which was quite difficult to move over safely in my crampons. Their shiny new coating was now a road map of scratches from the abuse of moving steadily up the hill. Just like the days before, the time between starting to walk and my ankles loosening up was an agonising affair, made worse by my lack of balance and the jarring path that would lead the way home.

After about half an hour I was over the Geneva Spur, approaching the Yellow Band with the massive void of the Western Cwm opening up to my right. The camber of the path was now reversed that so my right foot was no longer at an awkward angle, but it was taking the majority of my weight being down-slope, so I was in a lot of pain. Still. Feeling the exhaustion of the previous day's adventure, I stopped often to rest along the path. Still attached to the safety lines, I sat down and pulled off my right glove to begin the unshouldering process to remove my bag. Without thinking I placed the glove carelessly on the ice and began to dig through my bag. Out the corner of my eye, I noticed something move and watched in horror as the glove started to slide into the abyss. But as gently as it began, the glove came to halt about one-and-a-half metres in front of me and I felt the blood drain from my face. I quickly got redressed and carefully shimmied down the slope to the glove, pouncing on it like I was stalking a rabbit.

That was a polite reminder that I was still in the Death Zone, a reminder that I was still far from home and that this was not the time to let my guard down. I was still a trespasser in Madame Everest's kingdom and my welcome had come to an end. For the next few hours I stepped prudently from one fixed rope to the next, going through the motions, talking aloud to myself through each transfer from one anchor point to the next. *Unclip Safety one. Clipped. Unclip Safety two... and clipped. Wrap arm and go.* It would force me to pay full attention to the process and it also punctuated the never-ending descent down the glistening ice wall of Lhotse.

Every so often a sharp pain would jolt from beneath my ankle bone, causing my leg to buckle and ultimately leave me hanging on the fixed lines, having tumbled a metre or two down the face. My frustration turned to anger and a flood of tears, but I was not home yet. And so I would stand up, rub my knees which were throbbing from being bashed into the ice, curse my life and carry on until the next fall.

There will come a time in your life when all you want is to give up. But you can't; there are no other options. So just keep going.

Over the last few hours the weather had started to deteriorate, and banks of clouds began building up over the skyline of Nuptse. This was the motivation I needed to get back onto my feet and continue my slow journey home.

I limped into Camp 2, in worse shape than I had been on the way up. I'd endured eight long hours of arm wrapping, getting weaker with each change-over as one rope length gave rise to another in an unending trance. Arm wrapping is a technique used to cross steep ground by wrapping the fixed lines in a spiral around your forearm and through your hands in order to provide friction and control your speed downward. It is faster than abseiling or rappelling, but it is riskier and tiring. The fixed lines had burned lines in my gloves and sleeves as I had become more dependent on the rope and less stable on my feet. Nearing the last few pitches of the fixed lines, it became incredibly difficult to differentiate between the white of the ice face and the white nylon ropes that protect the steep face. I found myself squinting at the anchor points in an effort to find the blue strands woven into the safety line, completely exhausted but still aware that a mistake would make the last few months of hard work and effort for naught.

Eventually I welcomed the end of the Lhotse Face. About 300 metres from the pearly gates of Camp 2, I slumped onto the side of the path to catch my breath, my axe digging into my side. I remember lying there feeling the throbbing in my legs, all the way down to the indescribable cluster-fuck that were now my feet. As I lay there motionless, I was oddly grateful for the sharp spike in my ribs. It was my only incentive to get up and carry on.

To my surprise, just metres behind me were New Zealand's finest – the guides – and Lazarus, the walking dead. Chris. How slow was I if the dead guy had managed to catch me up? As Chris had descended with the guides he'd immediately started to recover and feel stronger, especially as the air got thicker and his body was under considerably less stress. Once in Camp 2, Chris managed to change into his other clothes and clean himself up and, to his extreme delight, sit on a proper toilet, even if it was a barrel with a toilet seat attached. As we all began to feel more human in the relative comfort of camp, I could feel both gratitude and relief that my teammate and good friend had survived possibly the most hazardous sixty hours of both of our lives.

It is not my intention to embarrass Chris, but to rather tell this story in a way that explains the events that took place and illustrates the savage nature of an attempt to summit Everest. Chris Macklin proved himself in the most relentless of environments where all factors and risks are increased by a factor of ten. This man was, and still is, a good friend who I respect and admire for his strength, courage and tenacity. The fact that he supports the English rugby team is a discussion for another time.

CHAPTER 31

VICTORY AWAITS

We woke up in Camp 2 at 4 am. I must have slept deeply.

The air was thicker and clean, and when the alarm pot went off I was severely disorientated. It took every ounce of strength to convince me to stuff my swollen feet into my icy boots, to face another day of death on two legs, but this journey was the last trial before victory was truly mine. I eventually got dressed once more, gagged down some breakfast and set off into the minefield.

We now faced the urgent objective of getting down to Base Camp before the sun hit the icefall. When the valley heats up as the season progresses, the ice seracs and hanging glaciers perched on the walls of both Everest's West Shoulder and Nuptse on either side of the valley become more unstable. They are still as large as soccer fields, houses and school buses, still weighing hundreds if not thousands of tons, still capable of shifting without notice, obliterating anything in their way.

In the years that followed, these seracs would be responsible for many more deaths, including the catastrophe of 2014. That dark day was Everest's biggest tragedy; sixteen Sherpa climbers were killed en route to establishing higher camps and ultimately it closed the season to climbers on both sides of the mountain.

In 2015 an earthquake would destroy Nepal's capital and wreak havoc across the country, triggering landslides and avalanches in

Everest Base Camp and the rural villages leading to it. There were massive efforts made to rescue climbers stranded above the collapsed icefall in the largest rescue operation in the mountain's history.

As the icefall empties into the Khumbu Valley, the terrain flattens out considerably. The last twenty-five minutes took forever to complete. My backpack was packed with everything I had used on the summit rotation, my clothing soaked to the bone from the last six hours of sleet, snow and mist. The weather had kept its promise. As we got closer to the tents, the murmurings of life and activity broke the silence of the icefall, which was now gratefully behind us. The relief of knowing I would never need to go back up there again was palpable.

It is tradition to welcome the climbers back home into Base Camp by grabbing all the pots and pans from the kitchen tent and clanging them together in a joyful ruckus, each team member returning to a deafening celebration of life.

And that's what it was, something to celebrate. I arrived in camp to a barricade of every person in our team armed with anything that made a noise, whooping and cheering like I'd come home with the Webb Ellis trophy under my arm. From between the mob, John emerged in his orange and black down jacket and we hugged like brothers reunited. One welcoming hug followed another as I was met with familiar faces: Lance Fox, the snowball-chucking American veterinarian; Big Jim Holliday, who I was so happy to see had recovered after we had said goodbye to him four days ago; Monica the expedition doctor, Valerio De Massimo (Italian royalty); Kirsty Mitchell aka "Camera Babe". Anyone within arm's reach embraced me in a flood of tears, regardless of how my sodden gear smelt.

A camera set up on a tripod filmed our rowdy homecoming and all I could muster when asked how it felt to be "home" was 'It's done! It hasn't quite sunk in just yet, but it's done!' My broad smile creased my burgundy face and cracked my lips.

And it finally *was* done.

To quote Ed Viesturs, "The summit is optional but the return is always compulsory."

CHAPTER 32

LIKE SOLDIERS BACK FROM BATTLE

I don't remember much about 26th May and I can confidently say that not many of the clients in the Himex Everest 2009 team do either. The day dissolved into a night of celebration. We drank like soldiers back from battle, like men who were happy to be alive. The Tiger Dome was heaving with noise and merriment, which was mostly swigged straight from the bottle. I browse the photos from that night of debauchery and apparently more happened than I remember. The evidence shows snapshots of me dancing with Alix, Valerio's now wife. It was a mixture of the Spanish Paso Doble, the waltz and gum boot dancing, which ended with a spectacular finale face down on the carpet. John was involved in a round robin of arm wrestling between the clients and the Sherpas and there are blurred visions of Hiro, our Japanese guide, screaming 'Domo Domo!' at every opportunity. What that actually means is still a mystery, but it is hilarious provided you point to your crotch with both hands while yelling.

At one stage during the night, I somehow noticed John was missing. I stumbled out of the Tiger Dome, calling like a lunatic in a hurricane. When I found him he was kneeling at a table in the mess tent, spooning instant yoghurt into his face, rambling on about how it was the most incredible thing he had ever tasted. But judging by the toilet paper wrapped around his head and shoulders courtesy of Moises, our "Mexicanese" teammate, John's judgement may have been slightly impaired by alcohol. At one stage, John had somehow landed up on his back while Moises poured champagne into John's puckered face.

Out of fear for my best friend's life, I convinced him to leave his beloved yoghurt and make his way back to the warmth of the party going down in the Tiger Dome. I reached the door of the tent only to realise John was gone again. I turned around to discover that he hadn't gone too far but had decided to nap in the deep snow among the remaining bottles of champagne. The scene reminded me of the Roadrunner cartoon where the coyote plummets to his doom, leaving a perfect silhouette in the ground. There lay John, face up like a snow angel ... without the wings and robe. I managed to get him to his feet and we eventually collapsed onto a chair in the relative safety of the crowded party tent. Well, evidence later showed that John managed to find the chair and I found the green carpet again. The photos show John sprawled out on the bench and me lying on the floor under his feet, curled up like a Labrador, holding onto his foot, most probably in an effort to stop the world spinning.

But day turned to night and we eventually staggered to our tents to pass out. All of us drunk, rowdy and dishevelled heroes. All of us united by the success of living to see another sunrise.

CHAPTER 33

RUSSELL'S FINAL TRICK

I firmly believe Russell Brice's impeccable attention to detail and planning knows no end. The morning after our victory celebration was a mad rush to pack our lives back into the barrels and duffel bags they had arrived in. Our departure from our makeshift home on the glacier, which could have been a rather drawn out and emotional occasion, was executed like the tearing off of a Band-Aid. Having failed to use the time before the summit celebration the day before, sentimentality went out the window as we stuffed the last scattered belongings in to any available gap in our gear bags and barrels.

The hangover that befell us the next day was the perfect distraction to sever the tie between ourselves and our home for the last two months or so. The blinding glare from the whiteness of the freshly fallen snow, together with a pounding headache and the sour smell of champagne in my sinuses, kept my mind off the sadness of leaving, a pain I would only feel later in the weeks that were to come. John and I started the long walk away from the barren wasteland of stone, sand and ice that we had both fallen in love with. Away from the rows of tents, the Sherpas, our guides and Big Boss. Away from "expedition life" and closer towards "real life". The sombre mood was punctuated by fits of laughter as one of our English teammates stopped every few steps to dry heave the last dregs of last night's champagne marathon.

Day stretched into night and Gorak Shep was replaced by Lobuche and Dugla by Pheriche, each village blurring into the next. By late afternoon John and pretty much everyone else, including the yak driver and porters carrying massive loads, were now far ahead of me. The one-and-a-half metres of snow that had fallen in the last three days had started to melt, turning most of the pathways into rivers of milky-grey slush which were difficult to negotiate. I was alone, in a trance following what I hoped was the right path, looking for a village named Pangboche or Dingboche or Tumboche. Something ending in "boche", anyway.

Darkness fell. In addition to my down booties, Oakley sunglasses, and a book about serial killers, I had left my head torch behind in Base Camp. It would have been very handy as the last of the daylight faded. I had no idea how far I still had to go; it could have been around the next corner or in the next valley for all I knew. Once again I found myself alone on the path, literally miles from anything familiar, my thoughts dominated by the familiar companion, the surging ache that had once again turned my lower legs into one mass of pain. The joy and novelty of my summit just seventy-two hours before was so far from my mind, it might as well have never happened.

I was no hero. I was still the chink in the armour. Nothing was different, and I hated myself for it.

By about 7:30 pm it was pitch black outside. John had reached the lodge at sunset and I was still out on the trail. The rest of the team were also home for the night, their boots drying around the lodge's yak dung-burning stove while I was out in the cold, fumbling and cursing my way home.

A very concerned John Black put on his famous orange and black jacket once more, grabbed his head torch and headed back up the path in an effort to find me and bring home, the last sheep once more. Walking in the dark had caused me to trip over every loose rock and tree root along the way, exacerbating my already inflamed ankles. I had reached the point of not caring and had reached the realisation that I would spend the night in the next village in whatever lodge or barn was available to me. But the flitting of a torch in the distance was such a relief, a relief doubled when I heard the familiar voice.

'Rob?!'

John had found me and cemented his name on my list of heroes forever. John tells me that on his way back up towards me, he came to a junction where the path split in two and flanks either side of one of the smaller Sherpa settlements. Remembering the journey down from hours before, John took the path on the left on the bet that I would choose the same way when I got there. Luckily that bet paid off, as the alternative would have had us missing each other and spending unnecessary time in the frigid weather, endangering both of our lives.

We chatted on the way back as we shared the tiny beam of John's headlamp, still tripping and cursing. But silently I fought back the tears. The lodge was another thirty minutes away, but I arrived to the team enjoying the stove in the dining room of the lodge. I was welcomed in as a seat opened for me like the parting of the Red Sea and some lemon tea magically appeared almost immediately.

One of the many nicknames I have for John is Joseph. It evolved from Joe, a shortened version of John (if that's even possible) but over the years John has on several occasions waited for me, walked beside me, guided me to safety and steered me both subtly and unsubtly, and in doing so he has lived up to his nickname. Joseph. Joseph the Shepherd.

But the night would not finish without tears being shed. When dinner was done and it was time to go down the five stairs to our rooms, I was unable to stand up. The day's goliath trek had caused my joints to swell as soon as I had sat down to eat. I tried several times to stand, but the pain was unbearable and I fell back onto the wooden bench, fighting back a surge of tears. They were tears of frustration, exhaustion and embarrassment. Tashi Tashi, the expedition team's assistant cook, approached and offered me a piggyback down to my room, just 40 metres and five stairs away. I tried to weasel my way out of it, but he turned around and squatted down in front of me, tapping his hands on his shoulders. Eventually I resigned to my crippled state and Tashi swiftly lifted me onto his back like a sack of flour. In my head, the newspaper headline read "Everest Hero Carried to Bed with Sore Feetsies".

Downstairs, the room John and I would share was cold and very poorly lit. I was glad it was.

I once more attempted to numb the pain with a stupid number of painkillers and anti-inflammatory tablets. Once settled in our beds, John wouldn't see the tears streaming down my flushed face. I lay there in the darkness and waited to hear the sound of deep breaths, signifying that John had drifted into a deep sleep. Then the barrage of tears flowed.

I am the chink in the armour. I am the Achilles heel. Still.

The next morning, I learnt that Tashi Tashi had arranged with the owner of the lodge to rent a horse to carry me to our next port of call, Namche Bazaar, for $35. I know more about quantum physics than I do about horse riding and the thought of the journey ahead had had me in a cold sweat. My hard cash included the services of a fifteen-year-old boy who not only led the horse on foot, but carried my backpack for the 18-kilometre journey to Namche. Once again the headlines popped up in my head, this time reading "Conqueror of the Mountains Rescued by Village Teen".

I have little to no recollection of the second day, the 29th May. Examining photos from several team members' cameras, I can barely recall a few snippets from the walk back to Lukla from Namche Bazar. Having been back along that path another three times since, only now am I able to arrange the memories chronologically, pinning them to a vague timeline. The first memory is a photo of Chris Macklin, fully recovered, smiling and with eyes as wild as the lion's mane now outlining his face. We stopped at the Everest Bakery for a cappuccino and slice of apple pie before the final trek back to the bustling airport village of Lukla, spring-boarding us back to civilisation.

The next morning was the last of our early wake-up calls. We rose in the dark, packing our gear like automated robots before making our way to the airport terminal, just a fifteen-minute walk in the first light of sunrise. We wanted to be on the first flights back to Kathmandu, ahead of the crowds of trekkers and the other teams. Once back in the city we checked into our hotel. The decision as to who got to shower first was settled with a hand of rock, paper, scissors. Ching, Chong, Cha. After twelve weeks in the wild, what was another twenty minutes? An eternity.

John and I spent the day ambling through the streets of the Thamel District of Kathmandu, scouring for souvenirs and an embroidery shop that could sew a memento of Everest onto the fleece jackets we had set aside. These skilled artisans could create exquisitely intricate pictures of almost anything onto fabric, and all for the equivalent cost of three loaves of bread back home. With one final dinner in Kathmandu, we bid farewell to our new-found friends. We shared wine, ate well and toasted our success.

The next day we would go our separate ways, back to wherever we had come from, each one of us returning to our lives of familiarity, to wrestle and fret and toss and turn. We were leaving the mountains behind, along with the busy, dusty roads of Kathmandu, the dream of the last fifteen years now put to bed.

Put to bed, but not to sleep.

CHAPTER 34

BACK TO LIFE

Walking away from the baggage carousel back home, I became emotional, welling up with tears as I imagined the moment the terminal doors opened. I knew my mom was going to be there as we had chatted when I was in Kathmandu, and she would not have missed it for the world. But I didn't know if anyone else would be there.

The glass doors of the O.R. Tambo arrival terminal opened, and the hall came alive as I received a round of spontaneous applause from the crowd that had gathered. My mother and brother Dieter were there, accompanied by scouting friends and a pair of journalists. Tanya Bennetts, now a close friend, was also there and with her were five children from CHOC, the charity I had pledged to support with my climb.

I was floored when I saw these young children of primary school age. Most of them had no hair and they were very pale, with dark rings under their eyes. But they were smiling. They stood shyly, holding boxes of biscuits for me. They were the ones who were not sure if they would see Christmas or their Matric dance, and here they were thanking me for walking up a hill in the cold to cross something off my bucket list.

It was at this point that I realised what I had done meant something to someone else. I realised that it was my duty to find the answer to that question I had lain awake with just days before. *You climbed the highest mountain in the world. But what did it mean?*

Within the blink of an eye I was back in the real world. I can't say I was home, because I had not felt that feeling for a long time. During the time I spent in Durban, I had isolated myself from people, never settling nor able to fit in entirely. I had had no idea what the outcome of the expedition would be. It had all been hanging in the balance.

Since our arrival in Lukla, the other climbers were the only people on the planet I could identify with, socialise with, empathise with or rely on. In the thirteen weeks we shared on Everest, these strangers became my "mountain family". Through exaggerated circumstances, shared suffering, fear and endurance, relationships form at an accelerated rate and within a few days we had forged bonds that I hope will last indefinitely.

And now the trip was over. Once more I found myself back at square one, starting from scratch.

'So how was Everest?' is the question I usually get asked, and I'm never sure how I should answer it. 'How much time do you have?' is usually my response.

It's as if someone were to ask you how high school was. In the five years most of us spent in high school, there were good times and bad times; there were new people, new ideas and new discoveries about ourselves and the world around us. In fact, the nervous mouse who arrived at the school gates and the young adult that emerged having graduated are not even the same person, which makes the question even more complex to answer. To compress my entire Everest experience into a few simple sentences can never do it any justice and is very often futile. Sometimes I escape a long and in-depth explanation with the flippant response: 'You know ... it had its ups and downs.'

The majority of people ask about the route to the summit of the mountain – how it looked, how cold it was or how many dead bodies I had to step over to get there. I am often quizzed about the awe-inspiring view from the highest point on Earth and about the food we ate, the weight of my bag and even how we do a "number two" up there. But nobody ever asks about the way down.

Descending Mount Everest, the journey home and everything that would ensue beyond would take me on a path I could never have expected and one I was certainly not prepared for.

One of the commitments of my sponsorship agreement with Roche Pharmaceuticals was a nationwide road trip to all nine provinces in South Africa, speaking to a range of audiences with a presentation aimed at creating awareness about the signs and symptoms of Non-Hodgkin's lymphoma and the benefits of early diagnosis. I had the privilege of meeting and speaking to the South African Minister of Health at the Mount Nelson Hotel in Cape Town, various church groups, patient support groups and school children of all ages.

One presentation I gave was to a primary school in the rural village of Cintsa in the Eastern Cape. The rudimentary school has only one electrical plug point on the entire property and the toilets were essentially long-drops built at the edge of the dusty playground. I spoke in a prefab classroom crammed with over a hundred neatly dressed sardines. The sweat trickled down my back. It was winter but the open windows did little to cool the packed classroom in that one-horse coastal village. My opening slide was a photo I had taken of a yak by crouching down and extending my camera out to the giant, an extreme close-up that left me wiping strings of bovine snot from my lens. The children exploded in fits of laughter and my story began.

While I spoke, the room was a collage of wide-open eyes, completely silent except for my voice and the teacher-cum-translator, as together we explained the alien landscape I had come from, one sentence at a time. At the end of the slideshow I connected the projector to my laptop's camera and for the first time, these school children got to see themselves on a screen. Within minutes the classroom erupted into chaos as one by one they realised what was going on. There was waving of arms and faces being pulled in every direction as the picture on the screen mimicked their every move. When it was done, I left through a gathered mob, shaking hands and giving high fives as I edged my way back to the rented car. I drove out of the village along the dusty path and eventually back onto the highway.

Within two kilometres of the main road I was forced to pull the car off onto the side of the road, and there on that sweaty afternoon I sat and sobbed uncontrollably, not able to comprehend the extent of what I had just experienced over the last four months, in the context of a village full of children who didn't realise people could own more than one pair of shoes.

I had spoken at gala dinners and national conferences before, at fundraisers and corporate road shows. I had received standing ovations as I held up the framed photograph of me on top.

I had done this presentation several times before but had never been affected like this. It was the realisation that what I had achieved on that mountain had the power to affect others.

It was starting to sink in. My success *did* mean something, and that day, along with the smiling children from the airport, was the first of many clues that were to follow. I was given the opportunity to live the dream of a lifetime and gained so much more than just awe-inspiring photographs and bragging rights.

Now I held the responsibility to use all that I had gained to make a positive difference in the lives of other people. That was a lot easier to say than do.

CHAPTER 35

THE IMPOSTER

While writing this book, I found a journal entry that I wrote sometime in May 2010.

"I climbed Everest to raise awareness and funding for people facing their own mountain: cancer. And ironically, nearly one year to the day, my father has been diagnosed with colorectal cancer. The same disease I fought against is now an uninvited guest. It snuck in the back door and is now sharing a bed with a family member."

I had visited my father in hospital several times before. When I close my eyes and think of him, his asthma pump is never far away. He wore a neatly trimmed goatee, which gradually grew more and more silver each time I saw him until the day he shaved it off completely and I felt like a sceptical child seeing a strangely familiar man in Santa Claus's red coat and a dubious strung-on beard. My father's history of gastro-intestinal issues went back to my childhood and in the last few years of his life, his weight fluctuated between 80 and 52 kilograms as the disease flared and calmed.

I found out from my brother that my dad was in hospital again and this time the news was, in no uncertain terms, as serious as it was damning. It was cancer. Not the "Big C". That euphemism was reserved for people that you didn't really know all that well. But this was fucking cancer. And it was going to kill my father.

We walked down the labyrinth of dimly lit hallways. One thing I always notice in hospitals is the families that congregate in the waiting areas and at the bedsides of their loved ones: sons in their stretched-out, oil stained hoodies, daughters stealing every moment to carry on texting their friends unnoticed. Jokes whispered between loved ones, flowers, chocolate and silver foil balloons in their hands as they cautiously hug the bedridden in an effort to avoid the awkward tension infecting the ward.

We filed down the passages that led to where my father, Billy, was to be found. People always asked why my two brothers and I referred to my father as Billy and not Dad or Daddy. The common response I learnt from hearing my elder brothers say it was "because that's his name." In retrospect I think it was my mother referring to him by his first name. Why, I don't know.

On his left side stood Sheena, my father's wife, and my brother Dieter was on his right. My new girlfriend Tracey and I entered the room.

Tracey and I had met about six months before. On my way to give another Everest slideshow for a Scout group on the side of town I grew up in, I decided to accept my brother's standing invitation to drop in for a drink after work one Friday afternoon. I had left early to avoid the afternoon traffic between West Rand and East Rand and had about an hour and a half to spare, so it was the perfect opportunity for an impromptu visit. And I'm glad I went. My brother Dieter had met Tracey Braithwaite through a mutual friend and had mentioned in conversation that his brother, Robby, was a graphic designer who would gladly design new business cards and a corporate identity for her travel agency, TTS Travel.

As the afternoon went on, I made conversation with this woman to whom I was immediately attracted. When conversation reached the point where two adults exchange phone numbers, Tracey told me that there was no point in doing so. Having come from a really difficult relationship, she was not ready for another and besides, after the second date I would never call again, because that is just how men are. Right there and then I extended my hand and offered to sign up for a three-date contract, and I was willing to shake on it. We did exchange numbers that night before I left for my presentation.

Time would pass and we would eventually go on our first date. I was struck by her soft beauty, her endless compassion and the fact that she too liked Vini's legendary Polo Pizza. I ordered extra asparagus on my pizza which was met with some strange looks, but hey, every new relationship has its issues to work through. She would turn out to be the person I wish I could have called from the summit of Everest.

That night in the Olivedale Clinic was the first time Tracey would meet my father, but also the last time I would see him alive. Had I known this, I think the conversation would have been entirely different.

By the time we had fought the Jo'burg traffic to get to the hospital, the doctors had already told my father the prognosis and his proposed treatment plan. The implications meant he would have to have large sections of his bowels removed, an aggressive radiation regime and a colostomy bag for whatever time he had left.

The visit crept by as my brother and I tried to lift the atmosphere, trying to dart that toxic elephant in the room. 'No matter what it takes, we will fight, fight, and fight. That's what we do,' I said bravely to the grey-faced man that was my father, his complexion blending all too well with the screen-printed linen he was lying on.

The salt in these gaping wounds was the fact that my father's financial situation was appalling and his chances of survival were overshadowed by the threat of not being able to afford any treatment of any kind. In his mind, the battle was lost already. We all assured Billy that we would all do whatever it took when the time came.

I left the room silently, but in my head I knew it was time to be a pillar of optimism. I was the founder of "The Climb of Hope" for fuck's sake! Hope, optimism and "climbing a mountain for those who couldn't" was what I was all about.

That night when I got home, I dug out a book that I had recently read from a drawer. The book had touched me from page one with a message of steely nerves and an attitude of victory as aggressive as the disease it stood against. Along with the book, I mouthed a speech to myself, rehearsing what would have been akin to Winston Churchill's delivery of "we shall fight them on the beaches". On Friday morning I put the book in my car along with my memorised speech, ready for deployment on the Omaha Beach of my father's disease.

The book I wanted him to read was Lance Armstrong's *It's Not About The Bike*. I read it in a time when Lance was deemed clean and I respected his worldwide campaign to live strong. His was a story of how his decisions and attitudes took him from his death bed to the finish line of the Tour de France. A story of how he shifted his focus from the problem to the solution, from pain and fatigue of unrelenting hillsides to the yellow jersey waiting at the end. A story of passion, aggressive positivity and an indomitable spirit to survive – no matter what.

Everything I needed for Billy to hear at the time.

CHAPTER 36

RESEARCH WELL EXECUTED

It was early afternoon on 27th May 2010. I had just come out of a meeting and was leaning on the edge of my desk, holding a notebook to my chest and laughing and joking with my neighbours in the desk cluster I worked in.

Shamima Thomas, the personal assistant to the company's MD, gestured to me from the other side of the open plan office, signalling me to come and talk to her. She looked panicked and I was immediately confused. She had a message from my girlfriend Tracey. After not getting through to me on my mobile phone, Tracey had contacted the main reception at Ogilvy Johannesburg and was put through to Shamima. My brother Dieter had also tried in vain to reach me after Sheena had called him in a panic, so he'd called Tracey.

I don't recall exactly what Tracey said to me, but the phrases "your father" and "no heartbeat" were what mattered and what sprung me into action. Being the closest person to where my father lived, I left my laptop and all my other belongings behind and sprinted out the front door, fumbling through the cluster of keys to find the one that would open my car door. I drove the 15 kilometres between the office and my father's house as fast as the little engine in my Suzuki Jimmy would go, mostly on pavements and in the emergency lanes of the streets of Northgate. During that time I managed to make two phone calls, one to return Tracey's call and another to my mother. Upon reaching the complex where my father lived, I burst from the car and up to the front door of my father's home. I drew a deep breath in an effort to compose myself. The door opened immediately.

'Where is he?' I asked in a calm voice.

Calm Robby stays calm.

In past incidents, Calm Robby has always managed to keep a solid head, assessing each component in the triage and doing whatever it is that needs to be done. That's what Calm Robby does – he stays calm.

Sheena greeted me and hurried me to the garage door. I paused for a moment, balancing on a razor's edge of not knowing what lay beyond that door and envisioning exactly what I was about to walk in on. My hand was shaking as I pulled the cold chrome handle downward.

My eyes scanned from right to left. My father's car was parked in the right-hand bay of the double garage of their two-bedroom townhouse. There was nobody in the front seat. For some reason I remember how clean the grey painted floor was. Everything was neat and packed in its place. There on the floor lay my father.

My heart was still thundering in my ears and my dry lips uttered an irreverent 'ah ... fuck.'

I sidled up to him as he lay face down on a small carpet, as if it was placed there for this very reason. Still my blood thundered through my veins, so much so that my tongue felt swollen, so much so that every effort to feel his pulse left me unable to know if it were his pulse or mine. I moved my face closer to his. There was a slight scent of apple cider vinegar, a scent that misled me to think he was breathing. In my desperation I tried to wake him up. 'Billy! Billy! Squeeze my hand if you can hear me.'

The cold and harsh realisation hit me. Kneeling next to him, every hope drained from me as I felt my face grow as cold as his clenched hand in mine. There was no pulse, no faint sound of breathing, just a thin line of spit leading from his blue lips to the small puddle of drool soaking his cheek. I then grasped his forearm briefly, feeling both how cold it was and how stiff the joints had become. I stood up and carefully stepped one foot over my father to get closer to the wooden workbench. There on the stained work surface sat a plastic container – like those that contain aqueous cream – a teaspoon and two glasses. The glasses were the ones everyone has, the kind with the handle that German mustard comes in, too quaint to throw away. One stood empty, the other was filled with a murky liquid, looking like salt water but reeking of the same sour apple odour I smelt on my father.

The wave of shock resurged through me as I remembered that I had almost attempted to resuscitate him with mouth to mouth. I knew exactly what had happened.

To this day it still astounds me how time, in a situation like this, seems to expand and contract. Split seconds of instinct, punctuated with astute razor-sharp moments of logic and clarity, screamed backwards and forward through my head as I attempted to absorb the tragedy that lay in front of me.

The battle of denial versus reason – even optimism – raged inside my head. One voice argued suicide against another scenario that was less sordid. A heart attack, an accident? Some pleasant scenario where my father lay down gently as death shadowed him painlessly and swiftly to a better place? But confirming my suspicion was the tub of white powder half-wrapped in a torn plastic Jiffy bag. The plastic bag had a knot in it as a safeguard against its contents. The container had been removed through a hole ripped in the side, with no intention of ever being packed away again.

The white label read "Potassium Cyanide – EXTREMELY TOXIC", ironically written in my father's handwriting.

A wave of nausea swept over my body as I had a flashback to a conversation I had had with him years before. We were speaking about booby traps for criminals when he mentioned this stuff. He told me how a quarter of a teaspoon was lethal and how he had to sign a register to obtain it.

Potassium cyanide is known as an antiquing agent. My father was in possession of this controlled substance purely for use on the knives he made. Dissolved in water, it turns steel black to create the illusion of tarnish, age and wear. Dissolved in water it is lethal, able to induce a coma within minutes, and death inevitably follows shortly thereafter.

I picked the tub up carefully and screwed its lid back on firmly, trying to prevent any further damage. I remember trying to get the lid on using the bare minimum of my fingertips when touching the poison, as if it was a coiled snake that was capable of jumping out and injuring me too. I stepped back and took the grey cotton dust coat hanging from the tool cupboard and covered my father's corpse from the waist up. My first memories of my father all have him wearing a signature dust coat, some white, some royal blue. He was a worker. Making knives was my father's passion, hobby and often obsession, and it supplemented his tool and diemaker wages. It also played a large role in the breakdown of his first marriage (to my mother), a lifestyle that meant our garage never had a car in it, but rather a milling machine, lathe, band saw and belt grinders.

The picture in my mind comprises my father's workbench, always a litter of sandpaper strips of the finest grit, hand sketches and an article stuck to the steel cabinet door, describing how a *Billy K* signature bowie knife was used by a woman to defend herself and her child in an attempted kidnapping. The yellowing news clipping's headline, still as clear as day in my mind, read "Man Wou Kind in Die Nag Steel" (Man Wants to Steal Child in the Night). The little girl's white-blonde locks contrasted against the sullen grey face of her murderous mother.

In our family garage, Billy K forged a name for himself as one of South Africa's most renowned knife makers and the honour of Master Craftsman from the Knife Maker's Guild of South Africa. My father produced several period pieces, each one a demonstration of historic accuracy, fine craftsmanship and an attention to detail beyond the grasp of the common person. His work is scattered across the world, collected and displayed. It's been used on all seven continents. One of his custom pieces, a skinning blade, was bought by a client for a hunting expedition to Antarctica in the 1980s.

As my father lay there, I noticed the deep purple veins in the back of his pale legs. Again, a snippet from my past reminded me of how I had always admired my father's calves as a young boy. Never having been athletic in his lifetime, I was surprised one day when I become aware of his muscular and well-defined legs. Sadly I think that was the closest I ever got to the cliché of children believing that their fathers are invincible. My father's occupation and hobby had him standing for twelve hours of every day. His calves were the result of standing behind a workbench, not the calf machine at the gym.

Calm Robby was calm. Sheena was sitting on the couch when I decided to leave the body in order to check what was going on back in the house. By now Sheena's daughter, Fiona, had arrived and was comforting her mother, who was crying heavily. Sitting next to the broken widow, I put my arm across her shoulders, but I was speechless. After a few moments I was able to find the words I hoped were as subtle as they were dreadful. 'He did it himself.'

As soon as I'd said it, Sheena clutched me, sobbing words of denial into my side as I sat cautiously on the arm of her couch. I explained the lethal capability of cyanide and from what I could see, suicide was evident. Minutes later Dieter arrived and we both made our way back into the garage. Dieter knelt next to my father's head and peeled back the grey coat covering his face. 'Ah Billy, what have you done?' he asked in a voice that exposed Dieter's softer side, the vulnerable side not many people have seen.

Suddenly a wave of anger swept over him as he rushed to his feet, his hands clenched in fists and ready to hit something, but it ebbed away as fast as it had arrived and Calm Dieter returned to the room. He knew there was business that needed taking care of. With one more look at my fallen father, we left him in peace and went to attend to the crisis unfolding on the other side of the door. The police and paramedics had been called and Fiona was kept busy trying to explain the gravity of the situation to her two young daughters, who had spent the day with their granny Sheena at the shopping mall. Sheena was now a quivering wreck, sipping whiskey on the couch.

'I wish I'd known that this was the last I would see of him, my Billy, my dear Billy,' she said in her lyrical Scottish accent, her voice shaking as she sobbed. 'It was just this morning. We went to the shops and I came back to find him on the floor.'

Despite having seen up close his lifeless shape on the floor, and having felt his stiff hands that were cramped in claws, I too was feeling the shock and disbelief. It was as if my real life had stopped and I was ejected into this nightmare.

But Calm Robby was calm.

The afternoon passed in an abstract blur as we waited for the paramedics and eventually the police to come and remove the body from the garage floor. The ER24 vehicle arrived and I flagged them to the scene. One of the paramedics walked up to the body and, with a carefully placed stethoscope, pronounced my father dead, confirming what I had discovered hours before. He felt my father's arm and rigid fingers and estimated the time of death to be several hours ago. He asked me if I had attempted to resuscitate him and I said no. He then explained that if I had, I would need to be hospitalised as a precaution due the presence of potassium cyanide. I too could have died or been severely poisoned from the liquid still present in his mouth.

A matter of hours after I had arrived on the scene, Sheena passed me a page from an A5 notebook, scribbled with my father's distinct handwriting in black ballpoint pen. Everyone mentions *a note* when the topic of suicide enters a conversation. This was that note.

Addressed to Sheena, the note explained that my father feared the surgery and procedures that lay ahead and that he could not live with himself as a burden to everyone around him. He loved her too much to be a millstone around her neck. This was the missing piece of the puzzle that Sheena had kept from me in a futile hope that it would make the situation any less tragic, but eventually she'd handed it over, thus confirming what I knew already. I was slightly angry that this evidence was held back, but now I can understand that it is difficult to think straight in situations as traumatic as that afternoon.

In 2015 I contacted Sheena once more and got a copy of the letter my dad had scrawled on the day of his death. Upon close inspection it is only too obvious to understand his frame of mind at the time. The date is written at the top of the page as "1235/05/2010". The five representing the month has been rewritten over a seven and the first four digits don't make any sense. My father's handwriting is large and erratic and the lines are not parallel. Even simple words like "being" were misspelled, an error my father would never have made under normal circumstances.

He mentioned not wanting to be a burden to "sundry and all", which stood out as odd. Despite his excellent command of the English language (even though it wasn't his first), that phrase was written anxiously and in a rush. There are several obscured scribbles along the top edge of the page and "A3" is written in large letters for no apparent reason. Reading the letter once more, despite the five years that had passed, still managed to cause my chest to tighten and it unnerved me for a while afterwards. One thing that does give me comfort is that my father concluded his letter to Sheena with three words I don't think I ever heard him verbalise: "I love you".

Despite the time that had passed between the first time I read the suicide note in the garage and examining the letter for research purposes for this book, that letter still flooded me with the same bewildering mixture of rage, pity, betrayal, acceptance and horror once more. On one hand, the familiar pattern of his handwriting was comforting, making me feel like he was close by for a fleeting moment. But in complete contrast, my father's final words also felt bare and distant. The harsh reality that scrappy piece of paper was the last thing my father would express before ending his own life.

Billy and Sheena were staying in a townhouse complex where the houses are racked tightly together, and so on the day of his death our private affairs were visible to all the residents as they arrived home from their normal days at the office. My car, Dieter's car and an ambulance were all crammed outside the garage door, making quite a spectacle. So we kept the roller door closed after a neighbour drove past at snail's pace, almost snapping his neck to get a view of what was happening.

Eventually the police mortuary vehicle arrived. The sun was setting and an officer asked the routine questions about the apparent cause of death, the identity of the deceased, and an account of the day's events, all of which were recorded on an over-copied faded form clipped into a grimy wooden clipboard.

The policeman then reversed the van up to the garage door and from under the canopy came a stainless-steel stretcher, cold and industrial. I'm not sure what I was expecting, but that cold sheet metal and welded frame wasn't it. Dieter and I then took it upon ourselves to load my father's body onto the stretcher and hoist it as cautiously and respectfully as we knew how into the back of the vehicle. Like two pall-bearers, we took the opportunity to bid a final act of respect to my father's body. I remember hoisting the stretcher in unison with Dieter to keep it level, and I was surprised but also saddened by how easy it was. My father weighed less than sixty kilograms and lifting his withered body was a painful reminder that he had started disappearing long before he finally departed.

After my father's body was taken away, we took a short while to wrap up the evening, and then Dieter and I left and went to our respective homes. I got back in my car, except this time I made my way home without the screeching of tyres or mounting of pavements. I entered the warmly lit living room after closing the front door. My mom was there, John and Natalie were there and Tracey was there. All of them were waiting for me as I shuffled towards them, feeling dazed and emotionally drained.

My home was full, a stark comparison to how empty Sheena's home would be from that night onward.

CHAPTER 37

EULOGY FOR BILLY

My father's funeral was in May, one week after his diagnosis. The leaves had started turning and the wind had a very fitting chill in its breath. I was sitting in the passenger seat of Tracey's car, counting the ResQ tablets in my palm. I used to take three or four ResQ tablets before doing a presentation or speaking in public; it calmed my nerves, but most of all it calmed the frog in my throat that tends to make an appearance whenever I speak about something emotional.

We had only been dating for a short while, but deep down beneath the gratitude I felt for having her sit there beside me, I felt guilty for making her endure this. One of the many reasons I can attest our relationship to is Tracey's unending support. As awful as those hard days were, they did help to cement the relationship that would eventually flourish into a very happy marriage.

Outside the church we parked the car and sat, not saying anything to each other. After half a minute I forced a smile at Tracey and reached back to grab my jacket. It is always easy to tell if I am on my way to an important engagement. I am usually most comfortable in cargo shorts or jeans, a T-shirt and running shoes. Today my shaking hands straightened the lapel of my jacket, which was deep grey, almost black. Very fitting considering what I was about to do.

As we stood at the steel gate that opened onto the corridor leading to the church, I looked across at the faces of those who had gathered to come and pay their respects to my father. The last time I had come to this church was the day my father married Sheena in 2007, not even three years before. I recall the day well. It was supposed to be my wedding day, but when my engagement was ended, the wedding was obviously cancelled and as it turned out my father planned his wedding to Sheena on that day. He didn't do it out of spite; it wasn't for any other reason than it was a lovely summer Sunday in February. At the time I thought it insensitive of my father to get married on this hallowed day, but in retrospect it is an overly sentimental detail not worth getting upset about. Those trivial details were furthest from my mind.

I recognised certain faces but others were like complete strangers, obviously a part of my father's life but not mine. I enjoyed a guilty smile when I saw Gert Muller, the opinionated German radical who had popped in from time to time to visit my father throughout my childhood. Come rain or snow, Gert wore khaki shorts and a ragged khaki collared shirt with a short-brimmed sun hat made from red towelling. Today Herr Muller wore a grey suit, his beard more white than ginger now, as every line in his hard face seemed to point downward. I reintroduced myself to Gert and his wife Lena, and in his thick accent he extended their condolences. I had lost a parent and he a friend. I smiled again as we parted ways. The abrupt and often radical "Crazy German" did have a heart after all and I got to see a glimpse of what my father saw in him.

To my right, walking along the paved sidewalk towards the church, was a grey-haired man, his jacket folded over his arm. As he approached and he came into focus, I felt the blood drain from my face. Within that fraction of a second, my mind convinced me that the approaching man was my father. There he stood. Everything was the same, from the way he took each step to the way the skin on his neck creased as he lowered his head to put his jacket on. But then just as quickly I was brought back to the gravity of that dreary day. As he got closer to me, I was able to see clearly that it was my father's younger brother Karl. He had come from Middelburg to say goodbye to his brother. I had not seen Karl in fifteen years and he needed to be reminded of which one of my brothers I was, but he was sincere and as approachable as ever. His pale blue-grey eyes and the profile of his lower face were identical to my father's. It was uncanny looking at Karl having seen that same face just days before, face down on the garage floor.

Standing together and talking quietly among themselves were John, Warren and my friend Dirk. These are the men who had been by my side in what I thought had been the toughest times of my life, the friends that became my brotherhood of the rope. In years past they had coached me, encouraged me towards summits and pushed me further than I ever realised I could go. But today they could not shelter me from the wind.

At one point I made eye contact with my eldest nephew Luke and forced that familiar "downward smile, raised eyebrow" expression we all make awkwardly to one another when words are scarce. In that crowded corridor outside the church, I felt truly alone.

We sat staring forward as the minister read a very truthful, and I'll admit, very reassuring message about suicide. From behind the podium Reverend Chunky explained that a successful suicide needs several factors to come together properly. The minister read them out like a long list of commandments.

The first was intent or reason to want to die. My father was diagnosed with final stage colorectal cancer after going to the doctor for a persistent fistula. As it was explained to me, the colonoscopy camera had discovered a tumour about eight centimetres in length, and the further the examination progressed, the more tumours were found lining my father's lower intestine. 'Eventually, they stopped the procedure,' my father had told me as he lay flat on his back in that Olivedale hospital bed. 'My guts are a minefield.' In the days that were to follow, a surgery schedule to remove sections of his colon and a treatment plan were drawn up. Doctors planned to remove the worst parts of the colon, fit a colostomy bag and administer aggressive radiation treatment to tackle this disease head on.

That was a week ago.

'Once the reason is there, the person needs to have the means to commit the act of suicide,' the Reverend continued, his collar tight around his jowls. All of a sudden it became apparent where the name Chunky must have originated from.

The conversation was clear in my head as if it had taken place just yesterday. My father and I were talking in the workshop where he crafted his knives. In his thick hand he held a 500-gram white plastic container of potassium cyanide, a white powder as fine as icing sugar.

'This same shit the Nazis kept in the lapel of their uniforms in the event of a capture,' my father explained, his cheeks dropping to emphasise the gravity of what he held in front of me. 'How do you think Heinrich Himmler died?' he continued, expecting me to know who that was. I assumed he was one of Hitler's commanders, but only because of the name. My father knew a lot about a lot. What he lacked in social skills, he made up for in general knowledge. I later researched Himmler's death and he did commit suicide on 23rd May 1945 – the same day I would summit Everest, some sixty-four years later.

'In the event of being captured or being tortured, the soldier could bite into the capsule and suck up the cyanide.'

'How long would it take to die?' I asked.

'About fifteen seconds, almost instantaneously.'

'Then how the hell did you get your hands on this, and why?' My initial reaction was a mixture of intrigue and harmless deviousness, like a kid smuggling firecrackers.

'You have to sign a register at the chemist if you want to get your hands on this. They ordered it for me, the guy on Webber Road, opposite Standard Bank.'

If I think back now, he took very few precautions. He kept the plastic tub at the back of the steel cupboard in the workshop and there was a piece of masking tape wrapped around the belly with a crude skull and cross-bones drawn on it. He'd scrawled the words "DANGEROUS – POISON" with permanent marker. That tub had enough in it to kill sixty people. It was never hidden under lock and key because it was probably taken for granted that people would obviously stay well away from it. It's potassium cyanide.

In the church I expected someone to stand up and object to how blatantly and matter-of-factly the reverend was talking about the commonly taboo subject of suicide, not to mention in a church, and at a delicate occasion such as this. But no one did. They understood.

'The third thing a person needs is the correct state of mind.' My ears pricked up as my instinct was to retort. Surely if he had the right state of mind we'd be visiting him in Olivedale Clinic, not staring at a photograph in the front of the fucking church? But his next words managed to calm me down as fast as he had got me worked up. 'A depression so deep and dark that they cannot see a way out. For this person, there is no hope of an answer. Billy was in such a state of mind that he was willing to hurt himself so badly he would die from his injuries.' It was a place so dark and terrifying that death was the better option. My face crumpled in a wave of sheer misery and my eyes welled up, blurring my view of the pulpit. For the first time, the extent of the fear my father had faced really dawned on me. We associate cowardice, anger and irrational panic with suicide, but never fear. A fear so brutal, so undiluted, that death remains your most attractive comfort.

It is sometimes said that suicide is the coward's way out. We struggle to comprehend self-harm because it goes against our instincts of self-preservation. Imagine this. Take the piece of webbed skin between your index finger and thumb and slice that skin with a piece of paper. The discomfort you imagine – the jolt of searing pain as the page cuts slightly into the leathery fold of your hand – causes you to cringe. Now consider the mindset – but more importantly, the courage – of someone willing to injure themselves to the extent of fatality.

My father was so far down a road of despair and hopelessness that physical pain and the fear of dying paled in comparison. As the years have passed since my father's death, I am still torn, not only by his absence but also the thought of the suffering he endured. It was a culmination of guilt, anger and the most concentrated sadness in the knowledge that death, and possibly the belief of eternal damnation, was the only option he could take. We feel deeply for those we love; our hearts break when our child grazes a knee. I am reduced to tears when I try to imagine my father's suffering, the misery of a broken man.

'Fourth and finally, the person needs time.' I became very aware of Sheena as her sobs grew heavier on the other side of the aisle where she had stood in unity with my father just three years before, her breath jerked as her children held her close. I looked across in consolation, but grief had consumed her.

Sheena felt that she could have somehow prevented my father's death. She had taken an innocent school holiday trip to the mall with her grandchildren for a movie and ice cream, and that was all the opportunity Billy needed to mix the toxic brew that would end it all. I know he planned it, and if it hadn't have happened on that Monday, it would have happened the next moment she stepped out of the house.

'I knew he was depressed, but I didn't think he would do something like this,' she'd said as she sat on the couch that day, metres from the body, the ice in her whiskey tinkling against the glass in her trembling hand. She was only gone for two hours. A movie and an ice cream for the kids, just as they usually did most school holidays. Those two hours were a gift. The plan was there from the moment the doctor handed down his prognosis. All that remained was the execution.

The moment had arrived and I found myself standing at the wooden podium, tapping my folded pages into alignment. I scanned the audience and swallowed hard. 'As you may know, I have done some very difficult things in my life, but getting through today is by far the hardest. To speak at my father's funeral is as much an honour as it is painful. Thank you to everyone for coming to pay your respects today. On behalf of my family and myself, we appreciate the love and support you have offered us and appreciate your being here.'

I had got through the introduction paragraph but my breathing was deep and laboured. Trying to remain in control of the frog perched in the back of my throat, I continued.

'My father took great pride in teaching others. And so in order to honour him today, I would like to point out what I have learnt, not only from him but also the life he led – and now in his passing.

Lesson 1: People are everything.

Within hours of my dad's passing, the support, love and open arms for me and my family has been incredible. If you look around the church today, the people who have come to say their farewells and celebrate the life Billy led, you will get a picture of the man he was. A father and grandfather, a brother, husband, loyal friend, an artist, mentor, the list goes on ...'

Years before I had saved the opening quote from the movie *The Bucket List*. I found it fitting to describe my father accurately despite not being wealthy, famous in any mainstream context or formally recognised.

"It's difficult to measure the sum of a person's life. Some people would tell you that it is measured by the ones left behind. Some say it can be measured in faith, some by love. Other folks say life has no meaning at all. Me, I believe that you measure yourself by the people who measured themselves by you."

If we consider the people seated here today as a reflection of who my father was, he was a man who was loved by great men and women, skilled tradesmen and apprentices, Everest climbers, teachers and explorers, regardless of wealth and age ... they all regarded him as highly as he did them.

Lesson 2: No one cares how much you weigh. The people who mind don't matter, and the people who matter don't mind.

One of my father's greatest gifts was that he was a born teacher. Many a man here today can attest to his gifted hands, his appreciation of the beauty in detail. My father was also an artist and a true craftsman. He could speak with anyone about anything from Roman history to Julius Malema's most recent pearls of wisdom.

When my father was diagnosed with cancer last week, I went through everything I wanted to say to him before the time came. I thought there would be a chance to tell him everything I was always too shy to say. Unfortunately, I did not get that chance.

My father was ill for a long time. As far back as I remember, my father used an asthma pump and later his stomach and digestive system was a constant yo-yo of problems. No two photos of him look the same and the belly I remember from childhood was later nowhere to be seen – but I think I now know who inherited it!' I smiled, rubbing my own stomach, a physical trait I have come to terms with, along with the round nose and a double chin that no surgeon's knife will ever rectify.

Lesson 3: It's never too late to change for the better.

My father was a teacher, but I am happy to know he was still able to learn. He told me a number of years ago of a saying that he had adopted, to my surprise: "Only profit matters". I was disappointed and saddened to think my father actually believed that. However, on the day my dad passed away, I saw a little wooden sign in his bathroom that read "Let your heart rule". Even through the sadness of that day, I was able to smile, as I was relieved to see he had changed for the better. I thank my stepmother Sheena for teaching my father to love more openly, to show some of the emotion he had inside of him and to teach him the joys of sharing.'

It was at this point I started to swallow hard, trying in vain to keep the knot in my throat at bay. I fumbled at first, stopped and I sucked down hard, calming myself and focusing on what I was here to do.

'In closing, here are some things we can all learn from Billy. Children, don't ever pass an opportunity to hug someone you love. Husbands, dance with your wives. Even if you think you look stupid because your legs are too short and you have no rhythm whatsoever. The truth is, you do look funny – but they really do appreciate and love you for it. Fathers, hug your children. Tell them you love them and that you are proud of them. They know you do, but tell them anyway.'

I looked up at the silent faces. Many of the guests were wiping their tears shyly, some staring straight ahead, but everyone was smiling. They were all suffering the loss, but for that brief moment I knew that each one of them was enjoying a personal memory of my father.

'Today we bury my father. The man is gone but not his legacy. Today we take a page or two from his book. Heaven knows he had volumes to offer the world. Today he has found the freedom from pain he could not find here on Earth, but so deserved.'

I finished with an exhausted "thank you" and folded the creased pages back into my pocket. I walked back to my seat where Tracey was waiting for me. As the service drew to a close, I felt proud, not of myself but of my father.

As twisted as it may seem, I had always wanted to be the one to speak at my father's funeral when the time arrived. I went as far as to write it on my bucket list. Beneath the sadness of losing my father and the incomprehensible whirlpool of emotions in the weeks that would follow, it was something I felt I had to do. I wanted to show the world the man I had only started to understand. I didn't want to justify his actions or the relationship we had struggled to have. I wanted him to be remembered not only for what we had learnt from him but for everything he had to offer.

Months later while sorting through files on my computer, I opened the document titled "Bucket list_RK.doc" and as I read through it I smiled warmly, highlighted the item half way down the page that read "Read my father's eulogy", and crossed it off the list.

CHAPTER 38

SAY WHAT YOU NEED TO SAY

I had not visited my father again in the three days after seeing him on the night of his diagnosis. I foolishly assumed that there would be time. I pictured a quiet afternoon sitting on the bed next to my father, the sun streaming in from a nearby window as I gave the book to him, showing him that cancer wouldn't win, telling him that he could ask for anything and it would be taken care of. I wanted to say everything I should have said several times during the past fifteen years. And I would have said something neither of us had ever said to each other before, something I have no memory of ever telling my father – I love you.

I have little memory of what I did with the sixty hours between leaving my father's bedside and finding his rigid corpse on the cement, but I can assure you that I have spent a hundred times that thinking about what I could have said – *should* have said – but now cannot. Not for all of Solomon's gold.

Months after the funeral, I heard John Mayer's hit song 'Say what you need to say' while watching *The Bucket List*. To this day, that song and movie have had a massive impact on the way I live my life and serve as a reminder that the privilege of time is not ours. Procrastination is said to be the thief of time. In this case it stole so much more. More than I will ever understand. So, say what you need to say and say it now. Don't wait one minute for that imposter named Tomorrow.

To quote a man who bears a strong resemblance to my father in his wise demeanour and offbeat sense of humour, Dr Gregory House, "Time changes everything. That's what people say. It's not true. Doing things changes things. Not doing things leaves them exactly as they were."

My father's body was cremated and his final wish was for Sheena to scatter his ashes in Scotland. "Spread my ashes near still waters, playing the pipes I have come to love so much." My father was Austrian by birth, with no sentimentality linking him to Scotland whatsoever. His final wish was intended as a gift to his wife to get her to go back home and visit the place of her birth and the land she adored. Sheena did relocate back to Scotland and I trust that she honoured my father's last request.

I would say it took about two weeks for me to finally fall apart. At the time of my father's death, I busied myself with the logistics and duties of contacting friends and family, many of whom I had to remind that I was Billy's youngest son Robert.

Over the weeks that followed I felt an insurmountable sense of grief and sadness. Not only was I missing my father, but I also had the heavy realisation that he was gone and with him went any chance of nurturing the relationship I could only wish we had had. I am often saddened when I think about my childhood and all the opportunities I missed. My father and I shared an ability to visualise and create with our hands, but he didn't have a lot of patience for mentoring. His workshop was just that – a place to work. A place he could generate income to fulfil his role as a father.

My parents were divorced in 1997 and for several reasons I went with my mother when she left and moved to a townhouse less than ten kilometres away. As the impending separation was brewing, my mother and I had several serious and rather taxing conversations. She would tell me her plans to end the marriage. She had her reasons. And so as the years passed, the distance between my father and I increased until our relationship consisted of nothing more than an awkward phone call at Christmas and on birthdays.

One thing I can smile at now is the phone call I received every year to wish me happy birthday on 13th January, regular as clockwork. I smile because my birthday is on the 12th, but at the time it cut me deeply that my father couldn't remember the day I was born.

During the times that we did see each other, the conversation was strained and bare. We had lost any sense of commonality and I'm ashamed to say that I wouldn't need to remove my shoes in order to count the times my father and I hugged.

And now it is all gone.

As the days after his death became weeks and the months slipped by into years, I found myself piecing together the bits of a puzzle. Some pieces are missing, some don't seem to fit at all, but there certainly is a clearer picture emerging. It isn't a bed of roses but I now have a better understanding of it. I feel I know my father better now than I ever did when he was alive. I have sought out reasons for some of the things he did or said and I can also forgive many of the difficulties we experienced in our relationship, having taken the time to find a better idea of where he was coming from, both geographically and in terms of his view on the world.

Willibald (Billy) Kojetin was a brilliant man in many respects, a man that – despite his exceptional intelligence and skilled hands – lived a life shackled by a mentality of scarcity, driven by the belief that life was about working hard to afford to live and a fear of not being able to provide. Disguised as practicality, these beliefs and fears would limit his every decision, governing his perception of the reality he lived in. My father believed that the world is a harsh place in which we will always struggle to survive, prosperity is dependent on luck and the few that do make any headway in life, probably did not do it honestly. Billy worked hard his entire life as a tool and die maker, a trade he took up directly after high school. His hopes of university were dashed by a lack of money, not effort, and he went about working, until the age of sixty, only to be boarded due to ill health. He died alone on a cold concrete floor in a rented two-bedroom townhouse with nothing to his name except for a well-stocked toolbox, a few books and not much else.

A fortnight or so after my father's funeral, his meagre possessions were divided between me and my brother Dieter. Sheena could no longer stay in the house, which was now only home to memories of sadness and pain. His pine bookshelf, varnished and yellow, was home to scores of books, some of which featured the knives he had made over the years. There were hardbacks and paperbacks spanning the last forty or so years. The titles were broad and varied, just like my father was. The garage was scattered with a selection of tools, unfinished knife blades and dry marker pens, all housed in dented and chipped steel cabinets and boxes. The value of his unfinished pieces pales in comparison to what they could have been worth as finished knives.

Among the belongings I took was a plastic milk crate of knife-making annuals and an old black leather briefcase, dusty and showing signs of wear. Looking at the brass locks, I began to think that perhaps the case didn't want to be opened. Or perhaps, it was me who was apprehensive of what waited inside. For months the briefcase lay hidden in the top of a wardrobe, its contents a mystery. The last remnants of evidence of Billy ever existing, the final piece in a puzzle.

I went about solving the combinations on the briefcase locks that were separating me from one last look into my father's life.

Billy's birth date. 4-7-0-7-0-6? Nope.

All zeros? Nope.

Then I tried 7-8-0-1-1-2, my birthday.

Nope. Worth a try, but the lock remained secure.

I resorted to prying the case open with a large screwdriver which, ironically, I had inherited from my dad, savagely breaching the neat brass levers from their locks until they snapped open. I felt an initial wave of guilt for desecrating a piece of my father's legacy.

Lifting the dust-covered lid slowly, I examined the black thread unravelling from the leather covering. I assured myself that the case was old and tattered and not worth replacing the latches. Inside were various personal documents and a transcription of a diary translated from German to English, which apparently belonged to my great grandfather. There were outdated policy documents from some or other financial institution. I scanned them thoroughly, partly to ensure I wasn't trashing anything of importance, but also in one last effort to find the clause where my father entrusted his secret fortune to his youngest, and most handsome, son.

And then there was a plastic sleeve, worn and matt from years of use. Within it was a low-resolution photograph, evidently printed on a household colour printer. A lump formed in the back of my throat. I swallowed and instinctively wiped the rush of tears that had already welled up in my eyes. I sniffed back hard, feeling the mucus sitting heavily in the back of my throat as I read the caption in my father's dynamic handwriting out loud. '23rd May, 2009. Robby – Everest Summi—' My throat clamped closed around that last word, forcing me into silence.

The photograph was of Lhakpa Nuru, my high-altitude Sherpa, and I sitting on the summit of Everest. The photographer was standing off to my right, about a metre in front of me. In it Lhakpa is aware of the picture being taken but I am facing off slightly to the right, my hands fiddling with the tether of my glove or something. It is evident how the weather had deteriorated as the three of us – me, Lhakpa, and the Buddha sitting in the painted wooden box – seem to be hovering against a white background, with nothing else to indicate that we are on Everest's peak. The top right and bottom left corners of the frame are marred by unsightly black triangles, which I later learnt was the camera's shutter, unable to open fully in the extreme cold. It's not the kind of image worth enlarging to hang on a wall. It documents a moment in time ... and not much more. I suspect he must have copied it from one of my many Facebook posts. The ink was faded, having soaked into the low-grade copy paper I imagine my father kept in his study.

As far as material mementos go, I have very little to remind me of Billy. This picture is my most treasured. I choose to believe it is a sign that my father *did* love me and *was* incredibly proud of me. He just didn't have the words, or freedom of expression to say it to me in words.

One of my greatest regrets is that I will never be able to thank him for the life he lived, motivated by a need to provide, overshadowed by the fear of failure; doing not what he loved, but rather what he knew would keep the wolf from the door – only to lose the battle after so many years.

At the risk of sounding idealistic, I believe my father could have lived an entirely different story had he allowed his passion and love of what he did so well to be his driving force. Confidence and self-belief in his many talents would have served him better.

At his commencement address at Maharishi University in 2014, Jim Carrey said, "I learnt many great lessons from my father, not the least of which was that you can fail at what you don't want, so you might as well take a chance on doing what you love."

CHAPTER 39

SURVIVAL

In the November of 2009, I went back to doing what I knew would pay the bills, spending more time sitting than sleeping, and all in the name of creating advertising campaigns that I'm sure most people have fast-forwarded through. I had climbed the highest mountain in the world, but now I was well on my way to becoming part of the furniture at another advertising agency that was very similar to the one I had escaped from just six years before, in pursuit of a life on my own terms. By March of 2010 I had accepted a permanent position at Brand Activation and was tasked to be one of the lead creatives heading up Castle Lager's participation in the 2010 FIFA Soccer World Cup. There was also talk of a promotion to the position of Creative Director, which lay in the outcome of how we handled this mammoth project.

It was during this manic period at work that my father had committed suicide, adding a whole spectrum of challenges which would disrupt how I processed his death as well as my availability to mourn. My work life overshadowed what was going on in my personal life, distracting me from the questions and trauma I needed to address in order to make sense of it, and more importantly how I felt about it. This delay would cause a lot more turmoil and emotional distress later down the path, resulting in me landing back on a leather couch, talking to another guy with glasses and a collared shirt.

June 2010 arrived and the sports fans came from all over the world to watch some soccer, drink an enormous amount of beer and then go home. And all that talk of a promotion turned out to be just that ... talk. Management at the agency changed hands and my progress never seemed to be up for discussion. My descent down the slippery slope – into becoming what I promised I would never be – had begun. This was not a life; this was just surviving. My life had become a survival scenario, punctuated by monthly pay cheques, beginning and ending each day with a sad sigh.

My state of survival was characterised not by the threat of hypothermia or falling into a crevasse, but rather campaign deadlines and client feedback. One day melted into the next, and all I could think about was just getting through it all, consumed only by my most immediate of needs and most urgent crises.

I had become a bottom feeder on Maslow's hierarchy of needs pyramid.

Any concept of the future was furthest from my mind because I had become so busy just coping with "the here and now". With my survival blinkers on, I was living my life on the back foot with no time to think or plan for anything, including anything better. The iconic theme music from *Carte Blanche*, a South African news and current affairs television programme that aired at seven o'clock every Sunday evening, announced the end of another weekend and initiated the familiar ache in the pit of my stomach. Regardless of my accomplishments or my intentions, I had slipped into a rut. I had become just another survivor, counting down the hours to five o'clock each day. "Survivors" just want to make it to the close of business, or just to Friday. Just to December. Just to their very own funeral.

When climbing Mount Everest, the concept of survival was ever-present and the difference between surviving or not surviving completely clear cut. In a mountaineering context, survival is defined by a climber's ability to stand upright and put one foot in front of the other. Survival means satisfying only the most immediate of needs: nutrition, warmth and shelter. And if you get that right, the result and reward is making it to the next day alive.

It is when we are within the safety and familiarity of our comfort zones that we slip unknowingly into a state of survival, concerned only with the right here and now – and nothing more.

One of humankind's biggest gifts is also one of our biggest downfalls. We have the ability to adapt. When our environment changes, we manage to alter ourselves in response and become accustomed to the new set of living conditions. The problem with this habit lies in that we are no longer scouring the bushveld in search of food and shelter. Instead we live comfortably in a house that we are buying one instalment at a time and a majority of our hunting is done on a fluorescent menu board outside the drive-thru at McDonald's.

When things change around us, we do whatever we need to in order to get used to it. Unfortunately, this includes the bad things too. When the demands of our careers turn our day jobs into day-and-night jobs, we get used to the idea of driving home from the office in the dark. When our relationships succumb to stress and fatigue, we adapt to the lack of conversation and find excuses why this is the norm and we accept that "that's just life". We lower our standards to increase our levels of (bearable) happiness and we recreate the idea of what it means to be alive. And what we used to call "living" is now a self-centric, rudimentary and very sad form of survival.

Just like everybody else, I too have a personal arsenal of one-liners I keep on hand for those occasions when people ask how I am doing. At one point or another we are all guilty of avoiding an in-depth or honest answer by responding to the "How are you?" question with one of the following quips:

'Oh, you know. Same old, same old.'

'Same shit, different day.'

'No use complaining.'

'Another day, another dollar.'

On the odd occasion, I usually throw in a "can't complain", implying that my state of being is neutral at best. But the reply that feels like fingernails on a chalk board every single time I hear it, is

'You know … Surviving.'

Survival is the most basic form of consciousness and is characterised by an absence of any positive emotion and absolutely no concern for anything that doesn't affect you directly. When we are stuck in "survival mode" we tend to grow blinkers, our peripheral vision transforms to tunnel vision and we are incapable of contributing to anything other than our own immediate needs. This limited view makes us useless in any social environment, be it within the constructs of the company in which we are employed, in a team and sadly family, relationships, friendships are not immune to the effects of this real-life "zombie apocalypse".

Modern society doesn't do much to help remedy this problem. It is easier to send someone an instant message than to actually talk to them. Emoji symbols on our keyboards are fast replacing our need to express real feelings when a laughing smiley face with tears or a happy poo will suffice. The radio stations we tune into while tuning out in traffic all blurt out the same bad news about other people's problems in other places, making you feel like these are now your problems and that they're all on your doorstep.

This epidemic sweeping the planet presents itself in varying degrees of severity, from mild discontent with one's life, to dire cases where people cry in their cars, sitting in traffic on their way to a job they hate, only to work late in order to avoid having to go home to someone they can't stand, sleeping badly and waking up to do it all again the following day in a never-ending continuum of mediocrity.

Being stuck back in an advertising agency, my happiness took second place and what was worse was that I was beginning to accept that it was "just the way things were". The scary thing is that not many of us are even aware of what it is that makes us happy, and if that is the case, how would we even know if it ever did come along? In this fast-paced, ready-made, too-busy-to-do-anything "age of information" we know less about each other and more importantly, less about ourselves than ever before.

CHAPTER 40

THE TRIGGER

'You? *You* climbed Mount Everest?' Steve said in a mixture of amazement and scepticism.

'Umm, yes. Last year May,' I replied bashfully. There was an awkward pause.

I'm not sure why, but for a long time I would become quite embarrassed when strangers would ask about Everest. I found it a challenge to feel proud of myself, to accept their reactions of surprise and their compliments. It's something I still struggle with to this day.

After everyone had gone back to their desks Steve Knapp, a hardened, straight-talking art director in his forties with a thick English accent and both arms tattooed in sleeves of skulls and flames, asked me that wrecking ball of a question: 'Well, what the fuck are you doing here then?' He didn't even take his eyes off his Mac screen.

I laughed and made some or other remark in an effort to keep the office chit-chat light and breezy, but in the back of my head the gravity of Steve's question had lit a fuse.

"What the fuck?" indeed. He was right. What was I doing there stuck behind a desk, advertising a beer I didn't drink? The job paid the bills, but my existence wasn't supposed to be just another survival scenario, dashing from one crisis to the next, measuring my life one irrational deadline at a time. I may not have been gasping for air in the Death Zone of Everest, but I was essentially just going from one day to the next and not much else – sitting in the same traffic, on the way to the same job in order to earn the same money to pay the same bills. Just like everyone else, I needed an income to live on while my amazing star-studded career as a motivational speaker was taking its sweet time taking off.

Oprah Winfrey is quoted as saying "Do what you have to do until you can do what you want to do" (which is a lot easier to swallow when you own your own television network). Freelancing as an art director and copywriter had given me the flexibility to manage my time so I could pursue the dream, but once I had signed on as a permanent employee, that dream soon found itself gathering dust in a drawer labelled "Someday". What defined that dream was not entirely clear, but it certainly wasn't spending ten hours of every day promoting casinos and alcohol brands. A large part of my disdain for the advertising industry, and my role within it, was a moral dilemma. It was my job to glorify a life of decadence and endless possibility that was just a roll of the dice away, to a target market that already weren't making ends meet before they had even dropped a single coin into the slot. I was also promoting the sale of alcohol by highlighting the friendships and memories that the product was all about. If we examine the issues of road deaths, domestic violence, unemployment and suicide, alcohol is involved almost every time. And no "social responsibility" line at the bottom of the page was going to help me sleep at night.

That afternoon's pep talk from Steve Knapp was the trigger I needed. After all, this was not the plan! I did not suffer the worst accident of my life and endure the physical and psychological anguish to defy all odds and realise a lifelong dream that 99.9% of the human population will never have the privilege of experiencing ... only to pack it all in and ferment behind the keyboard of a fifteen-inch laptop screen.

As harsh as Steve's "intervention" was at the time, I am grateful it happened. Typically, I would have carried on with a life I was not happy with, and for who knows how long? That moment – despite it just being a simple question from a work colleague – was a trigger, a defining moment that I needed in order to create a disruption. That disruption caused me to consciously stop and evaluate my direction, priorities and what exactly I was doing with my life.

Why is it that a majority of people need a doctor to tell them that their lives will end prematurely if they don't quit smoking, or lose weight or change their diet in order to start taking their existence seriously? Why does it take losing someone to a dreaded disease, barely surviving a tragic car accident or living through a brutal home invasion to re-evaluate the real value of our lives? These triggers are not always pleasant – in fact they seldom are – but they are necessary because they bring about change, and usually in three distinct steps.

1. Stop – even if just for a moment.
2. Think about the current situation you have found yourself in.
3. Make a decision to change direction.

The best analogy of a trigger is to imagine someone holding a gun to somebody else's head. I don't mean to make light of a serious topic, especially in the world we live in, but no matter what the victim was busy doing, regardless of what level of Candy Crush Saga they were in the middle of, when that gun cocks with the feeling of cold steel against their temple, it is safe to say that each and every time they will stop dead in their tracks.

By the time they have realised the full extent of what is going on, their brain is already assessing the situation, measuring the level of danger and preparing to deliver a full report on the situation ... and all in a fraction of a second.

From there, the conscious brain takes over and a decision is made regarding next steps. When faced with an unpleasant outcome, where, say, a gun is involved, human nature will most probably make that decision for you. And those next steps will be in whichever direction will get you as far from the source of danger and as fast as possible.

If I think back to that awful night of my accident in 2006, I can now confidently say that I needed to fall off that climbing wall and injure myself seriously enough to create a disruption. Nothing says "stop" like the sound of crunching bone. Things needed to fall apart completely to allow me the opportunity to take myself seriously enough. Only then were the apparent consequences "in my face" enough to force me to start taking steps to rectify my situation. Even if those steps required assistance and were very small and shaky at first, they were steps in the direction of something better, something closer to the life I wanted for myself.

These triggers will pop up from time to time in our lives and almost never in the way we expect them. There is no way to predict exactly how you will react to it when it arrives on your lap, but what really matters most is that you recognise the trigger for what it is.

How will you answer the question, "How am I going to handle *this?*"

CHAPTER 41

IT'S OKAY TO PEE A LITTLE BIT

In the October of 2006, about a week or so after I'd had my third surgery, I found myself sitting across from the surgeon in his little office for yet another check-up. The walls were filled with anatomical diagrams and degrees. The heavily laden bookshelf had plastic models of various joints, one of which was used to explain the procedure he had just performed on my ankles. He went on to explain to me and my mother that the initial extent of the injury had been underestimated, but the recent graft had been a success. He explained the complex nature of the ankle joint and the effect the injury had on it, as well as the limitations it would place on my movement. Despite the feeling of having someone standing on my chest, I took a deep breath and asked the question that worried me the most. 'And what about climbing?'

He looked down at the desk planner, tapped his pen against the desk, and in his thick Polish accent said 'This is bad. Walking? Yes, in time you will be able to walk. Maybe a little bit of a limp. But climbing? No, there is too much stress on the joint. Climbing and running? You can't.' He grimaced as if to say sorry.

They say the best way get something done is to tell a person it is not possible.

As the sun peeked above the horizon that clear April morning in 2011, the sea was flat and calm and the wind moved gently in between the crowds of people on the beach. It was the perfect day. The stillness was the exact opposite of what was going on inside my head and also my stomach. I stood silently, wringing my hands in anticipation as my breakfast made several mock charges at the back of my throat. It was 4th April and Paul Kaye's voice came over the microphone, announcing what would be the start of the SpecSavers Ironman Triathlon Port Elizabeth. And I was at the start line.

The national anthem boomed out of the speakers and within seconds there wasn't a dry eye on the beach. I felt a mixture of emotions – part patriotism, part pride, part fear.

The latex cap gripped tight over my head with the straps of my goggles adding to the pressure on my skull. I could feel the anti-chafe cream on my groin, armpits and the nape of my neck squelching with every movement. A trickle of pee ran a warm stream down my leg, seeping out the bottom of my wetsuit and disappearing into the sand of Orient Beach. A few routine, barely audible announcements over the megaphone put all 1,500 athletes at the ready. And then it was silent. My head was turning forward and back, quadruple checking every detail of my preparation for the day, as if I had the power to change anything now. And then ... GADOOM! The canon exploded, sending a shockwave of sound that hit me in the chest. And the race was underway. Months of preparation, saddle soreness, mind-numbing laps in the pool, swelling and pain during practice runs had all come down to that moment.

I started walking towards the water's edge. Everyone on the field had already begun to spread out. Wading out past the first few small breakers, I took a deep breath before diving forward into what was about to be the longest swim of my entire life. My head was awash with the thoughts of starting slow, fighting the anxiety in an effort to keep my breathing slow and steady, in complete contrast to what my heart wanted to do. Within a few minutes I approached the first buoy that was anchored about 300 metres from the shore. I lifted my face and began to tread water, watching the wrestling match of swimmers taking a 90-degree turn to the left around the buoy. The current of the mass exodus pulled me along and around the corner, allowing me to catch my breath.

And all of a sudden I realised that everything might just be okay.

I settled into a rhythm with each stroke, consciously breathing steadily and staying relaxed. Before long I had the shore on my right again and one more turn was separating me from the last stretch to the beach. One lap down, one to go.

Eventually I walked the 200 metres back to where I had begun forty-five minutes before and repeated the entire process. After an hour and a half I was tip-toeing my way out of the water and up the beach. Walking on my toes through deep beach sand had nothing to do with my racing strategy, but my toes had been pointed during the swim, causing my Achilles tendons to pull tight, just like they do every night while I sleep. I then entered the first transition tent, everything feeling like a blur. I shed my rubber seal suit in exchange for a helmet and a dry pair of cycling shorts.

Having left the race transition area, with my shoes clipped into my pedals, I tried to rinse the salt from my mouth with my first mouthful of energy drink. My ankles and feet were tight, which imposed a slow start on the 180-kilometre ride that lay ahead of me. For the next seven hours my iron horse and I would pass each kilometre by pacing ourselves on the uphill route past the very ironically named "Mount Joy" and taking advantage of the downhill slopes to stretch my lower back and take the weight off my tender tushie. The day was broken up into manageable bite-size pieces by the various refreshment stations, the cheers of the sideline supporters, their signs and their screams of encouragement.

One of my favourite signs from that day read "This is Ironman. It's okay to cry a little." On the second lap of the 60-kilometre route the sign had been updated with a black marker pen to read "This is Ironman. It's okay to pee a little." By the third time around, the sign was once more updated and now said in thick untidy letters "This is Ironman. It's okay to vomit a little." As funny and gross as it was, that message was a reminder of not only where I was, but also who I was. *You're human and it's okay to hurt. Hurt all you want – just don't give up and remember why you're doing this*.

At the end of each lap, the cycle route follows the coastline on a flat road that takes you past the transition area and past the majority of the supporters. In among the crowd were my supporters, who I am eternally grateful for. It's a very long and tiring day out for them and their addition to the Ironman formula is a very vital one. At each pass Tracey was there, brimming with encouragement and energy. Cheering alongside her was Warren Eva, the boy I had taught to climb, who in turn had taught me a lot about everything I am capable of, something that was once hidden behind a veil of preconceived beliefs. Completing the cheer squad were Wa's dad Milton Eva and his father-in-law Con Roux. Both are incredibly accomplished athletes with more Comrades medals than I have toes and a bronzed running shoe each, signifying ten Washie Ultra-Marathon finishes. (The Washie is a 100-mile endurance race run over twenty-four hours, a different kettle of fish entirely.) I was moved and humbled that these men stood by and clapped as I chugged along in a field full of real athletes.

As the afternoon began drawing to an end, so did my time on the iron horse. As grateful as I was for my bike – it was light and aerodynamic and made of aluminium and carbon fibre – by the one hundred and sixtieth kilometre it certainly did feel like iron. My lower back and shoulders were screaming and the last lap around the city of Port Elizabeth was a mixture of road cycling, free-wheeling and yoga. Doing the downward dog was a relief as much as it was a spectacle to behold.

I rolled up to the gate of the transition area where athletes' bikes were being racked by the volunteers. In all honesty I could not have cared less if I ever saw that bike again. I passed it to a complete stranger and limped my way off to go find my running shoes. The upcoming marathon was going to be an interesting one. The arches of my feet had tightened up in my cycling cleats and were now causing me a lot of pain. Plantar fasciitis, yet another complication I had inherited from my climbing accident. Though I knew I had damaged bones and tendons, it was only picked up years later that the fascia in the soles of my feet had also incurred some tearing.

The other factor affecting the outcome of the race – and I still had forty-two kilometres ahead of me – was that I had never done it before! The furthest I'd ever run was no more than thirty or so kilometres. But I left the transition fencing and turned right along the road. The afternoon seascape on my right was now turning grey and deep purple as sunset approached. By now the road was full of runners in all directions, most of them going faster than I was. But I eventually managed to settle into another lopsided rhythm, and over the next hour or so my feet and ankles eased into the new range of motion as I went on a quest to collect the precious elastic hair bands that proved you had completed each of the three 14-kilometre laps.

At some point during my *run / walk / limp* the sun went down, but the support and enthusiasm on the pavement only intensified. Tracey and I would share the odd update in passing and even a smooch or two, despite me looking and smelling like someone who had been sweating since sunrise. Warren would record videos chatting with all of our friends who were also competing that day. In one short clip, Warren and I chat for no more than half a minute and afterwards I start to run off in the wrong direction before realising and making an about-turn to carry on. Had I not already been red in the face, I would most probably have blushed. During one of the other pit stops I started to feel cold due to the drop in temperature after the sun had set and being wet from perspiration. I began pulling and tugging at my shirt frantically until eventually it peeled off of me. I bunched it up and tried to wring it out, expecting a puddle to be squeezed from it. I stood wringing and wringing it with no result, only to look up to see Warren in fits of laughter at my mission in futility. I slipped my wet shirt back on and continued to hobble, smiling from ear to ear.

There is a section of the running route, far from the well-lit streets of the Port Elizabeth beachfront that goes past the back of the university, that is a quiet and isolated piece of road, marked out in equal sections by the street lights. It was here that I looked down at my watch during my second lap and began to calculate how much time I had left.

Subtract the number on my watch from forty-two. That's how many kilometres I have to go. Now multiply that number by the number of minutes per kilometre, which is probably around nine or nine and a half.

My brain was as battered as my legs, and I felt a wave of disappointment and panic as my answer indicated I would not have time to finish. So I started again. It was only when I expressed my concern out loud to the buddy I had picked up along the way that I realised I should leave the sums for another day – we were going to be through the finishers' arch with time to spare before the seventeen-hour cut-off.

I have said on more than one occasion that the final fourteen-kilometre lap of the run that day was made possible by the bystanders who line the streets. These strangers with their signs, shirts and banners carried me on those final steps leading to the finish. Each athlete wears a race number on a belt around their waist with their first name on it. On that April night I was an exhausted mess, but the sound of my own name was the most exhilarating thing I'd ever heard. As each person shouted from the sidelines with words of encouragement and praise, I would choke up and often burst into tears, with much gasping and spraying of snot. But it was glorious. I was living a dream in the presence of friends, each one recognising that dream and what it took to complete it. And asking for nothing in return.

The winner that year finished the race in a time of 7:45:00, taking the title of Ironman 2011 to a rapturous applause. And I approached the finish line around ten o'clock in the evening, just over seven hours later. The final 50 metres of the course is on a red carpet, the apple of every triathlete's eye. On that carpet stood Paul Kaye, the voice of Ironman, standing and smiling as fresh as he sounded that morning just fifteen hours and 225.8 kilometres ago. As I approached Paul he reached out one hand and placed it on my shoulder, bringing me to a dead stop. Looking me straight in the eye, he said the words that would turn me into a flood of uncontrollable tears – and more snot. Tears of utter exhaustion, tears of overwhelmed excitement. Tears of joy – unashamed, raw and honest joy.

'Robby,' Paul said as my breathing became deep and jarred. 'YOU ... ARE ... AN ... IRONMAN!'

I nodded silently, looked across to Tracey and the familiar faces I knew were responsible for me being there in the first place, and then jogged the final few metres to stand under the towering gateway that proves you were there. As if the raw skin under my feet, the chafed patches of skin in my armpits and my throbbing body were not evidence enough. Adding to everything that made that day surreal was Chrissie Wellington, that day's winner who had also endured what I had. She had broken the ladies' record for the course and had also beaten the male winner's marathon time for that day. She was at the finish line long after her "work day" was over to greet the finishers and place our medals over our sweat-drenched heads.

From the finish line I made my way to the medical tent, wrapped in a foil emergency blanket, for a short lie down. My core temperature dropped rapidly and I began to shake as I climbed onto the massage bed. Within minutes there was a physiotherapist rubbing my calves and ankles which by now where seizing up from the day's exertion.

One of the things I cherish about the Ironman triathlon and the culture it has created is the fact that all finishers get the same medal as the winner does. There are no grades of Ironman – only finishers. Obviously there are the elite professionals, the age groupers and their times, for whom the records and performances hold an entirely different meaning, but for Average Joe it is essentially a competition with nobody but themselves. The decision to carry on or stop and the thresholds of pain and exhaustion are determined by the individual, and the concept of winning occurs the very moment that person takes one more step than they believed was possible.

Along with eternal glory and a lifetime of bragging rights, each competitor was entitled to a free Spur burger in the finisher's area. By the time I arrived there, I am sure that the chefs behind the grill were also as exhausted as the athletes and the burger I received was probably very far from their best work, but I distinctly recall thinking that it was the most incredible thing I had ever tasted in my life. I wasn't shy about sharing this with the world as I went about telling anybody who was willing to listen or dodge the flying chunks of bread and sesame seeds.

Once I was done, the rest of our group stayed at the finish to watch and cheer as the last few competitors battled the impending cut-off time. Eventually we all headed back to collect our bicycles and gear bags from the transition area, with the goal of hot showers and soft beds in mind. Leaving the bike shed I was met by Chrissie "World Champ" Wellington again. She noticed I was limping quite heavily as stiffness and inflammation of my ankle joints had set in (for a change). I congratulated her on her impressive win and she grinned widely, as she is known to do, and thanked me. Then she offered to help carry the kit bag I had slung over my shoulder. Having just won, breaking a world record and showing her face among the stragglers, she still had the energy and inclination to teach me a life lesson in being humble. Throughout her career, Chrissie Wellington garnered many critics who "saw through her signature smile" that she wore throughout her races and she was often criticised for her weight being "dangerously low". But regardless of the haters, she will always have one fan, and not because she can swim, cycle or run faster than anyone else she competes against – but because of *how* she does it.

I worked very hard for the medal I won that day, and it will always be very special to me. I plan to have it framed and placed on a wall as a reminder to chuck that habit I have of underestimating everything I am capable of, provided I apply myself and tackle any challenge in my path with focus, energy and hard work.

But what I would really like to have done with the medal is put it in an envelope with a small jar of KY Jelly and address it to the doctor who told me that I couldn't climb mountains and that I couldn't run. I appreciate what he did for me, but with all due respect, leave the decisions regarding my limitations to me.

CHAPTER 42

PRECIOUS CARGO

It was early July 2012. In a few weeks' time I would again be starting the whole process of pouring my life into a duffel bag and jumping on a plane. I was heading for the seventh time to Kilimanjaro. Except this time was different. Not only was I leading another group of people to the summit, but this time I was taking very precious cargo with me – my fiancée Tracey. As the departure date grew closer, my focus shifted away from my feelings of self-doubt and towards making sure Tracey had the best possible chance of summiting Kilimanjaro.

The trip went relatively easy with no major incidents. The group we were with were really great people and mealtimes and every moment in between was full of fun and laughter. Sadly, the entire team did not summit – I had to turn the youngest climber in the team back approximately four hours after leaving Kibo Camp. His pace had slowed considerably and his sense of balance was not good. I tried to be as objective as possible and used a pulse oximeter to measure his blood oxygen saturation level. On an average day most people should have a saturation level in the high nineties. As we gain altitude that number drops, usually to around seventy-five or so, and as our bodies acclimatise by producing more haemoglobin that utilises more of the available oxygen, that number improves.

I upped my pace to catch up with the youngster to test his levels.

From the look on his face I could tell he was tired and lethargic. He reluctantly took off his glove and gave me his index finger, onto which I clamped the pulse oximeter. Within a second or so the number flashed on the little digital screen, cementing his fate. Sixty-seven. That was dangerously low and I had the awful job of telling him that it was too dangerous to proceed any higher. Thankfully his father was standing next to me and agreed with my decision. I was both relieved and grateful to see his head nodding as I explained the situation.

'I'm sorry my boy, this is it. Let's go,' his father said, holding his son's gloved hand in his. After a short discussion the two of them left with an assistant guide to return to the safety of the tents, rest up and wait for our return. Of my nine trips to Kilimanjaro, there have been three such occasions where someone has not summited with us due to health reasons or exhaustion. Making that call for them – putting an end to their adventure and essentially crushing the dream they have been so focused on for so long – is one of the most difficult, gut-wrenching things I ever have to do. And it doesn't get any easier. It hurts every time.

The rest of the team regained their rhythm and continued the slow grind up the final, and steepest, stretch of scree leading to Gillman's Point on the crater rim, a mere two hours to the summit.

By now the sun had risen and the group had spread out, but I had resumed my usual place at the back of the queue. I was now walking with Tracey, who had done incredibly well so far but was now starting to feel the exhausting effect of altitude. With the sun came a scathingly cold wind that tore over the glaciers in the crater and straight at us. I immediately remembered the feeling from cresting the Balcony on Everest summit morning; it was still just as painful, scouring every exposed piece of skin and setting fire to my ears and cheeks. Just ahead, the summit posts stood among the crowd of smiling adventurers in the orange light of morning.

That particular summit of Kilimanjaro was extraordinarily special for me. Reaching the top is always an incredible moment, regardless of how many times you have been there before. Sharing the summit with the woman I was going to be marrying in seven months' time was beyond words. I hugged Tracey, trying to say something that expressed how proud I was of her and how moved I was to have shared this incredible experience with my future wife. I garbled something to Tracey as I hugged her, choking up as I did. But the reaction on her face was not conducive to the impassioned *Gone with the Wind*-like final kiss scene I had constructed in my head over the last few hours. Tracey gazed back at me, her mouth cracking half a smile, and before I knew it we were taking our summit photos before rounding up the team and heading back down. Heading back to the High Camp, I was quite ticked off at how unromantic the moment had seemed, but I have since realised that between the altitude, exhaustion and the wind, it was a miracle that Tracey had even heard me, never mind understood me. Whether I was stringing coherent sentences at the time is also not entirely clear either. But we had done this together, my teammate – the woman I now lovingly and proudly call my wife – and me.

CHAPTER 43

AMA DABLAM

John and I first set eyes on Ama Dablam in 2009 while on our trek to Everest. The path out of the village of Namche Bazar zig-zags its way onto the crest of a hill before descending into Khumjung, a small village where Edmund Hillary helped build the first of many schools and facilities for the Sherpa people of the surrounding areas. From the tiny stone-housed village, the peak dominates the skyline to the North. Ama Dablam, or the Mother's Necklace, stands 6,812 metres in height – just 18 kilometres, as the crow flies, from Mount Everest. The almost symmetrical shoulders of the peak come together gently before turning skyward, forming the outline of a head. At the base of the "neck" is a giant hanging serac, an overhanging bulge of snow and ice, completing the illusion of a necklace or locket around the snow giantess' neck. It is the second-most photographed peak in the Himalaya, next to Everest. It is a vision of absolute beauty and, for some, love at first sight.

Ama Dablam had me at "hello", but with our focus firmly on Everest, we had carried on with the objective at hand. It was only three years later when I returned to Nepal to lead a group of trekkers on that same path that the flame was rekindled and the idea of climbing "Ama" was considered in earnest. This mountain was the perfect challenge for us. Being a combination of rock and ice, this was another chance to climb in the Himalayas and the permit fee was just $400 per climber, as opposed to Everest's whopping $11,000 price tag.

When John is involved with any expedition, a conversation over a beer transforms into comprehensive research, cost estimates and subsequently the purchase of air tickets. Before you know it, you are shovelling yak-cheese pizza into your face in a tea house in Dingboche. Along with his planning skills, John also has an extensive network within the outdoor industry. As word got around of the first all-South African expedition to the peak, it wasn't long before The North Face, a leading manufacturer of extreme outdoor equipment, were on board in a joint marketing venture to aid re-launching the brand in South Africa. It was a dream come true to be "sponsored athletes" by a brand I had idolised since those days of hoarding tatty climbing magazines. It was as if Christmas had come early when we were asked to go onto the American North Face website and create a wish list of the clothing and equipment we thought would be suitable for the upcoming expedition. In comparison to our first experience of sponsorships, this was a shitload better than twenty-five kilograms of soya mince.

On the day the boxes arrived – stuffed full of backpacks, duffel bags, jackets, trousers, gloves, T-shirts and sleeping bags – we frolicked in the piles of new "stuff" like children on a bouncy castle, only with more squealing and jumping around.

As part of the sponsorship, we were also assigned a photographer to help document the expedition and get some decent photos to use in the advertising material for our new international sponsor. That photographer turned out to be Alex Treadway, a multi-award winner travel photographer and a wizard with a camera, specialising in remote cultures. John and I first met Alex in 2009. He was a friend of one of the climbers on the Himex team. He'd arrived in camp, hung around for a few weeks taking some photos for a book, and then disappeared down the valley again. The book he was working on involved shooting portraitures of the various team members, both before and after their ascent of Everest, as well as the spectacular surroundings of the Khumbu region. As previously mentioned, I have Alex to thank for my love of photography. I had been loafing around doing nothing when he sat with me and explained the basic functions of my camera, which up until now was set on fully automatic. In that single morning in the Tiger Dome at Everest's feet, he managed to clarify the relationship between ISO, shutter speed and aperture for me better than the three years at WITS Technikon did. Our lecturer, despite being incredibly talented with years of experience, left me clueless, submitting each assignment on a wing, a prayer and a sniff of bullshit.

Upon arrival in Kathmandu we met with Alex and arranged the first shoot in and around the Thamel region as we finalised the last few arrangements and bought a few last-minute supplies. There I was, feeling like a celebrity. New mountain, new gear ... same old ankles.

Alex had us walk up and down the same piece of road as he fired shot after shot in search of the right one. We posed in front of the many paintings of Ama Dablam, pointing as if we were choosing a climbing route and various scenarios in the midst of the city chaos.

With that out of the way, we could focus on getting onto the actual mountain. We were growing impatient, having travelled via Dubai to Kathmandu where we had been subsequently delayed for two days at the dusty domestic airport terminal due to bad weather, making the approach into Tenzing Hillary airport even more dangerous. Once safely in Lukla, we left almost immediately, but only after John had coaxed the rest of the team into having a cappuccino at the Starbucks, a small wood-panelled bakery and coffee shop with Wi-Fi and an array of baked goods. It was about as authentic a Starbucks as the "YakDonald's" restaurant next door.

With coffee removed from the top of our priority list, we followed the stone-paved pathway winding between the gear shops, souvenir stands and lodges, out of the village and into the forest. The expedition was finally underway and we spent the next three hours dodging yak trains, before crossing the steel bridge leading into Phakding for our first spectacular night next to the raging rapids of the Dudh Kosi River. It was incredible to be back here again.

For the first time in as long as I could remember I felt that my name belonged somewhere near the top of that all-too-familiar leader board in my head. This was the first time Allan and Warren had been to Nepal and I enjoyed the feeling of having the advantage of local knowledge. It gave me great pride to play tour guide for my teammates, with useless facts, route information and the odd Nepali phrase, one of which I would later learn was a description of one's parents' genitals and not the "don't worry, be happy" adage I was originally told it was on a previous trip.

Day two of our approach would end in Namche Bazar, but not before giving the guys their first sighting of Mount Everest. The clouds parted, giving everyone a good view of the world's highest mountain. Warren has always been adamant that climbing Everest was far too commercialised, and professed on more than one occasion that it would never be a priority for him. Until he saw it. Like Medusa, she casts a spell on all those whose gaze meets hers.

After a few compulsory photographs we continued up the steepened path that leads into the basin, which is home to Namche Bazar. As if it were scripted, John piped up with a suggestion. 'How about we find where we're staying and then hit the Everest Bakery for a coffee and some apple pie?

'And then go shopping!' added Allan.

I couldn't help but laugh. Al is famous for his ability to out-shop anyone, male or female, when outdoor gear and gadgets are concerned. 'You know that you can wash and re-use this stuff,' I gestured to the duffel bags.

'But Rob,' he justified, 'I just like new things!'

Our distinct sunshine-yellow duffel bags stood out against the grey-brown matted dreadlocks of the incredible beasts that had carried them to 3,440 metres above sea level over the last five hours. With our lodging taken care of, we stuck to the plan and made our next stop the Everest Bakery. Within fifteen minutes the ants in Allan's pants had him on his feet again in an effort to visit every establishment selling climbing gear and outdoor clothing in the greater Namche metropolitan area.

As the afternoon wore on, we would eventually all meet up at the village post office. A petite Nepali woman planted behind a wooden desk in a two-by-two room constitutes the postal service for the entire Khumbu region. I had been in shower cubicles bigger than this place. We crowded around the wooden counter sharing a chewed pen to scribble postcards before our "Post Mistress" licked and pressed each one with a stamp. I wanted to ask for my postcard back before it went into her out tray in order to write a health warning on it, but decided I'd rather not touch it again. It's become a bit of a tradition on our climbing trips to send a postcard home from whichever corner of the globe we are in. More often than not we arrive home before the cards do. This time would be no different.

The remainder of our time in Namche Bazar consisted of coffee, gear shops and more coffee, before we headed back for dinner, coffee, apple pie for dessert and eventually bed. Tomorrow would take us to the village of Khumjung via the Everest View Hotel, and the team's first view of our objective, Ama Dablam.

The afternoon mist was already rolling in when we arrived in Khumjung. With our luggage safely in our assigned rooms, the four of us set out in search of a bakery, coffee shop and / or both. A few metres from the lodge Warren opted out of the excursion and returned to the lodge to sleep off a headache. None of us said anything at the time, but I know we were all silently hoping that Wa's ailments weren't something more serious like altitude sickness. The rolling whiteout set the mood for incredible photos while we wound our way through the stone-walled maze of a ghost town, devoid of all life except the "tink-tink-tink" of a single stonemason chipping blocks to build another teahouse somewhere in the distance. The weather started to deteriorate fast, so after we had taken shelter in what serendipitously turned out to be a bakery, we returned to our lodgings for the remainder of the evening.

The next morning took us down the valley to the micro-village of Phunki Tenga before crossing a river to begin a torturous grind leading to the Tengboche monastery for lunch. We were all chomping at the bit, keen to get to Dingboche and finally Ama

Dablam's Base Camp. From Dingboche, the dusty path descends to a wooden bridge crossing the river before ascending the other side. One of the challenges of climbing large mountains in the Himalayas is the long distances covered to gain access to the base camps. We would only reach Ama Dablam's camp at the foot of the peak on the sixth day of our trip. It was located on a plateau surrounded by yak grazing land. Base Camp exists for three months of every year in a small basin approximately 400 metres wide and about twice as long.

As we were yet to find out, this mountain would also have a "Mr Miyagi" lesson of its own, another vital piece of education cleverly disguised within the folds of toil and hard labour. In the weeks leading up to our departure, a massive weather system moved across Asia, terrorising India before moving west into the Himalaya range. As the warm and moist air is forced upward over the mountains it cools rapidly, creating snow. A lot of snow. Most of the mountain range was buried by a metre of the white stuff in a very short space of time. Base Camp, being in a basin and only getting direct sunshine between 9 am and 3.30 pm, became a very cold place, frozen in time, thawing at a painfully slow rate. We would make our home for the next two and a half weeks on one of the exposed grassy patches, among chunks of snow and ice pillars in a surreal Salvador Dali-esque landscape – only the melting clocks where missing.

In the mornings we would wait for the sun to peer over the neighbouring peaks, flooding our tents with sweet sunlight. We'd congregate for breakfast in the communal dining tent. Each meal usually ended with all four of us slumped in our camp chairs that were placed in the sun and hopefully sheltered from the wind. The end of each day would bring with it bone-chilling cold. The setting sun released long shadows that crept across the valley, freezing everything they touched. We would dress in our warmest clothes and shiver our way through the hours separating us from our beds.

On most nights we would huddle around an iPad mini to enjoy a movie, John, Allan, Warren, Gunga the camp assistant and Bierbal the cook and me. Perhaps we would not have huddled that close to each other had *someone* not left the speaker back in Johannesburg! I was the culprit, and I was reminded of this ... often. But given the sub-zero temperature, the huddling was acceptable. For the first two weeks of the trip. With time, and the absence of showers or running water, the body odour in the tent became intoxicating to a point of nausea. By week three Bierbal, the guy responsible for preparing our meals in camp, developed an odour that could bring a tear to a grown man's eye and his dinner to the back of his throat. Admittedly we were all less than rosy, but this guy was on another level.

We'd wake up, eat, faff around camp, eat, faff some more, drink coffee, eat, watch a movie, go to bed. And wait. There was literally nothing more we could do.

Eventually it became too much. After more than a week of waiting and watching, we shouldered the backpacks we had loaded the day before and took our first steps out of Base Camp to go and establish our first of three camps en route to the summit. The path leading to the higher camps is usually a straightforward path of gravel and scree, snaking its way around the back of the ridge and up a steady slope out of sight from our tents in the basin. This year, some poor sod had had to forge their way through knee-deep snow all the way past Advanced Base Camp and on to Camp 1. As grateful as I am for said sod, the sun penetrated the snow and heated the rocks exposed by those first footsteps. Those deep foot holes in the snow eventually melted away and created a furrow, or more of an awkwardly thin path, about thirty centimetres wide in most places. Complicating things further, the narrow groove formed unevenly, almost diagonally due to the angle of the sun, forcing us off balance to one side between the leaning walls on either side of the path.

This made walking difficult. If I haven't made it blatantly clear by now, walking even at the best of times is not my strong suit. In fact, I am the first to admit I am downright shit at it. Add the weight of a fully loaded backpack and rigid La Sportiva Spantik mountaineering boots on the iced-up rock and gravel terrain and you have a recipe for a miserable day. Going up was not too bad; as we moved steadily forward, each obstacle was laid clearly in front of us and mostly avoidable. It was only on the return journey, heading back to Base Camp, when my composure, balance and my sense of humour went out the window.

The path hugs the contour of the mountainside before rising steeply to gain the main slope. A steady uphill across rocky ground leads to Advanced Base Camp, or Yak Camp, at 5,400 metres altitude. Further up the slope, Camp 1 is situated at 5,800 metres, poised on the edge of a sharp ridge overlooking Base Camp.

We arrived at ABC and pitched one of our tents. We stashed the contents of our bags before snapping some pictures and having some snacks before heading back down the icy path like lopsided train carriages. The glassy ice-covered rocks and slushy terrain slowed me down considerably as I slipped and skidded, jerked and jarred all the way back. *This could become a problem*, I thought to myself each time I jarred over the obstacles in the path. Turns out I was right.

We were greeted in Base Camp by Gunga, the assistant chef-cum-butler, who was in the middle of his daily routine of fetching water from the river just east of the camp. Each day he would take two 25-litre containers and walk the three or four hundred metres to the stream. Often he would reach midway and just stop. For fifteen to twenty minutes Gunga would stand motionless, doing absolutely nothing. Then, without rhyme or reason, he would reach down, pick up his containers and carry on. At first we thought he was taking a break from the weight of the bottles, but then we noticed him stopping on the way to the river as well, when his bottles were still empty. As strange as we all thought it was for anyone to do *nothing* for such a considerable amount of time, I believe there is a significant lesson in hitting pause on a daily basis and just being present in that very moment. I think you'd agree if you were to meet Gunga and see the size of the smile he wears at any given moment.

A day or two after our load carry to ABC, in an effort to break the monotony we decided to pack a few essentials and head back down the hill to the teahouse we had stayed, in Dingboche. We went for a night in a real bed, some decent food and hopefully a shower. Coincidently it was the same teahouse we stayed in the night John had ventured out to find me in the dark after leaving Everest Base Camp. I remembered the five steps separating the kitchen and dining room from the bedrooms on the ground level. The yak dung-burning stove was still burning, only this time the benches were empty. I could hear the noise of fifty conversations in six different languages and see the sunburnt faces on sardined bodies, and I remembered Tashi Tashi crouching in front of me gesturing for me to climb onto his back. This time the sun covered most of the floor, highlighting the barren benches. One of the dining-room walls had a bookshelf, neatly packed with a range of books left, borrowed, stolen and replenished by passersby.

Next to the bookshelf stood a glass-doored cabinet with a few pieces of mountaineering history, from a rusted crampon to an antiquated oxygen bottle dating back to one of the first expeditions of the 1950s. A frayed lock of rope and a splintered piece of a log that was used to cross the icefall were all labelled with their dates and origin on neatly written paper slips.

I had been in this room before, but last time I was in no shape to realise, let alone appreciate, these little gems from expeditions past. I imagined each historic piece in a box frame, mounted on a wall back home, but the sign scribbled on the back of a piece of a cereal box made it clear that these treasures were "no for sale".

A little after our first decent meal of the day our expedition leader Russell Brice and Japanese guide Shinji Tamura – along with two other guides – arrived at the gate of the teahouse's courtyard. They were on their way home, having had no luck on the lesser climbed North Face of Ama Dablam. Deep snow had made any progress above Base Camp too difficult even for these veterans, most of whom were professionals with impressive high-altitude résumés. We sat and chatted for a while, enjoying a flask of lemon tea, the sunshine and the company. Russell was quiet and reserved, more so than normal, possibly feeling the impact of aborting a commercial expedition. It was disappointing not only for him, but also those who placed large sums of money and their hopes in him.

'Save your fingers and toes and go home.' Russell's words landed like a ton of bricks. This was the man with forty years more experience than any of us. His educated advice stirred a mixture of emotions; some anger, some disappointment and a shitload of doubt. But I had a choice. Was Russell's advice an absolute fact, or just an opinion?

We bid our farewells and his entourage headed off down the path intent on reaching Namche by nightfall. When night arrived, instead of diving for my down jacket and gloves, I relaxed on a bench, read a copy of *Tuesdays with Morrie* and enjoyed the welcome change, the stove warming my bare feet as I waited for my yak-bolognaise with spaghetti to arrive. I chatted late into the night with my friends before we made our way down to our rooms. I smiled to myself as I walked those five steps on my own two feet.

A hearty breakfast was the perfect way to celebrate the lazy start to the next day. A few metres up the path, having bid farewell to the luxury of the one-star opulence, is an internet café, offering half an hour of Wi-Fi at the cost of a few hundred rupees. All conversation was replaced by the tapping of thumbs on phone screens. Cellphone signal from Base Camp was apparently possible from a rock, half a kilometre out of camp, while standing on one leg. Allan was apparently able to send a message home to his wife, making the rest of us look like insensitive and uncaring bastards.

An hour of text messages and the odd photograph flew past before it was time to disconnect from the lives we had back home and make the trip back to the cold of Base Camp – back to the waiting game.

Returning to the basin of the camp, we noticed how empty it had become. One by one even the biggest of teams were packing up, accepting defeat and heading in the opposite direction of the summit, leaving circles in the snow where their tents once stood. It had become starkly apparent that our expedition had reached a critical point. The days remaining for a summit attempt were slipping past and the need to make a decision was upon us.

There had been a lot of talk of a "plan B" as our chances of climbing our original objective had become slimmer. Warren began concocting plans to head further up the valley towards Everest and climb Island Peak, a 6,000 metre peak that has become quite popular in recent years.

'The way I see it, there are two possible options,' said John, sitting forward in his camp chair. 'We can pack it all in and head home, or try our luck, do what we came here to do and go for the summit.'

What would normally have been the obvious answer had been distorted by doubt and the frustration of waiting on weather conditions that were less than ideal. Ama Dablam lay before us on her death bed and we were gathered at her side, contemplating the decision to pull the plug on her. Were we to let her slip away quietly, or resurrect the last sliver of hope and carry on with brave faces? At what point would prudence and calculated risk meet the spirit of adventure? When does bravery become bravado? When does the quest to push the boundaries become a futile mission of endangerment? The thought of living to climb another day had crossed all of our minds.

'I say we go for it. We have to. This is what we came for,' someone piped up, cracking the tension in the tent. Whether or not it was the right decision, nobody knew, but at least we *had* a decision.

Committing to attempt Ama Dablam meant having to go back up that skewed path again to establish Camps 1 and 2, and then returning to Base Camp for more supplies before a final bid was possible. We risked putting in all of this effort, carrying heavy loads with no guarantee that the conditions after Camp 2 would be safe enough to summit, especially the Mushroom Ridge. It could all be a grandiose waste of time, money and effort. There is a name for this act of placing all of your bets on one pony with very little control of several external factors and influences, gambling for the hopes of a good result and the risk of losing absolutely everything without even a moment's notice ... it's called mountaineering.

We started with the date on our air tickets and began the process of working backwards, calculating an absolute worst-case scenario itinerary, which turned out to be quite tight with almost no margin for error.

23rd November: Fly out of Kathmandu and arrive in South Africa on the 24th.

22nd November: Fly out of Lukla.

21st November: Leave Namche and go to Lukla.

20th November: Leave Ama Base Camp and head to Namche.

19th November: Pack up and come down to Base Camp.

18th November: Head to Summit.

17th November: Climb from Camp 1 to Camp 2.

16th November: Load carry to Camp 1. Sleep at Camp 1.

So that was the plan. We went about separating and allocating loads in order to begin the process of ultimately establishing Camp 2, from where we would attempt a summit. We carefully scrutinised the tent, selected items of clothing, fuel, stoves and rations in an effort to minimise mistakes but, more importantly, minimise the weight of our backpacks. Anything going up the hill now was going on our backs.

The following morning was a repeat of the motions we had been through on the previous trip up to establish Camp 1. We followed the path out the basin, along the contour of the mountain, before heading up the steep slope, aiming for the orange VE25 dome tent we had put up nearly a week ago. The following day would be the highlight of the trip for me because this was where the real climbing would begin. In contrast to a lot of mountains that are essentially an uphill slog, moving to Ama Dablam's second camp situated high up on the knife-edge ridge required real technical climbing. With towers of granite, gullies and edging across sheets of rock, this felt like a proper climb and held an appeal that filled me with confidence.

Finally, I was feeling more like the hardcore climber everyone back home thought I was.

It is strange to think how the fondest and the worst memory of that trip both occurred on the same day.

Camp 2, or as we soon renamed it, "Camp Poo", exists atop a pillar of stone, a massive wart on the dragon's back, before the route turns upward to the summit. The cluster of scattered ledges can barely be classed as a camp, but with a fatal drop on either side of it, it is the only semi-level piece of ground for literally miles around. Photographs of tiny orange dome tents, clinging awkwardly to the granite outcrop like little mushrooms on a rotting log, were ironically a massive part of what appealed to us when deciding to embark on this trip.

Guided by our noses, we reached the ledges and began seeking out a suitable site that was level, free of bulges and bumps and large enough to accommodate a three-man, of which we had none – so we pitched the tent anyway. We found rocks the size of soccer balls to anchor the guy lines. The terrain leant off to the right where a shoddy rock wall made up that edge of the platform. Two corners of the hexagonal tent floor hung over the edge, just a metre or so above our closest neighbour, another barely-pitched deep green two-person shelter. What Camp 2 lacked in comforts it made up for in spectacular 360-degree panoramic views.

We made the cache of gear, piling it inside the dome in a semi-organised fashion in an effort to keep each of our belongings separate, but also to hopefully weigh the tent down. A strong wind up there would turn our shelter into a kite, delivering free camping gear to a village somewhere in India. Happy to have shed the weight we had hauled to this 5,900-metre-high perch, we buckled up and began the journey home one-and-a-half kilometres below us. As much as my confidence had been fortified on the way up, returning home proved to be a slow process. As each anchor appeared, it became a guessing game of which fixed line to use while the tangled clumps of ropes of varying colours and degrees of wear flitted in the breeze. More often than not I would clip my carabiner through three or four strands trying to justify my paranoia ... but never truly ease it. The near vertical sections of rock sometimes stretched across six or seven metres, making me wish I had the dexterity and friction of rock-climbing shoes with their soft and sticky soles. Instead, my rigid space boots skidded beneath me in search of a small ledge or crack to catch on to. With all of my weight hanging on the grey and faded fixed ropes, I looked down between my feet to see an icy blue glacial lake, its magnificence numbed by the thought of how far down it was.

Back at Camp 1 the ground had become less steep, and as grateful as I was to not be reliant on those dubious ropes, I almost immediately missed the undiluted thrill of the technical section. The inclined faces and bulging boulders were replaced by a series of slabs half-covered in snow and ice.

The going was still slow and the final hours of the afternoon were upon us. Despite my intentions, my pace remained slow and prudent. The stiffness of my boots together with the stiffness in my ankles had me scrambling from one slab to the next using my hands, knees, butt or whatever was available to me. The gap between me and the others widened.

Once again I was last on the path by a long way. Once again I was slipping and sliding, jerking and jarring over ice-polished rocks. Once again I was far from camp when the sun went down, leaving me to fumble my way back in the moonlight. My headlight is rechargeable, so when the battery runs flat, you can easily plug it in and charge it on any available USB port. *How convenient*, I thought to myself. Once again I found myself in the familiar dark hole. Once more my name was posted at the bottom of that leader board, kept in place by the mass of cobwebs. In the darkness I made my way down slowly and painfully. Each time my foot slipped over an icy patch, it jerked me off balance, jarring my already tender ankles, sending jolts of pain through my joints despite the solid support of my boots.

By now Allan and Warren's head torches had disappeared over the ridge and I felt truly alone. There was no fear of getting lost; the full moon lit up the snow in an enchanted display of every shade of blue, turning the world around me into a glowing cloud hanging in the still air. The inky dome of sky above me was a scatter of sparkling jewels. I thought back to the movie *The Bucket List*. The lady in the bar speaks of climbing Mount Everest, describing the sky as more blue than black, and the stars like pinpricks in the floor of heaven.

But out on the path, I had only Ben Harper in my headphones keeping me company, telling me to keep my head up and my heart strong. By this point, the pain in my lower legs was at a constant level now and no amount of jarring or straining made any difference. The only obstacle between my tent and I was the amount of time it would take to get there.

To me, the line "eyes like wild flowers, oh, with your demons of change" sounded like "eyes like wild flowers – just the demons I'd change." My head was up, my heart was strong! It was just the demons I would have changed, the demons that were in the process of turning the pain and swelling in my ankles into doubt in my mind. The demons I knew that would turn against me ... again.

About twenty minutes after the others had disappeared behind the ridge, a bright, piercing light appeared ahead of me, a shining star (but sadly no wise men to follow it). My lips contorted into a crumpled smile, my eyes welled with tears and I sniffed back hard on a tide of snot. Waiting patiently on the path and looking back patiently as I edged towards him like a towering lighthouse to a lost ship, stood John – Joseph the Shepherd – just as he had four years before. Once I caught up with him the two of us began to make our way back to camp, sharing the light of his torch. We just talked about nothing and everything.

Over the years our lives have become busier, with new priorities and everything that comes with "growing up". John and I spent the better part of two hours just shooting the breeze (talking shit) just like we used to before life got busy. It's always good to be reminded from time to time that these trips are not just about getting to the top.

Eventually we reached the relative comforts of our tents, now covered in a shimmering blanket of ice crystals. After dumping my backpack in the entrance of my tent I slumped down to take off my boots, which now felt like blocks of cement, and slipped my sweaty feet into my softer and much lighter trekking boots, before limping my sorry ass into the mess tent for something to eat. That night I was cold, tired and gatvol (fed up) and no movie would have remedied this, not even *Rock of Ages*. Among the expected "skop, skiet en donner" (violent and action-packed) movies Allan had loaded onto the iPad was a musical set in the eighties, with a soundtrack of rock classics including Def Leppard, Motorhead and Journey. It had us all secretly tapping our toes to cheesy covers by Tom Cruise and an expedition favourite Julianne Hough. To this day, Warren swears blindly that that movie was the worst hundred and thirty-six minutes of his life. Philistine!

When morning arrived, I was immediately reminded of the previous day's walk as well as every trip, twist and tumble I had taken on the way down. My right ankle in particular was that familiar shade of purple, bloated and round. The left foot was not as bad, but still stiff and tender, making my trip to breakfast slow and painful.

Before I had fallen asleep that night, I had already started coming to terms with what was going to happen. As much as I was hoping that a good night's rest would help me to recover, I had begun to resign myself to the inevitable. On the leader board in my head, my name was in stone last position with little chance of a comeback.

After breakfast we sat chatting about the movements of the next few days. Tomorrow the summit bid would begin, moving from here to Camp 2 where the tent was already pitched and a lot of the food, fuel and equipment was cached. The day after that, it would be Camp 2 to summit and back.

'I'm not going to be able to go with you,' I blurted out of nowhere, killing the conversation in its tracks. During the silence I noticed Allan and Warren looking down awkwardly. Just when I thought I couldn't feel any worse about my decision. Despite having turned the decision over and over in my head, words were still hard to find while attempting to justify my decision to the three of them. Their silence gave me the impression that my withdrawal had already been discussed. There were no expressions of surprise, no effort to talk me out of it, just disappointment.

Somewhere in the back of my mind, a man on a ladder was reaching for the plate with my name written on it. It was the one gathering dust in the bottom slot on the leader board. He slid it out, leaving an obvious blank space.

'Are you sure?' John asked, as if we were going over a script we had both rehearsed before. With a nod of my head it was done.

With his head hung low, John sighed in defeat, throwing it in the sand before walking away.

CHAPTER 44

IF THE CHINKED ARMOUR FITS

There are times when solitude can be instrumental in healing. The isolation and silence can be quite cathartic, a welcome pause in which you can gather your thoughts, review your decisions and make peace with how the dice have fallen. It can also be a deafening void, with nobody to help you absorb the impact of what you have done.

John, Warren and Allan left that following morning, leaving me alone in camp with Bierbal and Gunga, three crows and the last few remaining strangers in the neighbouring camps who hadn't abandoned their own expeditions. And a big stick. A big stick which I used repeatedly to thrash myself for my acts of cowardice and stupidity. For being a liability, a disappointment and so fucking predictable. I would be alone for the next three days as the team moved up to the summit. Once I realised I could not possibly remain horizontal in my tent any longer, I tried to occupy myself by dawdling between the camps, striking up superficial conversations with strangers and immediately regretting having done so as each encounter highlighted my failure to carry on with the rest of my team.

Night eventually arrived and I spent an hour or two hobbling around in the cold taking long exposure photographs of the mountain, perhaps in an act of solidarity with my friends who were undoubtedly also feeling the seeping cold perched on the top of the stone pillar that is Camp 2. With my fingers stinging from the sub-zero temperature, I retreated to the mess tent for one last cup of coffee before climbing back into my tent for a repeat performance of *Rock of Ages*. As the saying goes, "what happens on the mountain, stays on the mountain."

Once the credits began rolling up, I watched another movie for another hour or so before the iPad's battery was depleted. All the while sleep was keeping its distance. The feeling of desolation and acute sense of how far from home I was was like nothing I had ever experienced before in my life. And I hope I never will experience it again. The constant monologue of the bully in my head carried on as I lay there in silence until I eventually fell asleep, exhausted by the sound of the scathing voice in my head.

The yellow light of morning would eventually wake me. I rolled over, in no particular rush to deal with another day, when the realisation hit me. 'It's summit day!' I said out loud. It was 9.15 am and it was agreed that they would leave the tents in Camp 2 at 9 am once the sun was shining on the route. With the addition of strong winds on the exposed ridge, the temperature would plummet way below zero, so any additional heat from the sun would be greatly appreciated. I exited the tent, wheezing, coughing and limping in what must have been a pathetic spectacle. Adding insult to injury, I had developed a chest infection after coming down from the load carry two days before, which progressed to bronchitis. At least the mountain gods had a sense of humour.

Just behind our mess tent was a small chorten made from stones, crafted into a perfectly square pillar no more than a metre tall. That morning the campsite was clouded by the blueish white smoke coming from the large branch of green juniper that was burning at the foot of the pillar. Juniper is burnt as an offering to the gods, requesting safe passage when climbing. I was moved that Bierbal and Gunga had made this gesture on our behalf and I stood staring as the smoke drifted up and the prayer flags fluttered in the breeze.

At the dining tent I was greeted by the ever-polite Gunga. In his limited English and my even more limited Nepali, we agreed on a breakfast of egg on toast and coffee.

'Maji moto?' I asked him. His default smile turned into a look of confusion and I immediately realised my error. Gunga didn't speak Swahili. Right phrase, wrong mountain. 'Ah shit, sorry. Ah ... tato pani?' I said apologetically. With a toothy grin he nodded, pointing to the flask of hot water already on the table. I went about mixing the instant coffee and milk powder into what would turn out to be the first of many cups of coffee that day. 'Tato pani ... not maji moto! He's probably thinking this South African dickhead has lost his marbles,' I muttered into my plastic cup.

I took up my usual spot outside between the cooking and the dining tent, dragging one of the camp chairs into a patch of sun, facing the peak. And that's where I would stay, radio in one hand, binoculars in the other. The boys were up there and I was going to sit vigil with my attention focused on the upper slopes of Ama Dablam. Craning my neck, I scoured the route that they would be following, but without any luck.

From Camp 2 they would be heading further up the ridge to a rocky obstacle known as the Grey Tower before taking on the Mushroom Ridge. Only after the ridge would they be visible from where we were, so patience became the name of the game.

After approximately an hour I decided that the sunny and relatively windless conditions made for perfect shower weather. While Gunga prepared the pot of hot water, I dug out my various toiletries in a rush of excitement. The simple joys and comfort of washing with hot water is taken for granted until it is no longer available to us. In the mountaineering classic *Touching the Void* by Joe Simpson, his climbing partner Simon Yeates speaks in detail about how, after presuming he had killed his climbing partner, he loses track of time while washing himself in a nearby lake in an effort to try and cleanse himself of the guilt of having cut the rope, sending his best friend Joe to his death. As I carried my steaming bucket to where I would be "showering", I remembered Simpson's story with hopes that the process of washing my anger, disappointment and shame away would be just as cathartic for me.

Joe Simpson describes Simon's bath in the lake as a spiritual moment, an act of mourning and a cleansing of sins ... which I soon realised was a bunch of bullshit. Within thirty seconds the bucket of hot water had become tepid at best and my pamper session turned into a mixture of tap dancing and a Scottish highland jig in a frantic race against hypothermia. What I had hoped would be a soulful moment of respite became a whore's bath, barely skimming my "pits and bits" before diving to throw on the same pungent clothing from the weeks before.

Back in my lookout spot, while I was thawing gradually in the morning sun, Bierbal handed the binoculars back to me, pointing at a speck moving up the face, followed by two more specks slightly closer together. All three specks were moving upward. This was excellent news, worth celebrating with another cup of coffee and some lunch. An hour had passed since my brisk brush with hygiene and it still felt like my frozen nipples could cut through my shirt.

Slowly but surely the specks on the great white face made their way up the right-hand edge of the peak, keeping to the far right of the hanging serac that is the locket on the necklace around Mother's neck. The last pitches leading to the summit were the only things between the boys and success. The first anonymous speck was nearing the top, so I made another trip to my tent to fetch my mobile phone so that I could record the upcoming conversation from the summit.

While waiting like an expectant father, I paced the frozen ground repeatedly, checking that my radio was on and still working. I turned on my iPhone and opened a new voice memo, ready to hit the record button at a moment's notice. As the screen came to life, so did the radio with a bleep and a hiss, before falling silent again.

Record.

'It is almost three o'clock on 17th November 2013 ... we are waiting to hear the boys from the summit. We are watching them through the binoculars. They are cresting the ridge and we're about to chat to them live.

'Base Camp to summit team – do you read?' I asked, my eyes scouring the top again to count the three ants on the giant mound of ice cream.

In unison a rapturous 'Whoooooooooo!' came over the radio. Warren spoke first and I could hear the exhaustion in his voice.

'We are so chuffed to have made it here on our last possible day, after having to wait for weather and snow conditions. We're seriously chuffed. Very, very chuffed. We miss you up here, Rob. Okay, here's Allan.'

'Thanks, my man ... very happy. Very tired, but vvry vrry happy,' Allan managed to articulate. The exhaustion and cold had numbed his face, slurring his words.

We exchanged a few more sentences of congratulations, keeping small talk to a minimum. John had been up there, unsheltered from the wind for around twenty minutes.

'What I need from you now, is to turn around. Get down. All ten fingers, all ten toes,' I barely managed to get my words out as I began to choke up from a mixture of pride and relief ... but also regret.

'Copy that,' Allan sighed and the radio bleeped again.

The following hours were filled with a sense of relief and satisfaction, knowing that they had made it and were on their way home. But that relief was short-lived as the sun began to dip towards the horizon, turning the mountain its characteristic tones of ochre. Efforts throughout the afternoon to make contact with the team received no response. It took a constant, conscious effort to keep my internal wrestling match between rational thinking and panic under control as the argument began in my head, trying to contradict every "what if?" scenario with a logical explanation based on faith and trust in my teammates and their capabilities.

What if one of them has fallen? thought Panic.

Then the others would have radioed for help, replied Logic.

But what if all three of them have fallen? blurted Panic, doing what he did best.

Shut the fuck up, grunted Logic.

At nine minutes past seven the radio, now a permanent fixture in my hand, crackled and bleeped, jerking me from a daydream about having to head up on a search and rescue mission. John, Allan and Warren were safely back in Camp 2, dinner was on the boil and Warren had thrown my pot away – off the edge of the ridge and into oblivion – thousands of metres below. It was such a relief to hear from them that the news of my fallen cookware meant absolutely nothing to me. It had been a hard day staring up at those three black dots on the mountain, inconceivably far away, knowing I should have been up there too – and hating myself for it.

After eating small bits of the meal that had been prepared for me, I exited the tent only to bump into Gunga who tried his best to piece a question together about the guys up on the mountain together. In his face I could see the concern etched deep into the grooves of his shining face.

The intent of his question was lost in translation. Gunga was either concerned for the wellbeing of his new-found friends or disappointed that tonight would be the second night in a row without a movie in the mess tent.

I retired to my own tent for another night of tossing and turning from one sore hip to the other, to lie awake and examine the extent of that ever-widening chink in that familiar piece of armour, one that was now on the brink of being decommissioned.

All that was left to do now was to return home and complete the process of cleaning, repairing and packing away the clothing and piles of equipment ... and sharing the story. I'd had an expedition to Denali two years before that had failed, and just like that one, this story of failure was going to prove difficult. Re-telling a story of how everyone else had succeeded and I had not was going to be complicated even further by what was now becoming an inescapable spider's web and a little too familiar for my liking.

For the record, it never gets any easier. Ever.

CHAPTER 45

COMING DOWN

It has often been called "coming down from the mountain", that feeling that occurs when you have to return back to normal life, to readjust before hitting the ground running in an effort to fit in to everyday life, where nobody else had left. Most people will have experienced it after a major high point in their lives, be it a pilgrimage or long awaited holiday, a major occasion like a milestone birthday, a wedding, or even a high-energy conference filled with positivity and enthusiasm. The coming down occurs when something incredible has happened to you. You have seen the world from a high place or experienced life at its absolute fullest. But no one else has.

It's a combination of missing those people you have recently been in close quarters with on a daily basis, a feeling that there is now a hole where excitement used to be and a general disappointment in life back in the real world.

I often have to remind myself that during those sacred twenty-two minutes back in 2009, when the world stood still for me while I was the tallest man on Earth, everybody I knew was either fast asleep or ordering drive-thru. For them it was 4.30 am on a Sunday morning.

As much as I miss Tracey from the moment we say goodbye at the airport departure terminal, as much as I worry about her while I'm far away and coming home to her is always the best feeling in the world, I still feel that coming down. It's just as I imagine a heroin junkie feels as lucidity returns, along with the realisation that they are not in Kansas – or in my case, Kathmandu – anymore.

Coming down the mountain having failed, again, brought me back to terra-firma in what felt like a crash landing. The disappointment I felt in myself was made worse every time I retold my excuse of a story and presented the expedition slideshows on behalf of our equipment sponsor. It was salt in an open and very ugly wound.

Once more there were two voices in my head, hard at work. This time Hope was trying to assess the damage, sifting through wreckage in search of any signs of life, while Pragmatism weighed up the successes versus the recent failures.

Hope was trying to find forgiveness and understanding, making allowances for my injuries. Pragmatism looked at the hard facts. I hadn't summited a mountain apart from Kilimanjaro since 2010 (apparently Kilimanjaro didn't count any more). Perhaps my future as a mountaineer needed to be reconsidered.

Months would go by and the debate continued, Hope against Pragmatism. In the meantime, I would return back to ordinary life. Speaking engagements were few and far between and I began to question my ambitions. *Who the hell wants to hear from a mountaineer that doesn't make it to the top?* As life and my bank balance would have it, I found myself in the familiar seat of the advertising agency I had sworn never to return to at least ten times before.

The repeated act of tucking my tail between my legs and surrendering to The Man each time left me feeling like a failure and a hypocrite. It was never my intention to be a part-time speaker.

One of my greatest fears was approaching fast, and the anxiety of it often kept me awake at night in a sweat of doubt and panic while my wife lay asleep beside me, having promised to be by my side through everything. That poor, poor girl.

I called it the Four Fs. Freelancing at Forty and Financially Fucked.

Had the brave decision I had taken all those years ago – to leave the structure and safety net of secure employment behind me – finally backfired? Was this life less ordinary finally unwinding around my feet? I wasn't twenty-five anymore. Shit, I wasn't even thirty-five anymore! The ideal of speaking on a full-time basis worked for a few months at a time, but when the "cream" ran out I reverted to yet another freelance contract. Making ends meet and not much more. The very thing I promised I'd never do.

To create an analogy, imagine owning a fixer-upper holiday home at the coast. It is in bad shape at the moment, the foundations are fine but the walls need painting, the plumbing and electrics need redoing, but when it is done you will be able to use it to generate a decent amount of income from it, and one day it will be the home you can retire to. Sure, it is going to require a lot of time and attention before it can be lived in, but you really enjoy repair and restoration work and this is a project you see great value in and enjoy every opportunity you get to sink your teeth into it. Now imagine the frustration when it is only possible to work on this dream house for two or three weekends a year and when you do eventually manage to make some progress, all the overgrowth you had worked hard to clear from the yard has grown back and the repairs you have made have started deteriorating, leaving you not very far from where you started. Think of the time and opportunities lost! Given enough time and the right resources, you could really focus and turn this worthwhile project into a beautiful home that not only has financial worth, but is also the perfect setting for all of the good times and wonderful memories you envisage, not just for yourself but your family and loved ones.

Despite me not having an actual beach house to fix up, this was the battle I was facing on a daily basis when it came to creating a career as a professional speaker. I knew full well that it was possible to make a decent living from a speaking career, but my "product" needed to be developed into something I could sell, which required a lot of research, writing, crafting, rehearsal and time.

Unfortunately, my responsibilities and need for an income could not just be put on hold. There was no pause button to hit on my monthly expenses – not to mention the remaining debt from "the big sit-in of 2006" – while I went off to hack myself a new career path. Without a financial safety net, or fairy godmother, I had no option but to earn a living, paying the rent and keeping the wolf from the door just like most people do. If I have not made it clear enough yet, the advertising industry is fast-paced, where deadlines have the final word and the concept of leaving the office at five is often a far-off fantasy. But I was also to blame. It is within my nature to dig in and get things done, and my ability to multi-task as a writer and art director combined with my inability to say "no" results in me arriving home well into the evening, mentally exhausted after having spent an hour in traffic each way. I understand that a lot of people call that a day job. But weeks would bleed into months and any momentum I had gained on the speaking side of my career was lost in a cycle of rebuilding the foundation phase, like Sisyphus and his unrelenting boulder.

I am embarrassed to admit that the book you are reading now was started several weeks after returning from Everest in 2009 and has been gathering dust in a folder creatively labelled "THE BOOK" ever since. With large gaps of time, it was near impossible to pick up where I had last left off, and the lack of progress quickly turned into a lack of motivation and any sense of value in what I was doing.

In addition to the demands of working on a contract basis, I have on several occasions found myself up "Shit Creek" when my freelance gigs were prematurely terminated, often with less than a week's notice. And it becomes difficult to plan ahead or create some form of a strategy, because jobs often popped up and started immediately, sometimes lasting several months. Sometimes not. When times were good, they were good, but when times were bad, they were utterly awful. Never knowing when the next gig would come up, I was compelled to say yes to everything that came my way and the things in my life that held true value landed up waiting indefinitely.

To make matters worse, exacerbating my frustration with the situation was the fact that I had had a taste of what was really possible. I knew I wasn't chasing a unicorn and that making a life for myself as a speaker was entirely possible. I have a speaking portfolio of which I am very proud, having spoken for some of South Africa's biggest companies including Vodacom, Volkswagen, Liberty Life, Nedbank, Standard Bank and SASOL to name but a few. And my reviews and feedback have been nothing short of outstanding.

I had landed deals that had me present national road shows spanning all nine provinces and I, on one speaking contract, had earned in thirteen one-hour presentations the equivalent of three months' salary working nine-hour days as a freelancer. Even if money was not a consideration, speaking was and always will be something I am passionate about. I derive a sense of value from it and believe I add value to those I interact with. But money is not my driving force. I am motivated by the visible proof of my ability to make positive change in others. If that can provide a good life for my family and I, then even better. One particular quote that really influences my motivation to speak comes from a quote made at a press conference held when Samina Khayal Baig became the first Pakistani woman to summit Mount Everest.

"It does not matter that I was the first. What matters is that I can inspire someone to be second." Her profound words add fuel to my temperamental bonfire.

Did I have a marketable product? Absolutely. Credibility? Yes. Capability? Definitely.

Momentum?

Cue the tumble weed and the sound of crickets.

On the odd occasion my phone would ring, I would run outside to escape the hubbub of the studio, dropping whatever job I was designing or scripting, and if the person on the other end of the line was a potential speaking client my spirit would soar. They would enquire about my availability (which was pretty much all the time), we would discuss cost and then I would offer to meet with them to discuss the specifics of their upcoming event. I would hang up the phone and dance a little jig on the paving beside the duck pond before returning to my desk with the satisfaction of feeling one booking closer to "my ticket out of this place".

But not every call translated to a speaking engagement and I soon learnt all of the excuses. "The client has downscaled the event", "the dates have changed and we'll get back to you when we have found a new one" and, my personal favourite, "the client decided to go with a comedian".

My presentations were based on my life story, starting just before my accident and then taking people on the journey downward through my depression and then back up to a crescendo – reaching the summit of Everest. They inspired people with an illustration of determination and passion and limitless capability of the human spirit. The keynote was a personal story informally titled "A Boy and a Big Rock", named after a photo I had a stuck on the cover of the A5 journal I used to document our first expedition back in 2000. The photo is of a wiry young boy carrying a boulder which appeared on the cover of a Petzl climbing equipment catalogue. Immediately the image grabbed me and I saw a metaphor in the nameless youngster and his struggle with a large piece of granite. The talk managed to invigorate and encourage people and was laced with much of the lessons that I had learnt along the way so that my audience could implement them in their own lives. But I was just another adventure speaker from a very far-off place, with a tale to tell and an intangible goal that a majority of people will never truly identify with.

I needed to dig deeper and focus more on what my journey could offer to others. But what was it? This was not the first time I had wracked my brain trying to find something that would turn something good into something of real unique value. But as it turns out, the answers I was seeking were all right in front of me. Everything I needed to change had been said to me by various people throughout my life, on a number of occasions. I have since learnt that there is great value in the skill of being able to just stop and listen.

Too often we feel a need to provide an answer when the situation requires the opposite. Often we do not absorb the sage advice being served up to us on a shimmering platter because we are either not ready to implement it, or because it may lead to solutions that we don't believe we want. We often choose to ignore many options available to us, not because the opportunity isn't good, but because of our own list of reasons outlining "why not". Those reasons are always based on our own feelings of inadequacy and beliefs that have limited us and kept us warm and toasty in our comfort zones.

For years I had been hearing the same words over and over. When I meet people I have become acquainted with from various circles, I can be assured that I will be asked one of two questions: "Where the hell were you this time?" or "So what's next?". I'll usually answer them with a quick recap of my previous expedition, to which my answers usually evoke one of two responses. Either people will reply with something like "No way, you're bloody crazy!" or "You know I have always wanted to do that. It's definitely one on my bucket list!" Regardless of whether it was climbing Kilimanjaro or piranha fishing, everybody always connected with my spirit of adventure and a need to explore. A vast majority of people feel that pull of the world out there in some form or another. Whether they will ever act on it is another story altogether. In one form or another, whether we realise it or not, everyone has a list of things that have captured their imagination, a curiosity I believe is hard-wired into each and every one of us. Everybody has a bucket list of sorts, whether they call it that or not.

In the 2007 movie *The Bucket List* starring Jack Nicholson and Morgan Freeman, two men in their seventies from two very different backgrounds share a room in the cancer ward and become friends. Before long they embark on a list of things they wish to do before the time comes when they will inevitably "kick the bucket". This beautiful journey leads the two men around the world as they learn about each other and also themselves.

I won't spoil the story for you, but if you haven't seen the film it's well worth it.

In the back of my head I could immediately see an opportunity. There was definitely something in the idea. I recognised a lot of potential, something I could really explore – perhaps one day when I have time.

One Saturday morning in May of 2014, I found myself lying awake, a million ideas bouncing around my head, so loud I could not get back to sleep. As luck would have it, I had the house to myself. Tracey was away in the tiny holiday town of Clarens. I got out of bed and slipped on a pair of weathered cargo shorts. I cleared the kitchen counter and cued up the movie on my laptop. Jack Nicholson, Morgan Freeman and I began to map out the epiphany that had struck me awake at three o'clock that morning. Large pieces of flip chart paper, lemon-yellow Post-it notes covered the dining-room table and every kitchen surface available, like dishevelled roof tiles after a hurricane had passed through. I scribbled down random ideas, references, stick man drawings, and I connected concepts with arrows and lines. What was starting to emerge made me feel like that moment when Stephen Hawking's chalk boards began to animate into a swirling universe.

Okay, that's an exaggeration, but what I was putting down came naturally and my gut was telling me it was right. The kettle worked overtime that morning, and I worked into the afternoon and then the evening until I eventually stopped and stepped back from what was starting to strongly resemble "the way forward". If my life was made into a movie, this would be the montage with the epic Hans Zimmer instrumental overture playing, the entire day edited into what feels like a few minutes.

I felt as if I had completed six weeks' worth of renovations on my make-believe beach home in just a few days. And as the concept developed, so did my enthusiasm. I had started something that incorporated not only who I was and what had happened to me, but also a message that offered value and had the ability to create real positive change for other people. And what's more, this was something I could believe in.

I immediately began to redesign my website, and for the first few weeks the landing page read, in bold 36-point Helvetica type, "Ah S**t! Not Another Everest Speaker." The subheader went on to explain that I was now so much more than just another climber with yet another story of another mountain.

Mount Everest was no longer the core content of my keynote presentations. It was now a pivotal event that had led me on a particular journey, a testament to my approach to recovering stronger, mixed together with all of the chapters in my life that I had been downplaying up until now.

You climbed the highest mountain in the world. But what does it mean? I asked myself again. For the last five years the question had been echoing around inside of me, subconsciously present in every waking moment, and now it was finally edging closer to clarification. I was finally starting to understand that all of this had not been all in vain.

Somebody once pointed out that if people wanted to know about Mount Everest, they could read up on it online or watch a documentary. *You climbed a big mountain, so what? What's in it for me?*

For the first time I was able to portray my experiences of a life less ordinary to others in a context that made it relevant to the audience. I was now telling a human story. A story that people can empathetically relate to in terms of my challenges, emotions, doubts and failures. It was no longer about how high or how cold, it was now about what that meant to me and what it felt like.

And more importantly, how I was able to deal or not deal with each challenge.

The concept of a bucket list became the platform from which I could create a common ground with my audience, regardless of background or social stature. Only 4,000 people out of seven billion on Earth have climbed Mount Everest, but all of us – from Kroonstad to Kamchatka (look it up) – have or will have a list of things that we want to achieve. A list to live for.

If it were a list that had brought me thus far, then what if I were to use it to map the way forward? Control the list, control the story.

Three months later I had the pleasure of guiding a group of trekkers to Everest Base Camp. Sitting in one of the teahouses after a long day walking, I had the chance to share not only my story, but also the new content I had brought into my talks. Over the next few days, that conversation evolved into plans for me to address nearly 2,000 financial planners around South Africa, starting in the new year. I was absolutely elated and secretly relieved. As is typical of freelancing, ad agencies don't bring in contractors during the quieter months at the end of the year. It was going to be a very tight November and December, but come January, this speaking tour would open the floodgates on my financial desert.

When January arrived, I went on to present my "List it – Live it" keynote, fine-tuning the message each time and leaving the stage to a sea of smiling faces time after time.

This was the new wooden flooring in my little house at the sea.

This was what I wanted to do with my life. *This* felt right.

CHAPTER 46

SLOW LEARNER

I tried to avoid the conversations like the plague. A year and a bit had passed since we'd arrived back from Ama Dablam and just like clockwork, talk of another expedition had started doing the rounds among the usual suspects. When the topic of the next expedition arose, I would surreptitiously retract like a tortoise into its shell and dodge the ideas and suggestions as they were hurled around the table at our semi-regular boys' nights.

Since January of 2014, my speaking career had taken off, punctuated by the odd contract working at an advertising agency. I was able to make ends meet. It was only when I allowed self-doubt and fear to govern my decisions that I retreated to the safety net of formal employment, but at least there was some resemblance of a bigger picture, albeit in the distance.

I professed to John and the boys that this expedition was badly timed and, this time, I would be choosing to do the responsible thing by giving the trip a miss. I made the decision because I was intent on avoiding the loss of momentum of the progress I was making in my speaking career, which would once again suffer from an absence of four weeks away.

And I almost believed it too.

Alpamayo is a peak in the Cordillera Blanca of Peru. A pristine ice sculpture towering 5,947 metres high into the air, it is a beautiful white mass consisting of intricate ridges and furrows streaked down the main face. An ice climber's dream climb.

The real reason why I was not joining the team this time was that I was absolutely shit-scared of going to climb another mountain knowing full well that I was probably going to cock it up at the last minute with an excuse, or an injury, or an excuse of an injury. I had failed on a number of climbs over the years: Mount Kenya in 2008, the Denali Debacle, Ama Dablam's disappointment ... Going to attempt to climb Alpamayo was just another potential failure, and I was not ready for yet another layer of mud on my face.

I withdrew from the conversations that stretched into the night over WhatsApp. Links to articles describing the upcoming climb were ignored. As the self-proclaimed "weakest link" I chose to avoid the topic, the possibility of another failure had begun to shape my decisions.

But the planning continued. John, Warren and Allan were all on board, as well as two newcomers to the usual climbing crowd, Will Woods and Anthony Pringle. Will was originally one of John's wife Natalie's friends, who over time got roped into the things we were doing, from kloofing in the chilly river gorges of the Magaliesberg to the various triathlons we took part in, including Ironman. William also summited Kilimanjaro with the group of friends and acquaintances John had got together a few years earlier. Anthony was a scouting parent from when Warren ran a Scout troop in Benoni and they subsequently became good family friends, both working in the engineering field. Over the years they got closer, sharing several interests like hiking and climbing. This was to be Anthony's first real taste of altitude for which his mouth was already watering.

One Saturday morning in March, Tracey and I met with Allan and his wife Elizabeth for breakfast at Doppio Zero in the Sandton City shopping centre. While the women were chatting, Allan and I were chatting even more so, and the conversation inevitably turned to the upcoming trip to Alpamayo. Once again I tried using my "big boy voice" as I attempted to reiterate my reasons for not joining the team. It was a matter of finances ... and fear. It was about maintaining the momentum I had worked so hard to gain both as a speaker and in my regular day job (*still* freelancing). And fear. It was a convoluted pile of bullshit that was not convincing anybody, not even me.

The conversation hit a momentary pause, and in true Allan fashion, he raised his steaming cappuccino to his lips and drew a sip. Then looked me straight in the eyes and said, 'I hear you and I completely get that. But ja ... you should come!' As if it was a see-saw in my head that needed tipping.

As much as he was joking, Allan sparked within me the excitement of going on another adventure, an opportunity to revisit an old nemesis. And for the first time I allowed myself to actually consider the possibility of going. I looked across at my wife in trepidation, expecting the rolling of eyes and gnashing of teeth ... but it didn't happen.

'If you want to go, then you must go!' she said, unperturbed.

Tracey has never once been anything short of encouraging and supportive in whatever I have chosen to do, and this time would be no different. She knew all along that this was what I wanted to do, obviously seeing straight through my attempt to mask my passion with a thick layer of bullshit.

'I need to look at costs ...' I began, reloading my arsenal of excuses. But then I noticed the three sceptic faces around the table. 'Okay! Shit ... how much are we looking at?'

I had crumbled.

The discussion continued and I began to realise that the lack of support and confidence in my ability as a climber and as a valued team member existed only in my head and nobody else's.

As we were leaving, Allan stood up from the table and delivered his closing argument to the jury in my mind. 'Ja Rob, you know what?' I turned to face him, expecting him to tell me that at the end of the day, only I could make the correct choice and that he respected my decision, whatever it may be. 'You should come!' he said, slapping me his signature high five.

'Ja, maybe,' I said, the corners of my mouth turned upward. 'We'll see.'

In the car on the way home, Tracey and I discussed what it would entail should I choose to join the team to Peru. As much as I was hatching a plan, turning my options over and over in my head, so was Tracey. She had been witness to the repeated aftermaths of the last three failed summits and the effects that they had had on me. She had seen the self-doubt and self-hatred I'd felt as a result and the depression that had begun to dig its claws into me, dragging me to the bottom of the abyss. An abyss that made me horrible to live with. Tracey not only endured my self-destruction and morbidity, but she never left my side. And that is something I value and appreciate without end.

The next morning my wife unleashed her plan on me.

'If you're going to climb this mountain, you are going to do it properly,' she commanded, peeling the magnetic whiteboard from the fridge door. 'You are going to train hard and eat properly. No more shit. No more takeaways!'

I was startled at first, as I stood listening to Tracey's Rubicon address. At first it felt like I was being scolded in the same tone one would chastise a teenager for breaking a curfew, but I eventually realised that this was going to be the most motivating one-way conversation I had experienced in years.

'We'll get you to train with Calvin once a week. If you don't want to spend the money, I'll pay for it, but you're going. We'll get you fit and get your ankles strong ...' Now my mouth was hanging open in a semi-smile.

As she spoke, Tracey was writing something I couldn't make out from where I was standing. Finally she finished scribbling and revealed to me what would be my new set of commandments.

"Get fit! Get skinny! Get strong! Get summit! Get SEX!!!" This was followed by a stickman standing on the peak of a triangle with a flag in one hand. Sold.

At the risk of sounding like every male ever born, sex is a rather influential factor in many of life's most important situations. But that was not what had convinced me. It was the fact that my wife had taken the time and concern to construct a plan that was intended to give me the best possible chance at success. She'd managed to examine my past downfalls when preparing both physically and mentally for a climb, and the failures that resulted because of it. She had my back and now it was my duty to do the same.

The A4-sized magnet went onto the fridge where I would be able to see it every day (only to be hidden away when my mother popped around for dinner one night). We then went into the bedroom and I stripped down to nothing but a pair of running shorts ... to snap my "before" photos. These will not be included in the appendix.

Within the next few days I was booked, weighed and measured by Calvin McEnery, Tracey's – and now my own – personal trainer. In our first sessions I learnt so much about my strengths and weaknesses.

Calvin assured me that my legs were actually not weak at all. From the time I had spent in a wheelchair and how I had rehabilitated, my upper legs and calf muscles were doing all of the hard work, while my hamstrings and core were under-utilised and in need of some love, as Calvin put it. He also re-educated me about my ability to feel pain. The days that followed each training session were lessons in themselves. I learnt to appreciate the small things in life, like being able to bend my arms enough to brush my teeth or standing up without whimpering like a startled puppy.

But it was all part of a plan with one simple and clear objective. Along with training with our personal trainer, Tracey and I were also doing boxing fitness classes twice a week. Within weeks I was starting to notice a difference in the numbers on the scale as well as my confidence levels. My preconceived ideas about my limitations – as well as my capabilities – were being redefined.

In those twelve weeks leading up to the departure date I shed six kilograms, and the muffin tops bulging over my belt began to disappear. In the correct light, a hint of a six-pack began to emerge. Sure, my phone wasn't ringing off the hook with magazine cover deals, but it was better than what used to be there.

During our training sessions, I picked up on a phrase Calvin would use often before handing me a dumbbell that was five kilograms heavier than what I was expecting, or just before the third set of lunges. He would say the same three words.

'You got this.'

Whether it was Calvin's intention or not, I made a conscious decision to adopt the mantra and use it on a daily basis. Whether I was doing forty-second blasts of heart-bursting "mountain climbers" or squats on the Smith machine, those three words went a long way to getting me to the last repetition of the set ... and a little further.

The day arrived and we boarded the plane. William, being an employee of SAA, took his seat in business class, while the rest of us herded in with the cattle at the back. Anthony and I drew shortest straws of all and landed up seated across the way from a petite Chinese lady and her unruly two-year-old, who I soon named Shitface. The nine-hour flight to Sao Paulo crept past as Shitface went from comatose to a raging tyrant on a forty-five-minute cycle. At one stage I considered asking the mother if she would like me to call an air hostess or anyone with access to pepper spray for assistance. But we eventually landed in Brazil, and surprisingly, Shitface had not been stuffed into an overhead luggage compartment. I loaded my two duffels onto a trolley and said goodbye to the others for the next eighteen hours or so. My delayed decision to join meant that my flights to Peru would be slightly different to everyone else's and I left immediately to connect to Lima.

Will may have enjoyed the spoils of a business-class ticket as an SAA employee, but my marriage to a travel agent trumped his leather couches and Johnnie Walker Black. As if she hadn't done enough, Tracey had also arranged to put me up for the night in the Lima Marriot, which was a spoil I relished every remaining night of the trip. I enjoyed the walk-in shower and free Wi-Fi, thick carpets and several Spanish TV channels from the comfort of my king-sized bed, while the others bunked in two shoeboxes that were so small they had to use the pile of luggage to access the top bunk beds.

But that's where the four-star opulence came to an abrupt end. Later that morning we met in a dimly lit bus terminal to travel to the town of Huaraz at the foot of the Cordillera Blanca. Despite the luxury of lie-flat seating and all the dubbed comedy you could ask for, the eight-hour bus ride winds its way up to nearly 4,000 metres through the desert of rural Peru. The swaying of the double-decker bus made me heavily nauseous, so I downgraded myself to the rubber flooring outside the toilets in an effort to find the lowest part of the bus, making sure my on-board meal stayed "on board".

After what felt like an eternity, the bus finally huffed to a stop in the small shed wedged between an all-night convenience store and a dimly lit bar just before midnight. In among the crowds of reunited families and travellers stood our contact, Chris. Towering a head taller than the native Peruvian population, he was easy to spot, with a mop of chestnut hair showing from beneath his baseball cap. John had found Chris on the internet, an American climber who had come to the Cordillera Blanca, found love and never returned. For a fee Chris was able to arrange the logistics of our trip, along with providing local knowledge and the occasional translation. In the two days we spent in Huaraz, most of our meals were in the restaurant next door to the backpacker's lodge Chris had arranged to put us up in. We soon learnt that the restaurant was his own business and the lodge belonged to his mother-in-law.

After a good night's rest we spent the next morning trudging around the town, shopping for food to last us for the next three weeks, giggling like children at the tinned tuna branded "Fanny". In the market, we filed between the aisles lined with open-air butcher stalls that were well stocked with piles of cows' tongues, rib cages, pigs' heads (both kinds: salted and unsalted) and trays of gutted guinea pigs, locally known as *cuy*. As the day wore on, we found our way back to the hostel for another excellent meal at Chris's restaurant.

It had been exactly ten years since Warren and I had been to this town. That time we'd also been intent on climbing Alpamayo, except back then I think our approach was governed more by balls than brains and we were sorely disappointed by the news that the mountain was in no condition for climbing, ending our trip at Alpamayo's High Camp. It was a long way to come to just look at a mountain and buy a postcard with its image on it. It was a heart-warming experience to see how much I remembered from that trip in 2005, from the colourful stained glass windows of the disproportionately huge cathedral to the tiny courtyard lined with outdoor clothing stores and quaint little restaurants where I got to use all of my learnt Spanish – "Tres café con leche, por favor" ("three coffees with milk, please"). This time around, not only was I more experienced as a climber, but my Spanish vocabulary had literally quadrupled to almost nine practical phrases like such as "necessito un paraguas?" (which translates to "do I need an umbrella?").

But as much as I was enjoying the prestige of being the expedition's nominated translator, it was time to continue our journey closer to the mountains and further away from civilisation. The three-hour drive on the winding dust roads often felt like the typical start of a B-grade horror movie as the minibus we had hired clunked its way to the dusty hamlet at the park gate. Cashapampa is almost too small to be called a village, a place almost void of life, to the extent that some of the local prostitutes are still virgins. As dusty and desolate as it was, this speck of civilisation was where the start of the trailhead leading to our mountain began, with just a lone wooden post with an arrow reading "Routa de trekking Santa Cruz" (trekking route to the Santra Cruz valley). We were on our way.

Once the donkeys were loaded with our duffels, we began the trek into the valley alongside a river which would lead us to the first night's rest in Llamacorral. The further we hiked into the valley, the greener the terrain grew and the steeper the valley walls became. Some of the surrounding peaks had ice caps, creating the kind of scenery you'd find in an oil painting. On the right-hand side of the valley stands several stone walls which were once used to enclose herded livestock, possibly llamas, thus the name "Llamacorral". On the lush lawns of the valley, sheltered by a stone wall probably built hundreds of years ago, is where we made camp for the first night.

Despite the long day travelling, the team were upbeat and the excitement of being in the mountains carried on for several hours after dinner. I relocated to a large boulder a few metres from the tents to attempt to shoot photos of the night sky. Miles from anywhere, the air was clean and clear and devoid of any light pollution, turning the heavens into a glittering blanket striped by the faint cloud of the Milky Way.

Unlike when trekking or climbing in the Himalayas, we reached Alpamayo's Base Camp the next day. Our home for the next few days was in a grassy meadow, dotted with trees with a stream running straight through it which froze each night, creating an eerie silence, only to thaw just after 9.00 am each morning.

From the enchanted forest, our itinerary would take us up to an intermediate camp at the snow line and over a tough pass through a saddle on the left-hand side of Alpamayo. Over the next few days we completed the traditional process of carrying loads to halfway, to "Morraine Camp" which was perched on a rocky band at the edge of the glacier, before moving there for a night and on to High Camp.

It must be said that the day we climbed from Moraine Camp to High Camp was by far the crux of my expedition. The route leaves the rolling slabs of grey rock, ending abruptly at a distinct line where stone meets ice. The laborious task of putting on crampons was the first taste of the massive effort that lay in store for us. With fully loaded backpacks weighing in the region of thirty kilograms each, the process of stopping, removing your bag, putting on a climbing harness and strapping crampons to your already large and clumsy boots was not to be underestimated. And then the hard work started.

For the first time on this trip, the leader board in my head appeared. My name was in the middle of the field, but could slip down the ranks at any moment if I didn't watch myself. I clipped into the rope joining me to the rest of the team and began an internal pep talk in an effort to remind myself that this time would be different.

This time you're stronger and more positive and you know what you're up against. Robert, you got this! the voice in my head assured me.

We wound our way over and around the bulging mounds of snow, crossing dodgy bridges over yawning crevasses. Hours passed. This was nothing like what I remembered from last time. Each year, with varying levels of snowfall and the effects of global warming, the terrain is created, and over time the pass had grown steeper. Much steeper. In order to gain the High Camp, three steep sections of ice must be negotiated before cresting a ridge. As the ground flattened out the other side of the world appeared in front of me, disappearing into a blue-grey haze as mountain peaks stretched on forever. I knew how Jack must have felt upon reaching the top of the bean stalk, but the weight of my bag was digging into my shoulders, keeping my sense of awe in check. There was still a way to go before I dumped this buffalo on my back and set up our home for the next nine nights.

Mountaineering rule 12(b): Nothing is as simple as it looks. There was a path leading to the plateau where several tents already had laid claim to their own piece of paradise. The path traversed down the other side of the ridge before turning sharply to the left, where the Bolivians and the Taiwanese were. It would take about a minute before the deep snow gave way under my foot, toppling me over like an overloaded Venter trailer, sending me off the path and into even deeper, even softer snow. Digging myself out of each hole sapped my energy as every attempt to gain purchase proved useless. The best part of half an hour went by before I limped into camp, my sense of humour somewhere in the slush back on the path. But we were home, for now.

As mountain life dictates, there was no time to lick wounds. Tents were being pitched on freshly flattened platforms in ankle-deep snow. Anthony and Wa occupied one of the nylon igloos, then John and Allan, and completing the neat row of three, me and Will. With our bags inside, mattresses were inflated and sleeping bags lined the floors. With no Starbucks within a four-day radius, our focus turned to tea.

Over the next week and a bit, we lived on a flawless cloud of white. Each morning the sun came up from behind our waiting princess, Alpamayo, and each evening the setting sun set fire to the sky in a spectacular finale of every colour imaginable. The dying light of each day would shroud the surrounding peaks in a silk vale of pinks and blues that could fool the most hardened heart into believing that these mountains were alive. A final deep sigh would announce the fall of night, scattering everyone in the kingdom in search of shelter. Cold would take its throne until the first light of morning, when the story would begin anew.

CHAPTER 47

YOU GOT THIS

In the pitch dark of midnight, I began the arduous process of getting dressed. Will was busy doing the same, so I slid forward to the entrance of the tent to put on my boots and avoid a collision with one of Will's size 13 climbing boots. Once I was dressed, I went about the familiar procedure of lighting the stove to boil some water for our last-minute breakfast and hopefully a cup of coffee. Despite the summit attempt being the main reason for the trip, preparing for it is counter-intuitive and defies all logic. It involves waking up at midnight to have "breakfast" before slathering on a layer of sunscreen in the dark and getting dressed to leave the tents when every cell in your body is screaming to get back into your sleeping bag. At a time when you should be most excited, nervousness and anxiety suspend you on the brink of nausea. Against every instinct and shred of common sense, you consciously turn away from sanity and stability and head off in the direction of the monster. Willingly walking into the lion's den.

It was go time. It's always the same, that one last pat down from head to toe, making sure that you have not forgotten anything (it's more of a psychological habit than an actual check) followed by the zipping up of the tents and one final nervous deep breath before walking off towards the bergschrund.

The bergschrund is a gaping tear across the bottom of Alpamayo's face, caused by the downward movement of snow and ice under the force of gravity, and it marks the end of the 40-degree slope of knee-deep powder and the start of the face. In the previous days we had identified a small snow bridge spanning the two-metre fissure, our only means of accessing the ice face. Through the binoculars, what appeared as a fingernail-shaped crescent of snow forming a bridge turned out to be an awkward bulge of ice, a fragile bridge over which we tread with extreme caution. As the last of us literally tip-toed over the "crescent", John and Warren set up the first stance to which we would all anchor. The route to the summit from here on up was a solid sheet of ice at a gradient of about 60 degrees, steepening with every pitch or rope length, the closer we ventured to the summit, which was almost vertical. A slip here would result in serious injury and more likely death, with several other casualties. An unprotected fall would turn the ice face into a bowling alley, smashing and goring skittles in every direction before dumping all casualties into the bottomless gutter of the bergschrund.

My stomach was a knot and sitting uncomfortably high up in my ribcage. I willed myself to stop, forcing a few deep breaths and silencing the voice of nervous doubt. Turning back I craned my neck, concentrating hard to keep the front points of my crampons anchored firmly in the ice and my knees against the wall. The valley behind us no longer existed, swallowed into a world of darkness. The land was separated from the sky only by the absence of stars. Nothing else mattered for now.

Swivelling back to face the ice, I forced a smile of self-reassurance. *Rob ... you got this.*

In the interest of moving efficiently up the ice face, we split the group into two teams: Will, Anthony and Warren, and John, Allan and me. With the belay anchors in place, our team set off first, with the others just a minute or two below us. We would usually meet up at the end of each pitch. John led the way, placing each axe and crampon solidly as he rhythmically clawed his way up the face like a clockwork toy. Allan and I shared the job of belaying him, controlling the rope as he ascended, pausing from time to time while he placed protection for himself, screwing in a four-inch-long ice screw or hammering in a 60-centimetre-long aluminium stake or picket. John would move steadily upward, each move sending fragments of ice downward, showering on us until John reached the end of the ropes and our next belay stance. Once the rope was pulled taut between the lead climber and the belayer, John would set up another anchor before belaying me and Allan up, each on our own individual ropes, to meet him at the stance before starting the process again. It was like a sixty-metre inchworm making its way up a high branch over half a kilometre in length.

The other team was never far from sight and often we would share the belay stances, with Warren and John leading one pitch after another. Hours passed and before long, sunrise was not far away. The temperature was dropping noticeably as the first signs of light began to reveal more of the mountain, reminding us that we were making our way up a 600-metre slip-n-slide. All of a sudden there were panicked voices above us, screaming as the first few shards of ice began raining down on Allan and me.

When this happens, instinct usually causes us to look to wherever the warning is coming from. However, the spray of icy shrapnel was all the evidence we needed to know that something bigger was on the way. We both leaned into the face, tucking our heads in and down like shy tortoises in an effort to make ourselves as small a target as possible. The noise of the falling ice chips pinging against my helmet was interrupted by a loud crack. A piece of ice the size of a block of ice cream had hit Allan, glancing off the front of his helmet before ricocheting off his shoulder and out of sight below us. After a few seconds, the noise eased up and the shower subsides.

'Al?' No response. 'Allan!' I shouted again. Still nothing. Allan's head was still down against the wall in front of him and his eyes were closed.

'Allan!' I barked urgently. My pulse had doubled.

As I started to move towards Allan, who was no more than two metres away from me on my right, he lifted his head up and the words 'Ja, I'm fine' slipped from his mouth.

'Mate! I thought you were fucking dead! Jesus, are you okay?

You just had a chunk the size of an ice cream la nd on your head!' I rambled in a string of profanity.

Allan looked at me, his expression of shock turning to one of anger, a reflex reaction from a deafening blow to the head and the bone-chilling fright that came with it.

The ice block had unintentionally been dislodged by the other team nearly 50 metres above us, either from trying to find a decent ice-axe placement or from kicking footholds into the side of the mountain. Allan was stunned. He was visibly shaken, wringing his hands as he took the better part of a minute to compose himself.

'Allan, mate. Are you okay? Is your neck okay?' I asked, trying to gauge his level of consciousness.

'Ja, I'm fine. Just got such a fright!' His voice was calm but difficult to hear. His hands scanned the surface of his helmet.

'Fuck, dude. I thought you were a goner!'

After a moment to reflect and to feel grateful to be alive, we were ready to carry on up the face. The mood was quite sullen, despite my attempts to lighten it with a smart-ass quip – 'Al, if your head's a bit sore mate, you should consider putting some ice on it!'

It's amazing what a person can tell you with one half-hearted smile.

At the top of the pitch, both teams arrived simultaneously and dug in. Using the tethers from both ice axes and an additional ice screw, I was able to relax a bit and ease my weight into my harness, all the while watching for any movement in any of the three anchors. The topic of the flying projectile wasn't discussed for long before we began the process of climbing the next pitch. For the first time all day the runnel in the ice was visible, leading up for several metres before veering off to the left and out of sight. There was an all-too-familiar burning in my Achilles tendons and up my calves from the unrelenting pressure of standing on-point. I was actively ignoring it. Not today.

A few moments later, John took off up the face, clinking and clunking onward and upward without showing any sign of fatigue. He soon disappeared from sight and the only way we could tell what he was doing was by the movement of the rope. The tension was constant and the rope was pulling up at a steady pace. John was still climbing. Each time the pulling stopped, I could only guess that he was placing an ice screw or picket in the face to protect himself from an impending fall. Then the steady pull would resume for a few metres before coming to a complete stop.

Usually, once John had reached the top of a pitch, it took about four or five minutes to anchor himself safely before three distinct tugs on the rope signified that Allan and I could begin climbing towards him. It's like Morse code for climbers – "tug, tug, tug" translates roughly to "I'm ready for you. Hurry up and climb already – I'm getting cold."

Four minutes went past. Where Allan and I were perched was less than homely. The wind had picked up and we were still in the shadow of the mountain. My runny nose and numb cheeks helped me to estimate the temperature at around –10°C. Five minutes, and then six went by. Nine then ten.

'What the hell is he doing up there?' I asked Allan, who had shrunk into the shelter of his jacket.

I had visions of John basking in the sun on the summit, having forgotten about his two frozen friends below.

Suddenly the rope jerked once and then twice more. The furrow in the mountain side we were following had narrowed to about a metre wide, so I climbed ahead of Allan, absolutely paranoid about sending any shards of ice down onto Allan's already throbbing melon. The final pitch was by far the steepest of the lot and my chest was bursting with pride that I had made it. I felt impressed that John had led this pitch and grateful that it wasn't me. After several metres, I looked up to see John poised rather awkwardly as he belayed me and Allan towards him. 'Howzit Joe!' I smiled, happy to see he wasn't slacking off as previously assumed. 'Howdy,' he replied casually as if we were meeting for coffee, and not 5,947 metres above sea level on a vertical ice rink.

'John, you've ran out of uphill!' I managed between breaths.

'Ah no, bro!' he replied in his best New Zealander accent.

The summit of Alpamayo was nothing like any of us had envisaged. We did not manage to crest the usual ridge and stand proudly on top. John had climbed as high as possible, landing himself precariously on top of an awkward razor's edge of semi-solid slush. This explains what took so long for him to secure himself. Any attempts to place ice pickets were futile as they pulled out of the mountainside like a beach umbrella on a windy day. From where I stood, the piece of ice we were on was so thin I could see sunlight shining through the mountain. The final metres or so of the top edge were very brittle and so there I stayed, with my head level with the top of the mountain. Allan was not far behind and the three of us played a mixed game of vertical "Twister" and Tetris in order to find our own places on the summit of Alpamayo.

Within minutes Warren appeared below us in top spirits with the same expression he always wore in the mountains – his "mountain smile". His arrival was the perfect opportunity to take our summit photo, the three of us looking down at the camera for one of the most uniquely composed summit photos I've ever been in.

After a short discussion with Warren about anchoring safely, we began the process of abseiling back down the same way we had come up in order to give Warren, Will and Ant a chance to get up there for their own moment in the sun.

As I reached behind me to unclip my belay device from my harness, my gloved fingers caused me to release an ice screw from the gear loop it was attached to, which slipped between my clumsy hands. It bounced between Warren's boots like a shiny ball in a pinball machine before rocketing straight down the face, gaining speed instantaneously – directly towards where Will and Anthony were waiting.

'BELLOOOOOW!' I screamed at the top of my lungs.

The elation of reaching the summit was instantly replaced by the terrifying thought of a double murder. I forced the ropes through my abseil device, attached myself to the rope and began to make my way down the line as fast as prudence would allow. Exiting the final groove, I gained sight of my teammates. Both were alive.

Apologising profusely, I joined them on their frozen perch and made myself safe at the anchor. It turns out they saw something come screaming past but didn't realise it was an ice screw. I was ever so glad they were untouched. I hoped the Spanish couple below us on the route had been as lucky.

Anthony and Will had been stagnant in the same place for half an hour, in the shade, unsheltered from the wind and hypothermia evident in the colour of their lips. Will was frantically rubbing his gloves together, letting out a string of choice adjectives while Anthony's complexion was beginning to match the blue-grey ice we were standing on. With very little formality, the two immediately began to move in the direction of the top. Whether they were motivated by the thought of summiting the mountain or just getting into the warmth of the sunshine, they took off immediately, passing John on his way down.

Once John had joined us, we began undoing all of the hard work we had spent the last eight or so hours doing. We joined both of our 60-metre ropes together and threaded one end through the two pickets anchored in the ice, before throwing the coils of nylon spaghetti down the face. Allan and I each clipped our belay devices to a rope and abseiled simultaneously, each step cautious and deliberate, having just seen how much the snow pickets were moving in their holes. The tricky part of the abseil was trying to find the next anchor, most of which were a little less than obvious, often half buried or hidden in a depression.

The process was unnerving as we weren't able to trust any of the anchors entirely. On the last pitch of the abseil I was once again impressed and grateful. Incredibly, John managed to find the ice screw I had dropped from nearly 600 metres above. I was grateful that he hadn't discovered it embedded in a Spaniard's skull. Our final abseil went over the edge of the bergschrund we had crossed eleven hours earlier, and the relief was instantaneous. I could finally stand flat-footed on the ice, giving my exhausted calves a rest.

I unclipped from the rope and took great care when re-attaching my belay device to the gear loop on my harness, listening for the clink of aluminium on aluminium. With the relief of being off the face and having the summit in hand, the mood lifted immediately, as if clouds had parted after a heavy storm. I began stomping my way homeward, trying to place my footsteps in the fresh holes John had punched a few metres ahead of me.

It was done. The curse was lifted. I stopped for a moment and turned to look at the white mass, no longer daunting and fierce. 'Thank you,' I said under my breath, my voice quaking. As my eyes had filled beneath my snow glasses, so had my heart filled with gratitude for a successful, and more importantly, a safe day on the mountain.

The burgeoning weight had been lifted from my chest and I breathed as deeply as my lungs would let me. The cold dry air stung the insides of my nostrils as my chest expanded, before letting it all out in one hearty sigh. I turned to continue my way down the slope, smiling widely to myself, finally able to let go of the possibility of repeating failure.

For the first time in what felt like an eternity, I allowed myself to enjoy the feeling, an emotion I barely recognised: the warm glow of self-pride. This time I was not turning my back on a beast, having been found wanting. I was returning home victorious, a man worthy of his lofty dreams.

CHAPTER 48

THERE'LL BE DAYS LIKE THIS

Carl Jung, the father of analytical psychology, once said "I am not what happened to me. I am what I choose to become." It's a beautiful quote, making a person exempt from the burden of circumstance, giving them the hope and empowerment to pursue a destiny that is all their own. But there are days when those words are nothing more than just another quote. I could add it to a board on Pinterest, print it out for my office wall, hell, why not tattoo it into my skin? But it cannot change the fact that I have been broken, and all the King's horses and all the King's men will never fully put me together again.

There are days when I *am* what happened to me. When the enduring pain from a mistake of ten years ago has more power over me than the possibility of a better tomorrow. Every morning when I climb out of bed, it still takes a while for the tightness in my ankles and calves to ease enough for my heels to touch the floor. That's just how it is for me. I live with pain on a daily basis, the level of which is determined by the exertion of the day before. People ask me if I feel my injuries on cold winter days, to which I reply 'Yes, and also all the other days too.' When asked if I am limping or why, I just say 'That's how it is.' These are the days when I resign myself to the fact that I am indeed the chip in the crystal chalice.

And then there are days when I realise that things could be a lot worse, that I could still be in that wheelchair. There are days when the nagging pain in my feet tells me to be grateful that I have ankles to feel, that they are hurting because of something I had the privilege of doing yesterday. There are days when I have the presence of mind to make peace with what happened in my life, whether it's the scars on my ankles or those dark and bitter days of failure. Days when I can forgive myself for my human condition.

On these days I can accept all that I am, even if that is the chink in the armour, the Achilles heel. On days like these I can appreciate that there is a divide between *having* damage and *being* damaged. On these days, I am the sum of everything that has happened to me.

And these are the days I live for.

EPILOGUE

If I have learnt anything from this whirlwind of a life, it is this: no matter where this journey takes me, wherever the next adventure lies, I'm pretty sure I will be able to handle it the only way I know how. Left foot. Right foot. Repeat.

ACKNOWLEDGEMENTS

This book has evolved so much since its original inception. Each step of the way has been a lesson in humility, kindness and growing, not only as an aspiring author, but as a person too.

To Alex Treadway, Hiroyuki Kuraoka and John Black for your kind generosity with your expressive photographs. To Paul and Barbara Aarden, Jenny Paterson and Stephanie Cox for your care and patience regarding what I thought was good writing. To those who greeted my many questions, requests for favours, and ignorance with your time and talents. To my incredible wife and teammate Tracey, for your patience, your faith in me and endless support.

Lastly I want to acknowledge those whose names appear within the story that is my journey thus far. For carrying heavy, for kind words, for never doubting, for attentive belays, for pushing, pulling, cursing and kicking, for sheltering me from the icy gales and sharing the glorious days of sunshine.

Thank you does not seem enough, but I hope my gratitude to each of you is evident in the pages of this book.

I've said it before and I'll say it again ... You cannot climb big mountains on your own.

If you found this book interesting ... why not read these next?

Man Up Man Down

Standing up to Suicide

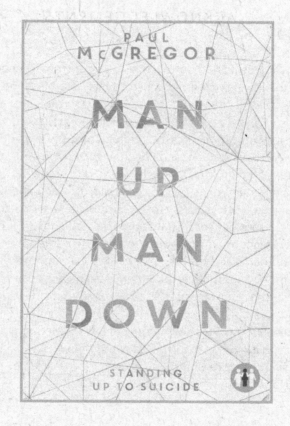

When his dad died suddenly by suicide, Paul was devastated. Now he's on a mission to change how we think about men's mental health and what it really means to "man up".

Must Try Harder

Adventures in Anxiety

After 30 years beset by extreme social anxiety,
Paula decided to change her worldview – one terrifying,
exhilarating challenge at a time. Paula shares her extraordinary
journey from recluse to adventurer.

Breakdown and Repair

A Businessman's Tale of Stress and Success

Succumbing to work pressure, Mark pieces himself back together after attempting to take his own life. But he soon finds that it's not so easy, especially when his daughter becomes ill herself.

TriggerHub.org is one of the most elite and scientifically proven forms of mental health intervention

Trigger Publishing is the leading independent mental health and wellbeing publisher in the UK and US. Clinical and scientific research conducted by assistant professor Dr Kristin Kosyluk and her highly acclaimed team in the Department of Mental Health Law & Policy at the University of South Florida (USF), as well as complementary research by her peers across the US, has independently verified the power of lived experience as a core component in achieving mental health prosperity. Specifically, the lived experiences contained within our bibliotherapeutic books are intrinsic elements in reducing stigma, making those with poor mental health feel less alone, providing the privacy they need to heal, ensuring they know the essential steps to kick-start their own journeys to recovery, and providing hope and inspiration when they need it most.

Delivered through TriggerHub, our unique online portal and accompanying smartphone app, we make our library of bibliotherapeutic titles and other vital resources accessible to individuals and organizations anywhere, at any time and with complete privacy, a crucial element of recovery. As such, TriggerHub is the primary recommendation across the UK and US for the delivery of lived experiences.

At Trigger Publishing and TriggerHub, we proudly lead the way in making the unseen become seen. We are dedicated to humanizing mental health, breaking stigma and challenging outdated societal values to create real action and impact. Find out more about our world-leading work with lived experience and bibliotherapy via triggerhub.org, or by joining us on:

🐦 @triggerhub_

ƒ @triggerhub.org

📷 @triggerhub_

Printed in the USA
CPSIA information can be obtained
at www.ICGtesting.com
JSHW031710140824
68134JS00038B/3613

9 781837 964055